Queenie of Norwich

LK Wilde

For Joanna and Gillian

PART 1

Ellen Hardy

Chapter 1

January 1906

Florrie's groaning beside me; writhing around like that time Arthur pinned a maggot to a cobble. We watched it squirm in anger, thinking it stood a chance against Arthur and his shoemaker's awl. It didn't look thrilled, and neither does Florrie.

"You alright?"

Florrie groans again. I shake her, and she turns to me. Still, she don't speak, so I run my hand across her forehead like I've seen Mum do. It's hot and sticky and I have to wipe my hand on the blanket.

"Is it your belly again?"

She nods her head. Poor Florrie's always getting sick. I'm made of sterner stuff, Dad says. Maybe it's that I sneak Dad's beer rather than drinking the stinking water from the pump. Florrie's always got a thirst on her, but the water she drinks is gloopy, sticking to the edges of her cup like shit to a stone.

"You need the pan?"

She nods again, and I fetch it for her.

"Here you go."

I put the pan beside her and help her stand. It's tricky 'cause she's bigger than me and flops around like a rag. She holds me tight and lowers herself down. I turn my head away and when she's done, she collapses to the floor.

"Ellen," she says through her tears.

"What's the matter?" I say, stroking her damp hair.

"There's some on my nightdress."

Florrie's shoulders bunch up with sobs, and I hug and shush her. We can't have Mum hearing us or there'll be hell to pay. She's as big as a heifer and never sleeps well when there's a baby on its way. I fumble with Florrie's nightdress and pull it up over her head. With no window and no lamp, it's a case of the blind leading the bloody blind. My fingers feel along the rough floor, looking for something to cover her. An overcoat will have to do. I wrap it over her shoulders and pull it tight around her belly.

"Florrie, get yourself into bed. I'll sort the pan."

"Leave it till morning," she says, but I can't sleep with that rotten stink in here all night.

Her breathing turns heavy. I tuck the dirty nightdress under my arm, then feel my way through the darkness. The hanky I've wrapped around my nose and mouth to block the smell isn't working. I can't hold the pan at arm's length, for my arms are little and the pan big. So, I have to clutch it to my chest, praying none spills onto me. It would be easier if the floorboards weren't curled up and down like waves on the river. I stick close to the wall, and don't disturb the sleeping bodies between me and the stairs.

Ten steps down, two to the door. Good, I've made it out without waking the yard. I stumble on the cobbles but twist my body in time and the filth splashes on the ground, not me. The privy is black as pitch. I do my best to tip the pan over the hole, but I'm sure some pours over the sides and there'll be cursing tomorrow when the neighbours use it. I shovel ash over the top till I'm sure it's covered enough for me to take off my hanky. Back in the yard, I walk twelve steps to the pump. I have to get my shoulder under the handle and push from my ankles up to get the bloody thing to move. It gurgles, then I hang on to it to pull it down, and dirty water spurts on Florrie's nightdress. With no lye, it's going to smell worse than before, but it's the best I can do.

I'm wringing out the nightdress when a foul smell wafts into the yard and I hear the clacking of horses' hooves. Bloody hell, it's the Honey Cart. I'm trembling, and for a moment I'm pinned to the spot. The sound of boots on cobble gets me moving, and I sprint to the nearest wall and press myself against it. I'm standing in the bloody drain, aren't I? My boots are filling with stinking water, but I don't care. I've heard stories of the Scavengers what drive the Honey Cart. Arthur told me they have three eyes, and Robert said they snatch kiddies what are out at night. *Oh God, please keep me safe*, I pray. Not that God's done much for me so far.

My heart's thumping as hard as Dad nails leather, but I do my best to keep my breathing quiet. There's two of them, I can hear them talking. They don't sound like monsters, but maybe that's how they capture you, pretend to be nice, then pounce.

The Scavengers' lamp chucks an orange glow around the yard. Tightly packed houses rise like monsters, the few windows glowing orange eyes.

"This there yard's one of the worst," says one man, lifting his lamp higher to get a better look. Light tickles my toes. *Please, no further, no further.* Loose bits of plaster poke into my back as I try to make myself melt into the wall. The light slips back over the cobbles. Bloody hell, that was close.

"Well I'll be blowed. That int right, it int," the other man mutters, trying to clear the mess I've left in the privy.

The yard fills with the scrape of metal spades as they shovel filth into buckets. I press hard against the wall. The stinking water flows fast, lapping at my stockings. After an age, the footsteps of the Scavengers disappear through the alleyway and onto the street. I wait for the clacking of hooves before I dare move again.

Back inside, I pick my way along the wall, stepping over the legs and feet of my family. How they didn't wake with Florrie's spurts and splutters is beyond me, but most were up at four and back after dark, so they're dead to the world.

I squeeze myself under the blanket beside Florrie and wrap my arm around her. It's wrong to say, but I love Florrie more than the others. I barely see the older ones with the hours they work, never see Dad, and Mum's always in a lather. Florrie's promised to always look after me, but it's always me looking after her. Not that I mind, she's the sweetest, most perfect girl I know. I'd cross hot coals for her if I had to.

My eyes squeeze shut, but thoughts of the Honey Cart jolt me every time I fall towards slumber. The others are stirring before I finally drift off.

***

It's hard to know where night ends and morning begins for it's so dingy in the house. But the room is empty, so it must be morning. I pick the sleep from my eyes and pull on my clothes. The fire is out, and I wear my coat over my dress to keep away the chill. My boots clatter against the bare boards of the stairs and as my hand sweeps down the wall, a patch of plaster falls out and I kick it to the bottom.

In the downstairs room, one piece of wood sits lonely in the fire. Dad's jumper and trousers are drying on the clotheshorse, but the timber is giving out more smoke than heat and I can't see them drying soon. Through the blur of smoke and darkness I see Florrie sat at the scrubbed table, bowl in front of her.

"You better?"

"Much better, thanks."

"That porridge?"

"Yes, there's still some in the pan if you want it."

I grab a chipped bowl from the table and ladle out porridge from the pan on the fire. It's good Florrie's eating. She needs to build her strength.

"Ellen..."

"Hmm," I say through a mouth full of sticky oats.

"Thank you for last night. I'm sorry about... about..."

She's choked up and I reach my hand across and squeeze hers. "You don't have to say sorry. I like looking after you."

"You're so grown up," she says. I don't know why, but she sounds sad.

"Course I'm grown up, I must be six by now!"

"I know, it's just girls what are six should play with dolls, not clean up filth while their mum and dad snooze away."

"What are dolls?"

"They're like small people, made from cloth and china."

"Sound scary."

Florrie laughs. "Yes, I s'pose they are a bit."

"Florrie... if I tell you something you got to promise, you won't tell no one?"

"I promise."

"Last night I saw the Scavengers."

Florrie's spoon drops from her hand and clatters against the table. "The Scavengers? You sure?"

"Yes, sure as can be. They weren't what Arthur says, though. They're just ordinary fellows scooping up buckets of filth."

"Were you scared?"

"No," I lie. "Is everyone at work?"

"Yes."

"Do you have to go in?"

"Not till noon, I'm on the late shift today."

"Can we play outside?"

"You sure? It's bloody freezing out there."

"It's freezing in here!"

"That's true enough. I need to head out to the washhouse. Will you help me?"

"You promise you'll play with me if I do?"

"I promise."

"Alright, I'll help you with the other chores too."

It don't take us long to sweep and make the beds, for our house is small. Even with nine kiddies and two grownups, no one makes much mess 'cause they're at work most of the time. Sarah will probably leave soon. I caught her kissing a chap from Reeves Yard and Mum says if she's not careful she'll get herself knocked up, or have a pea in the pond. I'm not sure what that means, but the way Mum talks it's like Sarah will soon be gone.

It's freezing outside, but there's plenty of folk about. I jump down the front step and away from our house. I don't trust it. The top half leans forward into the yard like it could fall on top of me at any moment. It also leans to one side, looking as squiffy as Dad does when he's sunk too many pints in the Queen Caroline. Our house might have been painted white once, but now it's grey with splodges of brown and green sneaking their way from bottom to top. It's almost as thin as Arthur, and I'm jealous of the Jeffries next door 'cause they got windows top and bottom.

"I thought you said you'd help?" says Florrie, her face red beneath armfuls of sheets and drawers.

"Give me some of that," I say, taking a bundle of cotton and tucking it under my arm. I need a hand free, for the neighbours have been doing their laundry, and strings of sheets and clothes hang from one side of the yard to the other. The last thing I want is Mr Morrison's drawers in my face. I hold back a grey sheet and let Florrie pass.

"You girls not in school today?" says Mrs Morrison as we walk into the washhouse.

"Too old," says Florrie.

"Too young," I say, though that's not true. I should be there, but Mum's not around to check and I know the other kids won't snitch.

"You done here?" Florrie says to Mrs Morrison, and she nods her head.

"You're good gals helping your mum out like this. Shame she has to go winding when she's so near her confinement."

We nod, and Mrs Morrison shuffles off. Most mums stay home, taking care of the house and the kiddies, but they still earn a few bob on the side. I doubt Mrs Morrison's laundry is her own, and I know Mrs Jeffries spends her evenings making dresses and trousers for local kiddies. But it's easier to take in work when you've a window to see by. No wonder Mum's often in a lather, working all the hours God sends, running a house and having so many kiddies to care for. I almost feel sorry for her.

We bundle our cotton mess into the copper and Florrie nips back to fetch the water she's been heating on the fire. It's a hard job on your arms, and our muscles ache from pounding out dirt. We don't spend as long as we should, for now Mrs Nicholls has appeared to hurry us up. By the time we've finished with the mangle, it's hard to say how long the whole lot's taken, for the sun never reaches us here in the yard, so it's a job to judge the passing of time.

"Can we play now?" I ask Florrie once the last dress is on the line.

"Go on then, fancy skipping?" I nod. "Alright, I'll fetch the rope."

Eddie and Dickie are sitting on their front step looking sheepish. They have a metal bucket turned upside down and are taking turns to bang it with a stick.

"What you up to?"

"A game for boys. Get you on, go on, shoo."

"Why can't I play?"

"You're a girl. Bugger off."

I stare at them and fold my arms. Florrie walks over with the rope.

"What's in that there bucket?"

The boys snigger, and Florrie gives Dickie a clip round the ear. For a moment he gets cross, then he grins.

"You want to know what's in our bucket?"

"That's what I said, int it?"

"Alright then."

Dickie jumps off the step and reaches his arm back to the bucket. With a bang, the bucket topples over, and a walloping great rat runs out. Florrie screams and I'm frozen to the spot as it races across my feet. Florrie grabs me and pulls me away from the boys.

"Idiots," says Florrie, "should've killed the bloody thing."

Florrie hugs me and waits for me to calm down. Mostly I like living in the yards, but the rats are one thing I hate. Their little feet patter round the floorboards at night and I find excuses not to clear out the fire, 'cause that's one of their favourite hiding places. They told us at school rats carry disease. At night I sometimes lie awake imagining them sneaking round, killing all my family.

Florrie lets go of me and ties one end of the rope to the doorknob. "Jump in," she says and begins swirling the rope round and round till it blurs against the grey buildings. Soon other little truants find us and it's a right old party we got going on. Doreen from Hawke's Yard's here with her sisters. They're poor little mites with only flimsy cotton blouses to warm them against the chilly winter air. Florrie would never let me go out like that in winter. Even if it means she goes cold, she keeps me warm. I bloody love Florrie, I do.

Chapter 2

February 1906

Mum was right to worry about Sarah having a pea in the pond. Her belly's got big, and her chap's done the proper thing and says they should wed. I don't give two hoots who Sarah's stepping out with, but I like what he brings with him. He's been slipping Sarah bits of meat from his butcher's shop and tonight we're having mutton stew for tea. The neighbours will be green with envy once the smell wafts through their fancy pants windows.

The mutton stew works a treat and like the Pied Piper, it's brought all the family running home. Dad's gone barmy with the candles and as one flickers away on the table, another two throw light from the space we call a windowsill, even though there's no window. Any other night, we'd be squinting away, trying to see by the light of one.

The candles stutter, burning down the wax. It's draughty in here and the flames jerk this way and that, lighting up patches of wall then throwing it back to shadow. Where two walls meet, a black splodge is creeping its way up from the floor and in some places, fur is clinging to it. Even the candle flames can't lighten it.

In places the black splodge hasn't reached, little beads of water cling to the wall. I ask Maria what they are, and she tells me it's from our breath. How could our breath stick to the wall like that? Makes little sense, but looks pretty, like Mrs Jeffries' string of fake pearls, what she wears every Sunday. Everyone is busy, so I play a game, stopping the water with my finger as drops race down to the floor. Pearls gather on my finger, then dribble down my palm. I wipe my hand on my skirt and look round the room.

Robert and Arthur huddle on the stairs, talking about their latest floozies. Maria, Sarah and Ethel are talking about wedding business, *girl's business* they call it, but they won't let me join in even though I'm a girl too. Ethel's face is burning brighter than the candle and I know they're talking about rude things, even if they won't tell me what.

Dad sits in a dark corner, rolling baccy from his tin, trying to ignore the mess of everyone squashed together like fleas on a rat. He's quiet, but that's nothing new. Dad's always quiet. I sometimes wonder if he has a brain in his head for the little he has to say. But then he'll surprise me and say something about the weather, or work. "Cold out," he'll say. Or "Boss was a right bastard today." Man of few words, I've heard Mum call him. Dad must have a brain to be a good shoemaker, so perhaps it's that with so many kiddies there's already enough noise going on. I could count on one hand the times he's spoken to me, but sometimes he'll walk past and ruffle my hair.

Mum has her bum in a chair and feet on a stool. Her ankles are nearly as big as her belly and thin purple lines creep up her face, like when she's shouting, only now she's quiet, picking out grime from beneath her nails. Mum looks up and I give her my best smile. She frowns and looks away. I don't know what I've done this time, but I always seem to have done something wrong, however hard I try to be good.

With Florrie busy stirring the stew and everyone else ignoring me, I'm left with no choice but to find Albert. He's escaped the noise and is playing with marbles on the sloping upstairs floor. He don't even look up when I come in, just stares at his marble, rolling drunkenly down the wonky floorboards.

"Can I play?"

Without looking up, he shakes his head.

"Why not?"

Another shake of the head.

"Cat got your tongue?"

I don't know why I bother, Albert never speaks to no one. It's only 'cause he's clever as hell he gets away with being so rude. It caused a great upset at the school when Dad took him out to begin work. They said he could've gone far, whatever that means. He don't like helping Dad at the factory, but Dad says he works faster and better than a grown man, so it looks like he'll have to stay. Maybe he's not as clever as they think. If I were him, I'd do shoddy work and get myself sacked and back to school. I hate school, but I reckon I'd hate the factory more. Everyone says me and Albert look alike, same blue eyes, same dark hair, but I don't want to look like no boy. Especially not a boy like Albert.

"Albert?" I say, waving my hand up and down in front of his eyes. Nothing. "Albert?" I grab a chunk of hair and pull his head back, so he has to look at me.

"Bugger off," he says.

"Bugger off yourself," I say. Just for good measure, my toe clips his pile of marbles, sending them spilling like ribbons of water across the scuffed floor.

"Ready," Florrie calls.

I run down the stairs before Albert can trip me up or push me. All that time Florrie stood stirring, and the stew is shoved into gobs as quick as it hits the bowls. The room fills with the sounds of chewing and spoons scraping on the mishmash of bowls, plates and cups we're eating from. Mum makes me wait till last, so I only get one ladle's worth, and it's full of burned bits scraped off the bottom.

There's not enough chairs for us all, and Mum's taking up two. The boys lean against the door frame and the girls by the fire. Me and Florrie sit ourselves down in the only bit of space near Dad's feet, the floor cold against my bum, the wall damp against my back.

Dad's trousers brush my cheek, and I shuffle closer to Florrie. He'll be so tired by now, I don't trust him not to forget I'm there and put a boot in my face. His trousers are fraying at the bottom, and there's a musty smell coming off them. If the light was better, I might even see it. I bet it would float green or brown through the air. His boots are the only smart thing about him, for a shoemaker can't have grubby shoes. Bad for business. His fingers reach down and scrub against his leg. He stretches out, and I get my head away just in time. Arthur reckons Dad likes to fuss about his dodgy leg so we don't forget he was a soldier. I don't need no leg to remind me, not with Pretoria as my middle name.

"You won't be getting no meat once I'm married," pipes up Sarah, her mouth stuffed with stew. "I'll have my own mouths to feed."

"And we'll have one less wage coming in," mutters Dad.

"Send Ellen out to work," says Arthur.

"Ellen? She's too little, only turned six this week, a right old waste of space."

Mum's words make everyone go quiet. They fidget, looking at the floor, the walls, anywhere but me. Florrie reaches over and takes my hand. I squeeze hers back to let her know I'm alright. Did I really turn six this week? Mum never said, but I s'pose she's no reason to lie.

"I can't help being little."

"Can't see you being much use when you're big neither," says Mum.

Ethel collects up the dishes, and for a moment everyone forgets about me. She's like that, our Ethel, plain to look at, quiet as a church mouse, but she's a fixer, always trying to avoid rows and smooth things over.

I stare at Mum. My belly churns as she nibbles a dirty nail and spits the end out onto the floor. She's wrong about me being useless. The words spill out before I can stop them.

"If you're worried about dosh, you could always go to the pub less." I clap my hand over my mouth, but it's too late, I've gone and bloody said it.

"What did you say, girl?"

The lines on Mum's face turn dark purple, and bubbles of spit sit on her lips. I have to choose, keep quiet, or stick up for myself.

"It's simple 'rithmatic, really," I say. Florrie digs her nails into my palm to get me to shut up. It don't stop me, I'm on a roll. I look up at Dad, who squirms in his seat. "Four pints a night over seven nights is about nine bob. Go to the pub less and we'd not be so hard up."

Mum lifts one leg after the other off the stool and eases her way to standing. She waddles round the table and crouches in front of me. Her hand whips across my cheek. I reckon it stings more than a hot poker.

"You see this life? See the hours I work? All you have to do each day is go to school and you can't bloody manage that. Who are you to tell me that after a day of toil I can't join my husband for a drink or two?"

That shuts me up. I've said too much already.

"Robbie?"

Mum cocks her head towards the door. Dad nods and follows her from the room, ready to hand over his weekly earnings to the landlord of the Queen. It takes a minute or two before the room breathes again.

"You're a wild one," says Maria.

"She's an idiot," says Sarah.

"Who told you all that about the dosh?" says Arthur.

"No one told me, I just knew."

"How? You truant more than you go to school."

I shrug. "Numbers are easy," I say, and Arthur squints at me like he don't know if I'm telling the truth.

The others scarper in all directions when it's time to clear up, so it's just me and Florrie left with the dishes. She manages the pump better than me, and I hold a bowl underneath to catch the spilling water. We don't bother heating it, there's only one log left to burn. She gives the dishes as good a scrub as the water will allow, then passes them to me for drying. My cloth is more of a rag; torn in that many places, I have to fold it plenty before it will soak up any water. I scrub at the wet plates and bowls, but can't rub off the pump water's grease.

"You know," Florrie says, staring into the bowl. "What you said to Mum was rude, but funny." She turns to me and there's a twinkle in her eye. Her lips are twitching like she's trying her hardest not to laugh. "Did you really think that up by yourself?"

"Yep," I say, keeping my face straight. I've not given much thought to the brain in my head. It is what it is. They wonder why I hate school; it's dull. Too easy. Being clever is all well and good, but it don't change nothing. Mum will have me winding silk as soon as I'm big enough.

"Florrie?"

"Mm."

"Why don't Mum like me?"

"Ah, don't pay any attention to her when she's in a lather."

"But she's in a lather with me more than the rest of you."

"Yes, but you're the littlest. It's always the littlest what gets it worst. The littlest can't work, the littlest reminds her of all the mouths there are to feed."

"Were you the littlest once?"

"I was. Listen, they'll be a new little one soon and things will get better, I promise."

By the time Mum and Dad get back, I've been scraping numbers and sums onto the dirty floor for hours. I wasn't lying when I told Arthur numbers are easy, they are. Easier than people anyway. I hear Mum trip over someone's legs and curse loudly. I rub out the numbers and lie still, so she thinks I'm asleep. My breathing stays regular, even though my heart pounds as her steps get closer. I can smell beer as she gets down on her knees and moves her face near mine.

"I hope you go to sleep and never wake up," she says.

I keep my eyes tight shut. She may know I'm awake, but there's no way I'm letting her see the tears bubbling under my lids.

Chapter 3

March 1906

Mum hasn't gone to the mill today. She hasn't got up at all. Is she dead? I feel a terrible guilt at the cheer that thought brings. Florrie comes running down the stairs and fills the kettle without speaking.

"Florrie?"

"Sorry, Ellen, didn't see you there."

"Is Mum alright?"

"Will be, she's having the baby, I think."

"Oh."

"Look, Ellen, I'm sorry, but I have to leave you to look after her. She's supposed to be winding today, and if I don't cover for her, she might lose the work."

"Please don't," I say, but I know there's little point arguing.

"It will be alright. I've asked Mrs Jeffries to call in often, and if there's any problems go next door, and they'll send for the doctor. Think you can manage that?"

I don't think I can, but I don't want Florrie to worry, so I nod my head.

"Good. Once this water boils, take her a cup of tea with some sugar. She'll need her strength, so get whatever she asks for. Sarah's going to drop round some bread on her break, and I'll get back as soon as I can."

Florrie gives me a quick kiss on the head, then before I know what's happening, she's grabbed her coat and is out the door. Bloody hell. A day with Mum is bad enough, but she'll likely be in even more of a lather than usual.

I take my time finishing my porridge. With more care than usual, I rinse my bowl and make the tea. When I can think of no more excuses, I trudge up the stairs. Mum has her blanket flung down below her knees and her massive belly sticks high in the air. Her grey hair lies like spindly fingers above her face, her skin is like ash.

"You alright, Mum?"

She turns her head and groans when she sees it's me she's left with. I hand her the hot tea and she takes it without a word of thanks. The cup wobbles in her hand and tea burns her arm. She must be bad, for she don't cry out. I kneel beside her and, after blowing on the tea, gently lift the cup to her dry lips. A quick nod of the head says she's drank enough, and I tuck my feet beneath me and smooth the blanket over her puffy legs.

"Anything I can get you?"

She shakes her head, cups her belly with a grimy hand and turns onto her side. Her face creases in pain and her body curls tight, like a beetle what's stranded on its back. Blobs of sweat have gathered on her forehead and I dab at them with a rag, whipping my arm back each time in case my fussing makes her mad. But her fight seems buried under pain; she lets me get on nursing without the usual slaps and scowls I'd get for being near her.

Mum's tatty nightdress is wet, damp half-moons beneath her arms and clinging fast to her back. I hover the back of my hand over her neck and let it rest. Her leathery skin feels cold, though there's sweat pouring from it. I rock back on my knees, wondering what the bloody hell I should do. Is it too soon to fetch help? Her face smooths and that tells me yes, it's too soon.

"I'll fetch some water," I say. Mum nods and shoos me away with a limp hand.

Out in the yard, I take big gulps of air. A breeze messes my hair. There's a fair bite to it, but winter is in its last moments and spring should gobble it up soon.

"How's it going in there?"

The voice belongs to Mrs Jeffries, leaning out of her downstairs window.

"Don't know."

"Well, how is she? How often is the pain coming?"

"Every ninety seconds."

Mrs Jeffries laughs. "And you can count that far, can you?"

She's laughing at me, thinks I'm a liar. I move closer to her window. "One, two, three, four, five, six, seven...." I get to fifty-six before she holds a hand up to stop me.

"Well, alright then. Ninety means it might not be much longer. When it gets to sixty, fetch me and I'll come and check on her."

"How long will it take to get to sixty?"

Mrs Jeffries laughs. "No way I can say, love. You kiddies have a mind of your own, keep us mummies guessing while you're on your way into the world. Mind you, her last few were as quick as shelling peas so I don't expect it will be much longer."

She closes her window, and I catch my reflection in the glass. Bloody hell, I look like the girls from Hawke's Yard. I forgot to brush my hair this morning and my fringe is sticking out here, there and everywhere. I hate to say it, but I know what they mean about me and Albert looking alike. I'll run next time Mum comes near me with the scissors. If I'm lucky, my hair will have left my ears for my chin by summer.

There's a splodge of dirt on my cheek and I'm going to rub it off, but I don't think Mrs Jeffries is keen on me using her window as a looking glass, so I head over to the pump. I wedge my shoulder beneath its handle, but the bloody thing won't budge. Mrs Jeffries must still be watching me, for her window opens once more.

"Need some help with that?"

I nod and in a few moments she's beside me, yanking the handle, sending mucky water bubbling into my bowl.

"What you getting the water for?"

"I reckon Mum must be thirsty. Also, she stinks."

"Ah, I see. Well, a wash down might do her good, but she'll need something stronger than that water to drink. Wait here."

She appears moments later carrying a glass bottle filled with brown liquid.

"What is it?" I ask, and Mrs Jeffries winks at me.

"Medicine. Give her a nice big glass full of that and the pain will feel better in no time." She winks again. I thank her and head back to the house.

I can't find no clean cups, so I rub one on my skirt till it looks alright and fill it to the top with liquid from Mrs Jeffries' bottle. I spill a bit on the stairs and crunch my boot over it a few times till it melts into the wood. No harm done.

Mum always tells us kiddies not to be greedy, but she breaks her own rules as soon as she gets a whiff of the cup and its stinking brownness. She near enough rips it from my hands and glugs it down in three gulps. There's dribbles running down her chin, but she don't care. The drink makes her dozy, and she chucks a sleepy smile my way. Still, every ninety seconds her face twists up all ghoul-like, and I know the pain is still there, but she don't seem to feel it as much now.

That fat belly of hers is moving up down, up down, up down. Was that a snore or a fart? I creep across to Albert's bed and lift the floorboard beside it. He thinks he's so clever with his little hidey hole, but we all know it's there. It's usually the thought of rats what keep me from digging around in it, but with nothing doing and time to kill, I could do with some fun. My fingertips settle on soft cotton and I grab the bag of marbles.

It's hard to play Ring Taw on your own, but I like pretending, so with my coat on I'm Ellen, without it I'll be Jeffrey. Jeffrey sounds like a right posh boy, and maybe I'll marry one of those one day. My nail scratches a circle in the dust and dirt covering the floorboards, and I gather up the marbles inside it. Me and Jeffrey take turns, flinging marbles into the circle to push the others out. Jeffrey wins, of course. Posh people always do, Mum says.

Mum groans, and I gather up the marbles and stuff them back under the boards. One, two, three, four... I count to seventy before the pain comes again.

"Do you want me to wash you down a bit?"

Mum nods and I pull the bowl and rag across the floor to her. There's not much room to work, with mattresses spread across the room, almost touching. I push Albert and Arthur's together, so I've got more space.

I've washed no one but myself before, and I don't want to see Mum's rude bits, so I work around her nightdress. Lift, pull, lift, pull. I start with her arms and legs. Her legs are rank, covered in spiders' webs in blue and purple that creep from bottom to top. Yuck. I hope my legs never look like that.

Her hands are rough and her nails dirty, but there's not much I can do about those. I wipe her arms so gently I'm barely touching. It must soothe her, for her face gets less creased, and she closes her eyes.

Her back is tricky. I can't pull the nightdress down far. I wipe around her neck and go as far down as I can. The wipe, rinse, squeeze, wipe, rinse, squeeze calms me too. I need to do under her arms. I lift one arm up and a mighty stink fills the room. Bloody hell. I turn my face away and wipe harder than I did in other places. Mum heaves herself round and I do the other side.

I count again. Still seventy.

"Thank you, Ellen. It's a long time since anyone took care of me."

Did she just thank me? I'm that surprised, all I can say in return is, "More tea?"

Mum nods and I carry the bowl filled with water and dirt downstairs. I tip it out in the drain and call over to Mrs Jeffries.

"Seventy now."

"Alright, love, won't be long. You know what to do."

The kettle squeals, and I'm making the tea when Sarah appears with a loaf of bread.

"How is she?"

I give her the latest, and she seems satisfied. "You staying?" I ask, and she shakes her head.

"Can't, only got half an hour till I need to be back. Keep doing what you're doing, Ellen," she says, then she's off.

I cut a hunk of bread from the loaf and look for something to put on it. All I can find is an empty jar that once held sugar. I lick my finger and run it against the bottom, gathering a fine layer of white as I go. My mouth is watering and screaming at me to keep it for myself, but I ignore my belly's grumbling and run my sugar-coated finger across Mum's bread.

Mum picks at the bread and seems more uncomfortable than before. I count again. Sixty. Sixty seconds between the groans and twisted face. I clatter down the stairs and out into the yard, banging on Mrs Jeffries' door.

"Sixty seconds," I say when she opens it.

Mrs Jeffries nods and follows me over to our house. I wait in the corner, while she lifts Mum's dress and checks around her private parts.

"Ellen, tell Johnny to fetch the doctor."

I run downstairs, into the yard, and bang on his door.

"Johnny? Johnny? Your mum says you're to fetch the doc."

Johnny opens the door and runs out so fast he almost knocks me to the ground.

"Thank you," I shout as he disappears into the alleyway and sprints out of the yard.

***

I'm holding Mum's hand and wiping her forehead when the doctor from the clinic arrives. I can't remember holding Mum's hand before. With mine the only hand on offer, she has no choice this time. Every now and then, she grips so tight, her nails leave dashes on my skin.

The doc is old, but his face is kind, and I trust him. He's wearing a woollen suit and tie that keep the cold of the room from reaching his bones. I like him even more when he says nothing about the smell, just starts taking shiny silver bits and bobs from a shiny leather case.

"We'll be fine here child. You go out and play."

"You sure you don't need me?"

He gives me a wide smile, all sparkly eyes, and straight white teeth.

"What's your name, child?"

"Ellen."

"Well, Ellen, it seems you've done as good a job as any of my nurses, but I can assure you your mother is in safe hands. Have a break, I'm sure you've earned one."

I want to hug this kind man, for rescuing me from Mum, and for... well... just being kind. Outside in the yard, I consider my options. Where will the truants be today? Hawke's Yard would be the most likely place, but there's old men there what scare me. They sit all grizzled and grim on battered chairs outside battered houses. Baccy has turned their fingers and teeth yellow, and they hack up globs of slime from deep inside before spewing it onto your shoes if you're not careful.

I decide to wander along Oak Street and try my luck, see what yard's got the best doing. Right down Oak Street I go till I get to Dial's Yard. There's not likely to be many kiddies in this one, but I like to look at the big old house there and imagine the fine people what once lived in it. It leans over the street, covered in timber planks and grey plaster. One end is crumbling, and it don't look safe enough to go in. Instead, I peep through the broken window and see the finely carved walls where people once had posh dinners with plenty of meat.

Saw Mill Yard, Sun Yard, Greenland Fishery Yard, Betts Yard, Unicorn Yard, all nothing doing, no kiddies what would welcome me anyhow. I poke my head into Dolphin Yard, but there's a woman in there fiddling with a bucket and drains. She has a proper skirt on her bottom half, but on her top, she has a thin blouse and one of her boobies is poking out. She should probably be in the madhouse. I'm not hanging round long enough to find out.

I run past Key and Castle Yard. Arthur told me the landlord of the pub there murdered his wife and cut her into tiny pieces. He said her ghost still roams the yard, wailing and banging on doors. Bugger that. I'll not be meeting her today.

I find myself playmates at Horton's Yard. My friend Alice what lives here, is at school, but her little sisters are happy to let me join their skipping. It's posh in Horton's Yard. Some houses have front gardens, some even have flowers in the gardens. There's even a bloody tap. A tap! What I'd give for a tap, no more heaving myself up under a rusty pump what more times than not sticks fast. It's clean here too, front steps painted white, windows with clear glass in every house. Still stinks like all the other yards, though.

The girls disappear into their house. I think Alice's mum likes me, but not enough to let me inside, so I don't try my luck. Two boys let me join in playing with their spinning top and the sun is slinking down before I say my goodbyes.

My steps get quicker the closer I come to our yard- Queen Caroline's. I don't think no queen ever lived here, can't imagine queens like sharing a privy or working a pump. I'm expecting a new brother or sister to be waiting for me, but I find Florrie, Sarah and Ethel round the table, drinking tea in silence. There's a scream from the upstairs room.

"She's not still going, is she?"

"Fraid so," Sarah says.

"Is the doc still here?"

"Yes."

"I might pop up and say hello."

Florrie grabs my arm and pulls me back into the room.

"Best not. Things aren't looking good up there. Dad and the boys have gone to the Bess O Bedlam to get away from it all."

"How long will it take?"

"No idea," says Sarah. "But if it goes into the night, the doc will cost us half a crown, which we can ill afford."

Florrie pours me tea and I settle myself cross-legged on the floor beside her. She hands me a crust of bread and I gobble it down. Sarah tries to distract us with talk of her wedding, but time drags and drags.

"Why don't you try to get some sleep, girls?" says Sarah. "I'll stay up and tend to Mum if she needs me. It'll be good practice for when it's my turn." She runs a hand up and down her swollen belly. "Best sleep down here though, I doubt you'll get much rest with all the squawking going on up there."

Me and Florrie creep up the stairs. The doc don't even look up when we walk through the room. He's taken off his jacket and rolled his shirt sleeves to the elbows. Now and then, he runs his arm across his forehead before feeling Mum's belly once more.

With arms full of blankets, me and Florrie tiptoe back across the room. Once downstairs, we make our beds up against the far wall. The last thing we want is Dad and the boys treading on us when they get back from the pub. I don't expect to sleep well with the howls and hollers coming through the floorboards, but the day's events must have caught up with me, for I'm asleep in no time.

Chapter 4

March 1906

There's a heaviness in the air that makes the hairs on my arms tin-soldier-straight as soon as I wake. What is it? Sleep is blurring my eyes, so I give them a rough scrub with my palms. I remember now; I slept downstairs. Maybe that's why it's so quiet? Boots slipped on, I take the stairs two at the time. The baby must be here by now. But there's no baby held to Mum's chest, or lying in the bed beside her. It's just the girls here. Florrie, Sarah, Ethel, Maria all sat round Mum's bed talking in whispers.

Bloody hell, what's that? A drawer is out of the old dresser, the only piece of furniture we own apart from the table and chairs downstairs. Something's lying in it.

"No," says Florrie, rushing towards me and holding me back. I push her arm away and drop to my knees beside the drawer. There's something in it, something ugly, scary. Eyes, nose, mouth; it even has hair, but the creature don't seem human. Its skin is waxy and grey, wrinkled and torn. Stripes of sticky blood run like ribbons from its hair to its chin.

"Meet Maude," Mum says and lets out an angry laugh. Why is she laughing? The others are grim faced, not in on the joke.

"Come away, Ellen." Florrie's words reach my ears like they're smothered by blankets. The room is blurry, and everyone seems a long way away. I try to stand, but my legs slip from me and Florrie tucks her arms under mine to hold me up.

"Had enough of a gawp, have you?" Mum's voice is hard, but wobbly. She's propped herself up on an elbow, her straggly hair unpinned and hanging across her face. She blows a strand away and glares at me with her little button eyes. I want to ask what happened, why the kind doc couldn't save Maude, but I don't dare. Mum's eyes turn to the baby and her shoulders scrunch up like she's going to cry.

"Come downstairs, Ellen."

Florrie's voice couldn't be more different from Mum's. It's soft as cotton, like a cuddle, and tells me she loves me with every word spoken. Her hands are rough from winding, but her long fingers curl around mine and she leads me back down the stairs.

Florrie don't go to the mill today. She stays with me, distracting me from all that has been and all that will come. Somehow, she makes the day bearable, and time passes quickly. At nightfall, I glance to the room above. The baby is still here. I thought she'd be away by now. Florrie says we have to keep her with us till morning when Mum's well enough to take her to the morgue on Barrack Street.

"Want to sleep down here again tonight?" she asks.

"Yes. Will you stay with me?"

"Course I will," Florrie says and wraps me up in her arms.

***

Last night I slept badly. Not 'cause of the hard floorboards beneath me, or the cold that filled the room once the fire died, but 'cause of the dead baby. All night I kept remembering that dead baby lying in the drawer, just above my head. I couldn't get her candlewax skin from my mind, however hard I tugged at the memory. I 'spose it will stay with me forever. A tiny body, who only got dealt a tiny life of one or two seconds. One, two... those are small numbers, too small for all the effort of making it into the world. I would've liked a little sister. I could've cared for her the way Florrie cares for me.

There's a clattering on the stairs and Mum, Sarah and Maria come into the room. Mum is unsteady on her feet, clutching her belly and wincing with each step. Maria holds a carpetbag to her chest, and I know it's filled with dead baby. I curl back further into the room and wrap my arms around myself to still the shaking. I don't want no one knowing I'm scared. *Keep that bag away from me, please God, let them keep it away from me.*

I look down at the floor, waiting for them to leave.

"Get your coat, we han't got all day," says Mum, and when I look up, it's me she's talking to. Bloody hell, why can't they leave me here? I don't want to be near the baby. Florrie hands me my coat and takes my hand in hers. My feet stay stuck to the spot. Florrie tugs at my hand. It's a gentle tug, but one that lets me know I have no choice but to follow her.

There's a fierce wind whipping its way round the yard, carrying with it dirty pieces of snow. Florrie pulls me closer, and we keep our heads down, fighting the wind. We make our way along Oak Street, coats flying behind us, snow stinging our eyes. Sarah spots a bus and holds out her arm. The horses don't seem to enjoy the weather much neither. They whinny and shake their manes to scare off the snowflakes. Their eyes glare at us for making them stop. Maybe they think the flakes are white flies?

The sensible folk have gathered themselves on the inside benches, so there's no room for us. Me and Florrie climb the curling stairs to the top deck. We look down and see Mum, face screwing up with each step, taking an age to lift her legs, one after the other. The conductor is getting impatient.

"Hurry it up there, love, it's not the weather to be dallying."

"Bugger off," says Mum, and the conductor goes back inside.

Maria only has one foot on the steps when the horses move. We lean over the railings, praying she can hold her nerve and not drop the baby. She grips the rail tight with one hand, bag in the other, and falls into Sarah on reaching the top. We all sit down, and I keep my back to Maria and the baby. I know it's all closed up, but I keep imagining a little arm or foot poking out and I can't bear to turn around.

I want to look out at the streets, for this is the furthest I've gone from the yard, but the snow don't let up. It's coming down in thick chunks, settling on my coat before soaking in and freezing my bones. My coat is on the small side and the cuffs are above my wrists, so I sit on my pink hands to stop the cold setting in. The roofs we pass are turning white, the bus juddering and skidding this way and that on the frozen ground. I need a wee, but don't want to bother Mum.

"You alright?" says Florrie.

I nod, and a drip falls from my nose. Florrie snuggles me up to her, wrapping her own coat around the both of us. Icy flakes soak our hair, snow sitting on Florrie's head like a nightcap. With my cheek pressed into her neck, her breath warms my skin. I close my eyes and dream of a warm fire, steaming cup of tea in my hands.

The bus moves on down narrow streets, wide streets, streets where houses sit tight together like matchsticks, streets where grand buildings lean over the road, warm light spilling from big windows. Now and then we turn a corner, or pass a gap in the buildings, and I spot the river. Wide grey water follows us on our miserable journey. A bell jangles.

"Get a move on," says Sarah, and I see her, Mum, Maria and Ethel heading towards the stairs. Maria gives the carpet bag a light shake to rid it of snow before pressing it to her chest once more. The purple lines on Mum's face have disappeared beneath a blanket of red, her beady eyes looking out from it like raisins. I have to feel sorry for her as she shuffles back down the stairs. She must hurt bad.

Stepping off the bus, I see we're beside the river. The wind has whipped away the smell and jiggles the grey water into little curly lumps. It goes on forever; like a shoelace, winding round the streets, separating us in the yards from the money of the city. Ethel yanks my elbow, and I follow her down closer to the water. There's some right big ships here, 'Wherries', Sarah says they're called. She whispers it, so Mum don't notice I'm distracted from the job at hand.

The snow is laying thick and already reaches above the toes of our boots. Our sorry little bunch leave a trail of footsteps as Mum leads us down to a grey building. There's a thick wooden door with a brass knocker that she raps three times. A man appears, dressed in black, from his top hat down to his shiny shoes. Maria steps forward, undoes the buttons of the carpetbag and opens it for him to see. He nods in understanding and opens the door wider for us to go in.

Before I can step through, Mum holds an arm out to stop me and Florrie getting past.

"Wait out here," she says, and signals for the man to close the door. As he does, a stench wafts out, filling my nostrils and leaking down my throat.

I turn to Florrie for an explanation, but she shrugs her shoulders and begins searching the grey stone walls of the morgue for any corner what might give us shelter. I sigh, and my breath pours out in a wispy cloud. I do it again, chasing the ball of breath away with my hand.

"Come here, Ellen."

Florrie has found a stretch of wall facing the river where the wind is less biting. I turn my face to the sky, where cobble-coloured clouds race above my head and the air is full with falling snow. Across the river, snow covers everything white. Next to us in the boatyard, white lumps of boat lie beneath masts that point like needles into the sky.

"I need a wee."

"Well, there's no one about on this horrid day, so fill your boots. Or rather, don't fill your boots or Mum will go mad." Florrie chuckles and the sound bounces off the stone beside us, chasing away some lurking ghosts, I hope.

With my skirt held up to my waist, I crouch down and feel a wave of relief as yellow burns through the snow. I give my bum a shake and watch as steam dances up into the air. A few drops land on my boot, but the snow will see to that.

"It's spooky here," I say. Florrie nods and shivers. "You reckon there's ghosts around here?"

"Well, there's enough dead bodies nearby," she says. My face must look scared 'cause she keeps talking. "But I don't reckon they come out till it's dark. We'll be alright here for a bit."

We don't have to wait long. There's a creak as the door opens and a soft thud of footsteps. We head back to see Mum and the girls walking out in the snow. Maria still carries the carpetbag, but it's crumpled now, empty of baby and sadness. I reckon she should chuck the bag in the river, but she clutches it as tight as she did before.

"What happens to the baby now?" I whisper to Florrie.

"Don't know. Maybe it will be burned or chucked in the river."

I shiver. Neither of those sound like a good way to go.

Chapter 5

April 1906

It's funny how a few weeks ago the yard was covered by snow, but now the sun is trying to sneak through any gaps in the roofs it can find. Yesterday, when I was playing down in Horton's Yard, I saw little green spindles poking out of the ground. My friend Alice said they'll turn into flowers soon. She reckons it's a sign of spring. About time too. This winter has dragged its feet too long for my liking.

Everything seems more cheerful now. Even Mum. She's not happy Sarah is leaving us, but the wedding excitement has reached even her miserable bones. Not long to go now. Just as well, Sarah's belly's blowing up like a pig's bladder that might burst if she's not careful.

"You coming?" calls Alice, standing at the entrance to the yard. She won't come no further in. Her mum's warned her to stay away, stay in her posh yard with its little garden and white front step. I don't blame her. I'd swap places with her in a heartbeat, as long as Florrie could come too.

"Coming," I say, and shove my feet into my boots.

I've been going to school more since the baby. Much better out of the house than in. I thought the teacher would be pleased, but she don't like my joking around, says I get the other kids in a lather. The kiddies are glad I'm back, more fun when I'm there, they say.

Alice has a satchel slung over her shoulder like a proper lady. I don't know what's inside, she won't tell me. I bet there's nothing in it, bet it's just for show. We walk along Oak Street together and through the iron gates into the playground. The teacher sees me and folds her arms.

"Will it be a good day today, Ellen?" she asks.

What am I supposed to say to that? Surely, it's up to her if it's a good day or not? I'm not the one stood in front of the bloody class! I nod my head, then run away, giggling. A gaggle of kiddies gather round me, and I get to choose what we play. Today I pick doctors and nurses. I'm the doctor, though Billy says girls can't be doctors and I should be a nurse. I pinch the skin on his arm so hard he runs off crying. No one else moans I'm a girl doctor. I make the kiddies lie on the ground and go around fixing them up. Alice is the nurse, and she helps me. I'm halfway through helping a baby out into the world when the bell rings and we have to line up, girls on one side, boys the other.

Me and Alice find our desks at the back of the room, hers in front of mine.

"It's not right," I whisper to her.

"Shush," she says over her shoulder.

"Why do the poshies get the front seats?"

Alice ignores me, so I reach over and flick her back.

"Alice? S'not fair, is it? They get all the good stuff."

Alice reaches a leg back and tries to kick my shin, but she misses. She might not say nothing, but I know it makes her as cross as me. Her yard *is* posh, but not enough to earn herself a front seat.

Teacher has noticed my whispering. "One more peep out of you, Ellen, and you'll be off to the headmaster."

Does she think she scares me? That old goat in his smoke-filled office don't scare me neither. Just as well, 'cause I'm in that office by noon. He makes me stand by his desk and moves around it so he's towering above me.

"Back again so soon, Ellen? And what have you done this time?"

I shudder when he speaks. His voice sounds like a hiss and bits of spit fly from his mouth as he talks. His face is shiny and his moustache twitches like a caterpillar when he's cross. It's twitching now.

"Miss said I didn't do no work."

"And why would she think that?"

"Cause she's a bloody liar, that's why."

The caterpillar on his face is wriggling round like nobody's business. His greasy skin has turned red, and he keeps smoothing down his thin hair.

"Show me your slate," he says.

I hold my empty slate out in front of him. "I did the sums in my head," I say.

He peers down at me. "I will not tolerate lying in my school, Ellen," he says.

I don't know how he gets the sound out 'cause he clamps his teeth together as he talks.

"I wasn't lying, sir, I did 'em in my head. It's Miss what's a liar, not me."

"I WILL NOT TOLERATE LYING OR INSOLENCE IN MY SCHOOL, YOUNG LADY."

Bloody hell, he made me jump out of my skin. I know what's coming, so before he can even say it, I lay my arms out on his desk, palms facing up. I don't need to look to know the cupboard that creaks open is the one where he keeps his cane.

For once, I don't count. I don't want to know how many times he's hit me with that bloody thing. When he's done, my palms are red raw. My skin may weep, but my eyes are dry. He's expecting me to cry. I don't.

"Don't let me see you in here again, Ellen," he says.

"No, sir," I say, then just for good measure I give him a big grin before running out of the room. That will show him.

***

I keep out of trouble all afternoon. Under the table I sort through the cigarette cards I pinched from Arthur's jacket and keep my hands busy, and mouth shut. Alice's been ignoring me since lunch, afraid I'll get her into bother. I should be more careful, for her mum won't let us be friends if I drag her into trouble one more time. And I like Alice. I like her yard too.

The bell rings and we rush out, ignoring the teacher's cries to walk, not run. Our little gang gathers by the gates and plans out the rest of the afternoon. Sometimes as many as eight of us gather and head onto the streets 'up to no good' some say. Today there's only four; me, Alice, Jack and Samuel.

"I reckon we should sneak a look in the Malthouse," I say.

"How about the graveyard at St Martins?" says Jack, but Alice shakes her head.

"I know something better than all that," says Sam, and beckons us to follow him. He leads us out of the schoolyard and heads up Oak Street.

"Where we going?" I ask, but he winks and says nothing. I tug at his sleeve. "Tell me where we're going, Samuel."

"Don't like surprises, Ellen?"

"I don't trust you to think of good surprises, that's all," I say.

It's usually me in charge and I don't like Samuel playing boss. Maybe I should give him a pinch, like what I did to Billy. But then I'd have to go home, and it's too nice an afternoon to be stuck at home or in the yard. I hang at the back of the group, dragging my feet.

"Stop sulking," says Sam.

The little bugger's laughing at me. He'd better watch it, or I'll punch him in the nose.

"We're here," he says, leading us into Unicorn Yard.

"So, the surprise is your yard, is it? That's a rubbish surprise," I say, turning to leave.

"You don't want to see what Dad's got in the shed then?"

I turn round. I can't help myself. We don't have sheds in our yard, so I've no idea what could be in there. "It'd better be bloody good," I tell him.

"Oh, it is, you'll see."

We sit on Samuel's step as he goes in the shed and closes the door behind him. There's banging and the sound of metal objects being knocked over.

"You alright in there?" says Alice.

"Need any help?" says Jack.

"Nah, be out in a tick," comes Samuel's muffled voice.

The shed door flings open and we all stand gawping as he appears with a shiny bicycle.

"Bloody hell," I say.

"Told you it was a good surprise," he says.

"Whose is it?"

"Dad's. The shop's been doing well, so he got this. Like it?"

"Not half," says Jack. "Give us a go."

He grabs the bicycle from Sam's hands and tries to climb up. He falls off three times before he gets himself on by leaning it up against a wall. His feet just about reach the pedals. They've gone round two circles before the bicycle wobbles and he's on the cobbles. Alice rushes over to him, still playing the nurse. She pulls a hanky from her pocket and dabs it against Jack's grazed knee.

"I thought we could go up Mousehold," says Sam, and we all gawp again.

"You know how to get there? You know how to ride that thing?"

"Course I do. Dad showed me. You keen?"

We all nod. Sam tries to get us all on, but it's impossible and after several times trying, we all have cuts and bruises for our trouble.

"I reckon I can get Ellen and Alice on here. Jack, you run alongside."

Jack looks disappointed but nods his head at Sam's idea.

Both boys hold the bike still while Alice perches above the back wheel and I climb onto the handlebars. Sam's bum won't reach the seat, so he swings his leg up and over and stands on the pedals.

"Alright, Jack, let go," he says.

The bike wobbles in all directions over the cobbles, and I'm sure we'll fall off again. But Sam gets the hang of it and before we know it, we're out of the yard. It's a fair old way to Mousehold. Sam says he takes fifteen minutes most times, but today we take forty. Sam says it's 'cause he's got two great heifers either end of his bike. Cheeky bugger. Twice, me and Alice jump off when Sam's panting gets loud enough for us to know we're not welcome. The downhills are the most fun.

I'm pleased I nabbed the front, for I get the wind in my hair and a fine view of the streets we pass through.

We reach a scrubby patch of land that goes on forever. Sam tells us we're here and shoves his bike behind a gorse bush so it don't get pinched. He leads us up a hill and we're all red in the face by the time we reach the top.

"Turn around," he says, and we do as we're told.

Bloody hell. I've never seen nothing like it. The sun is bright, so we rest our hands above our eyes to block it. Jack lets out a whistle. I would too if I knew how. We can see the whole of Norwich from up here. Rooftops and trees, a giant spire stretching to heaven.

"Blimey, looks better up here than what it does down there," I say, and the others agree.

I take such a deep breath; my shoulders almost reach my ears. The air's different here, it tastes nice in my mouth. The stink of the river's too far from us and the soot from chimneys has long disappeared. I lie down on the grass and stretch my arms and legs out; it's comfier than my bed, I can tell you!

"Get your lazy bum off the ground," says Sam. "It was me doing the hard work to get here, not you!"

He reaches a hand down and I grab it, letting him heave me from my comfy spot.

"I reckon we should play..."

Sam interrupts me before I can finish. "Shut up, bossy britches. It was me that got us here, not you. Today I choose what we do."

I want to argue with him but know I'll never find my way home without him, so I'd better not. He picks Cowboys and Indians. Him and Jack get to be cowboys, me and Alice have to be the Indians. Alice sulks for a while 'cause she wanted to play Mums and Babies, but I don't mind. I won't admit it to the boys, but I reckon Cowboys and Indians is more exciting than Mums and Babies.

Jack takes off his jersey to mark their base, and I use my boots to mark ours. There's no rules about where the base must be, so I find a tree with a thick trunk and shimmy up there. I love it up in the tree, it's like a proper den with a giant green roof. I could happily sleep up here, the trunk is that wide. Alice int happy, for she takes an age to get up to the branches. We sit and wait; the boys have disappeared, and I'm growing suspicious.

"Aaaaaah!"

The boys run out of the gorse, twisting long grass stalks, and pelting us with the heads that fly off them. They try to climb up our tree, but I use my feet as weapons, knocking them down with my bare toes. My nails are long and sharp, good for scratching. They can't get past my jabs and tell us we're cheating.

"You never gave us no rules," I say. But that makes them more cross.

"If our bullets hit you, you're out," they say, and I laugh. I'm good at ducking and diving.

Alice gets hit straight away. She tries to lie and says it missed, but we all saw. Once she's made it down the tree, the boys march her over to their base. They pretend to tie her hands up and tell her not to escape. Jack comes back, jerking his head this way and that while my feet kick out at him. The boys play a good game. While Jack has me distracted, Sam climbs up the other side and gets to our base. It's time to admit defeat, but I've learned my lesson. I'll win next time.

Chapter 6

May 1906

"What time is it?" I ask Florrie, as she shakes my shoulder and pulls blankets off my bed.

"Four. Time to get up or someone'll spot us getting the blossoms."

Stealing the blossoms is what she means. Today's the day Sarah gets wed and Mum said she'd sort the flowers. By *sort* she means sending me, Florrie and Ethel out to sneak what we can from other people's gardens. And she don't just mean blossoms neither. Whatever we can lay our hands on, she said. We'll have to go a good way from the yards, as nothing much grows around here, except in the churchyard, and it wouldn't do to take from there.

Ethel's waiting for us downstairs and hands us each a cuppa when we appear. She don't look best pleased about our morning task. Goes against every goody-two-shoes bone in her body, I'll bet.

"Come on, let's get this over with," she says, downing the dregs of her tea and wiping the cup with a rag.

We pull on our coats, for although spring is here, this early it will be chilly out.

"Where to?" I ask, and Ethel points away from the river.

"I've seen some big houses up that way, so's probably our best bet. Hopefully, everyone will still be in their beds."

We pass rows of brand-new terraces with neat front gardens. By the end of the fifth row our basket is ablaze with pink, purple and yellow. My gut twists at the thought of the poor women who tended these flowers, expecting to gaze on them all summer long. Ethel's worse than me, blubbing away about cops and robbers. Florrie just keeps walking, eager to be done as quick as she can.

We're about to turn back when I spot a huge red house. How one house can have so many windows, I don't know. A long brick wall runs in a curl behind it, and I spot blossom-covered trees poking out above.

"Look," I say, pointing to the wall. "I reckon I could get over there."

"Don't be daft, Ellen," says Ethel.

"We still need blossom," I say, "and from what I can see, there's plenty there for the taking."

Florrie wanders over to the wall and stands on her tiptoes, inspecting the bricks.

"She can't climb it herself, but I reckon if we give her a leg up it's do-able."

"You're both as barmy as each other," says Ethel.

"Come on," says Florrie, taking my hand. She looks behind her to where Ethel is pinned to the spot. "Ethel, if you help us, we'll be done much quicker. If you stand there like a statue, it will take longer, and they might catch us."

Ethel huffs and puffs as she walks over to us. She's glancing up and down the road, but there's no one about and she seems to relax a little. There's a branch resting on the wall above, pink and white blossoms just out of reach.

"Here," says Florrie, cupping her hands and making a step.

Good thing I'm so little. Florrie lifts my foot easily and pushes me right up to the top of the wall. I perch myself on top, one leg dangling either side, and begin breaking off branches, passing them down to Florrie, who hands them to Ethel to put in our basket.

"I reckon we've got enough," says Ethel. But there's an explosion of petals just beyond my reach and I'm sure if I stretch a little more, I'll get to them.

"Hold your horses," I say, grabbing hold of a branch and pulling it toward me. Just... a bit... further. Bloody fool I am. I lose my balance, don't I? My hands grip the branches as my legs slide off the wall, but the wood is too thin and snaps in two, sending me hurtling to the ground. I sit in a crumpled heap, hearing Ethel's sobs from the street. Well, my hands are alright, just a few scratches. There's scrapes down my legs, but they're not too wobbly to stand on.

I glance behind me as a light comes on in one window. "Florrie," I hiss. "Florrie, quick, help me up, I reckon someone's coming."

Ethel must have given Florrie a leg up, for her head pops up above the wall. Leaning over, she holds her hands out to me.

"Careful, Florrie, you could fall too."

"S'alright, Ethel's got a good hold of my feet. Take my hands."

I grab her hands and shimmy up the wall till I've got a good grip on the triangle tiles at the top. I'm almost over when we hear the shout.

"You there, you are trespassing on private property. Come here and explain yourself or I shall call the constable."

I jump down beside Florrie and Ethel.

"Run," I say, and we sprint back through the streets, angry shouts bouncing off walls behind us. Ethel drags us into a yard, and we catch our breath. The shouts have stopped, we're safe. Ethel won't let us go until she's poked her head round the yard entrance to make sure the coast is clear. She gives a thumbs up and we make our way to the street. There's a trail of colour from where we've come. But although it's tempting to pick up our lost treasure, the risk of getting caught int worth it. We've got plenty left in our basket to go around. Mum should be happy enough.

***

Back at home, the copper is in front of the fire, big pans of water sitting above the flames, heating for Sarah's scrub. She'll have a job to fit herself and her belly in that tub. We lay the flowers out on the table and the room fills with brightness. I've never seen our house look so cheerful. Mum gives us a smile when she comes in and sees our haul.

"Good girls," she says. "No trouble?"

"No, Mum," says Ethel, blushing and shooting looks at me and Florrie that tell us to keep our gobs shut.

"Grab yourselves a bite to eat. Sarah's first up for a bath, but I want the rest of you in there too so don't be disappearing on me."

"No Mum," we say.

Sarah don't like us hanging around while she's in the nud, so we eat our breakfast out in the yard. Ethel nabs the front step so me and Florrie find a bucket to sit on. A window opens in the house beside us, and Mrs Jeffries pokes her head out.

"Got your dresses in here when you're ready."

"Thanks, Mrs Jeffries, but Mum wants us scrubbed first," says Ethel.

"Pop in when you're done then, love."

"Will do."

I'm excited about my dress. Sarah's chap Syd gave Mrs Jeffries a few bob to make us all matching dresses. They'll be cobbled together from Syd's mum's old curtains, but Mrs Jeffries is a whizz with a needle and thread so no one will ever know.

It takes an age before it's my turn in the tub. Littlest goes last, that's the rule. Stupid rule if you ask me. Mum collects the scum from the top with a jug and chucks it out onto the cobbles. I whip my clothes off and jump in. Mum curses when I spill water on the floor, but it's hard not to. I've no idea how the others fit in here, for it's a squeeze for me and I'm little.

Mum hands me some lye and I give myself a good old scrub. Even my hair. I'm quick about it, for the water has lost its warmth by the time I get a go at it. Mum's not about to heat no more. It was enough effort dragging bowl after bowl from the pump the first time. In and out, that's the way to do it. No dallying.

Mum makes me stand up in the tub till most of the water's dripped off me. Then, I give myself a good old shake.

"You're not a dog," says Mum.

"How am I s'posed to dry myself then?" I ask, and get a clip round the ear for my cheek.

Mum drags her fingers through my wet hair, so it dries flat. It's that tangly, I worry she'll pull most of it from my head. Despite my wriggles and squeals, she tugs just as hard. She's eager to make a good impression at the church, I reckon. Us Hardys aren't churchgoers, and I've only heard her use God's name as a curse word, but I s'pose she wants to avoid hell as much as the rest of us.

Alice took me to Sunday school with her once. It was alright until the priest came in at the end. He was too friendly with the kiddies for my liking, took me into a back room and held me on his knee. His hand tried to make its way up my dress, so I bit his shoulder till he yelped like a puppy dog. I never told Alice what happened in that room, and I never told her why I wouldn't go back there. Probably not all kiddies get away like I did, poor sods. We're all so scared of the Scavengers, but it's the men in fine robes what read from the bible we should watch out for.

"Ellen, stop your bloody daydreaming and help me empty the tub," says Mum.

Between us and our pots and pans, it don't take long to chuck the water outside into the drain. Mum don't say much, but she's twitchy, rushing round, button eyes darting this way and that. She must've had her bath last night, for her hair's not so greasy, and her sunken cheeks are free of grime. She don't get no new clothes today, but Mrs Morrison is lending her a smart hat and Dad's got her a pair of heeled shoes from the factory.

"You girls ready yet?" calls Mrs Jeffries as we're swilling the last of the water from the copper.

"All done here," says Mum. "I'll send Ellen over for them. Ta, Maggie."

"No bother, Mary, your girls will look a picture in their finery."

"Some of them will," says Mum, cocking her head in my direction and giving Mrs Jeffries a wince.

"You're a cheeky bugger, Mary. Your Ellen is as pretty as a petal. Come on, love, I've got the dresses in the kitchen."

I leave Mum and head through Mrs Jeffries' open door. It's funny what a difference a window makes, and a small one at that. All that light makes everything more shiny, roomier, cleaner. Her kitchen's not much bigger than ours, but there's an easy chair in one corner and enough wooden chairs for all the family to sit. It's spotless in here, not a speck of dust to be found, however much my finger traces the mantel to find one.

"You got clean hands?" Mrs Jeffries asks.

I hold out my hands and she inspects them. "Humph," she says and takes me over to a bowl of water. She plonks my hands beneath the water and scrubs my nails with a tiny brush. She dries them on a cloth and inspects them once more.

"Much better," she says. "Now can I trust you with my hard work?" I nod. "Hold your arms out then."

I do as I'm told, and she covers my arms with layers of pressed fabric. It's heavy, but I keep my arms still.

"Now, you be careful getting those back to your place, we don't want no dirt getting on them before the wedding, do we?"

"No, Mrs Jeffries."

"Good girl. Now shoo, it's only an hour till you need to be at the church."

***

Me, Florrie, Ethel and Maria stand outside Mrs Jeffries' door, twirling round. Her hands cover her mouth, and she has tears in her eyes.

"Oh, girls, pretty as a picture you are!"

"Thanks, Mrs Jeffries," we all say.

We're proud as punch of our dresses. Red roses with green stems swirl over our bellies and arms, floating and flapping around our legs. I spin round to show how far the skirt sticks out and Florrie catches me when I stagger round dizzy.

"Better for dresses than curtains," says Mrs Jeffries. "With that much swing to them, they can't have kept out many draughts."

"Ta, Maggie, you've done a fine job with this lot," says Mum, coming from our house and wobbling on her heels.

"You don't look so bad yourself."

She's right, Mum looks nice. It's not her clothes, it's her smile. Mum don't often smile. It'd be a better smile if she had teeth in her mouth, but we're all pleased she's happy. Means an easier day for us.

Sarah comes out, all lace, ivory, and belly.

"Oh, my!" squeals Mrs Jeffries, rushing over and flinging herself on Sarah.

"Watch out, Maggie, you don't want to be wetting her with your tears," says Mum.

Mrs Jeffries dabs her eyes and holds Sarah at arm's length. "What a beauty," she says.

Sarah does look a beauty. Smiling, carrying blossom in her hands, no one would guess she comes from the yards.

Dad and the boys step out of the house, hair slicked down, shirts pressed. We make our way across the road to the church. I shiver as we walk through the porch. The air's warmth don't reach through the thick walls of St Martin's. The light do though. It makes a coloured carpet for us to walk down, shining through the bright pictures of Jesus and his pals built high into the church walls. I try not to step on the reds, blues and greens, but it's hard not to. We all gather at the front, Syd's family grim-faced at his marrying down in the world.

I stand at the back of our group, holding my posy of other people's flowers. Before you can blink, it's all over. I reckon it takes Dad longer to cut a piece of leather than it does to wed. Sarah and Syd walk out hand in hand and we traipse behind.

How Mrs Jeffries and Mrs Morrison turned the yard round so quick is a mystery, for when we step through the alley-way it's transformed. All the neighbours have brought their tables out and they fill the length of the yard from top to bottom. Plates of food cover the tables. Where they got it all from, I can't say. Kiddies run round squealing in excitement. There's a cheer as we come through the alley, and people rush forward to congratulate the bride and groom.

Syd's mum and dad look shifty among the yard folk, but his brother John mucks in, joking around with Robert, Arthur and Albert, pint in hand. I catch Maria eyeing him up. She's not best pleased Sarah beat her down the aisle and seems determined to right that wrong.

Chapter 7

October 1906

I wriggle free of blankets and stretch my arm to the wall. A tiny movement, but one that leaves me breathless. My fingertips are almost there, I pull one arm with the other, grit my teeth, but those tips tease me, dusting the wall then pulling back. I collapse in a heap. *If at first you don't succeed, try, try, again.* My teacher's words ringing in my ears, I give it a go. This time I shuffle further up the bed and can hold a flat palm to the damp stone. Cool stone brings a bit of comfort, so I keep my hand there till I've caught my breath.

Beneath my mattress, I've hidden the pebble Florrie got me. Smooth end between my fingers and ragged edge pointing out, I chalk a line through the chink in the wall. Sixteen. That's sixteen days gone, eighty-four to go. Hundred-day cough is what I've got. I'm not sure I'll last the full hundred, but the lines on the wall keep me going. Each day a victory. Two fingers up to the Grim Reaper. He comes to me in my dreams, but his face mixes with Mum's and I can't tell which is which. Mum would blow her top if she knew I'd carved one hundred scratches in the wall, but it's so dingy in this corner I don't s'pose she'll ever find out. I add a little cross above my line. Five. Five days since I've had grub.

My bed's a bundle in the corner and the others have pulled theirs as far from me as they can. Mum has made Florrie sleep by the door. She's the only one not had the cough, and she's too good a worker for Mum to risk her getting sick.

No one's allowed near me, only Mum. She says it's saving the others from sickness, but with the hours she works, it means most days are spent alone. She checks on me twice a day but she's a rubbish nurse. Alice could do a better job than Mum. I know I shouldn't, but I cough her way in the hope she'll catch sickness, have it rattle her body the way it rattles mine. Then she might understand, and at least I'd have some company. She keeps me watered, but it's from the pump and between the coughing and spluttering from my arse, my belly aches like hell.

***

Thirty seconds. Thirty seconds is all I need. Hold my breath for that long and I can sneak past the others without being spotted. My belly growls like an angry dog, and I shove fingers into the hollow space in my middle to make it stop. Don't work.

Bugger. I can feel the tickle rising in my throat. I squeeze my mouth shut and hold my breath till my eyes are watering but it's no good. Just in time I fling myself face down on the bed and the grimy blankets soak up the coughs and splutters. Between coughs I suck in air, making a squealing noise that scares me. Thank God Florrie's not beside me. She's a useless liar. Even when she tells me I'll be better soon, the lines on her forehead tell me the truth and those lines get even deeper when she hears my coughs and splutters.

My breathing gets more regular, and I know it's now or never. I wipe my damp face with my sleeve and take as deep a breath as I can. Go. Lucky I'm a good hopscotcher, for you need to be nimble to pick through the tangle of feet on the floor. At the end of the room, I'm careful to skip the last floorboard, I've learned from experience its squeak is enough to wake the room. I take the stairs quicker than I'd like, but I can feel the tickle rising again and know my time's running out.

I've only just made it downstairs when the coughing bubbles up again. Bundles of nightdress shoved into my mouth muffle the sound, but the drags from my lungs pull the cotton down too far and I think I'm going to choke. I yank it free of my mouth and feel the slime of sickness sticking to it. There's bugger all water in the jug, so I rub my nightdress against the crumbling wall, leaving more plaster on me than sickness on it.

The catch on the larder door lifts with a quiet click and I inch the creaking door open. My hand runs along the dusty top shelf until it settles on a candle. There'll be no hiding its burnt tip, but if I'm quick enough and it don't burn down too far, maybe no one will notice.

With the candle lit from the fire's embers, I return to the larder. My belly growls again and my mouth fills with spit at the thought of food. How long is it since I ate? Six days now? Time has turned liquid with its melt and flow since the sickness nabbed me.

The candle sheds a dim flicker on the larder shelves. Calling it a larder could almost be a joke if the bare dirty shelves were funny. A bag of oats sits high on the shelf, scattered remains of a rat's feast lying in a trail beside it. I can't make porridge, too noisy by far, and besides, the embers in the fire aren't enough for heating any water. My hand reaches further back on the shelves and something hard fills my palm. I pull it out. One stale chunk of crust from a loaf long forgotten. Bugger, this will do nothing to salve the growling dog gnawing away at my insides. I take a nibble and spit it out again.

I lean my back against the wall. My weak body would leave me angry if I weren't so bloody knackered. It must be cold in here, but my skin is burning, my hair damp to the touch, and even amongst this squalor I know it's me who reeks. Summoning all the energy I have left, I return to the pantry and take a pinch of hardened salt from a greasy jar. With no butter, this is the best I can hope for. I know I have to eat something. I take a few quick nibbles, but it catches in my throat and I'm forced to wash it down with a few drops of pump water. My belly will pay for that tomorrow. I can't risk any more coughing, so I carry the rock-like bread back upstairs and hide it under my blanket for the morning.

With no clock I can't be sure, but my sleep can't be more than ten-minute bursts. In the early hours I try bashing myself in the chest to stop the coughing; it don't work. All night the others throw out sleepy shouts, as my hacking wakes one after the other. I learn some new curse words, but my brain's too foggy by morning to remember them.

During my final titbit of sleep, I dream of the baby. The dead baby. I wake soaked in sweat, worse than any caused by my fever. Am I alone? I squint through the half-light and see the outline of Mum in the corner. Her hands are moving quick and steady, so she must be mending. With Mum distracted, I take the stolen bread from beneath the blanket and hide myself under the covers. Florrie's tried getting me food, even Albert had a go, but Mum stopped them each time. She says it's best to starve a fever, but I think it's me she wants to starve.

I crack the bread in two with a loud snap. My ears strain for sounds of movement, but I don't think Mum heard. It will be too noisy to crunch my way through, so I shove a chunk in my mouth to soften it. My plan would work were I not so ravenous. Before my spit can get to work on softening the loaf, my body takes over, my jaw working like a puppet, pulled by strings.

Bugger. The scratching, clawing tickle in my chest is bubbling up. I try to hold my breath, but it's useless. My puppet body works against me and goes to suck in a big gulp of air. Only, my mouth is full, and it's bread sucked down instead. I try to cough it back up, but it's jammed fast. My heart is drumming, sweat now coming in rivers instead of trickles. *Breathe, breathe, breathe.* No air gets through. I throw the blankets off me and Mum rushes over. My face is burning red, the room swimming in front of my eyes. It looks like Mum will help me, but in my distress the uneaten half of crust has tipped off my mattress and onto the floor. She picks it up. *Please*, I want to scream; *I don't have time.* She holds it in front of my eyes, which are now bulging so much they might fall out.

Something happens to Mum and it's like she becomes a statue. The bread falls from her hand, but she don't move to get it. She stares into space, frozen to the spot. I tumble onto the floor, squiggling and squirming, clutching my neck. Tears rush down my cheeks and my shallow breaths sound more like screams. Tears blur my sight, but I know the room is growing darker. They can't put me in a drawer, I'm too big. Will they just bury me in the ground? Maybe Mum will throw me in the river before the others get back? The last thing I hear are footsteps on the stairs, then darkness overtakes me.

My sight returns in flashes, light-dark, light-dark. The room is jumping and turning. I see Mum's feet level with my head. What's happening?

"Harder, Arthur!" I know that voice. It's Florrie. She's screaming. "Please, Arthur, help her!"

The room is jumping again. My head feels hot and heavy, my hair is swishing above me. Something eases in my chest and a slimy mix of bread and water flies from my mouth, skidding along the floor and making a puddle. The room spins and I find myself held in Arthur's arms. Now I'm level with Mum's head. Her face is still, mouth set in a line, eyes staring wildly from her skull. Arthur is cradling me, rocking me like a baby as coughs come so fast, I'm not sure they'll ever stop. Florrie has her hand on my wet hair, stroking and stroking, kissing and kissing.

The coughs ease off, and Arthur settles me onto my bed. He props me up so my back is against the wall and I can breathe easier. His eyes are shining, staring deep into mine. I've never seen him look like this before, it's like he's seeing me for the first time. He turns his head and his face changes as he looks at Mum.

"Sit with her," he tells Florrie. In three steps he's crossed the room. His hand wraps round Mum's neck, and he lifts her high, pressing her into the wall. She's trying to call out, her fingers scratching at his arms, but his hands are big, and grow tighter still.

"How does it feel?"

Mum tries to answer him, but it's all she can do to breathe.

"How does it feel, hey? This is how Ellen felt. Like it, do you?"

Now Mum's whimpering like a child. Feet banging against the wall, hands flailing against Arthur's back.

"I didn't know what to do. I didn't know what to do. I'm sorry, I'm sorry, I'm sorry."

As quick as it tightened, his hand releases and Mum tumbles into a heap on the floor. Arthur looks down at her, his face red with rage. He makes a gagging sound, then spurts a lump of spit onto Mum's head. A whimper escapes my lips and Florrie pulls me close.

"I didn't know what to do," Mum whispers.

"Didn't know what to do? If you were any sort of mother, you'd have helped her. You near enough left your own flesh and blood to die. Near enough killed her yourself. No, you're no mother."

Mum curls up in a ball, eyes hidden by her palms. Arthur comes over to me and takes my face in his hands. Gentle hands that only moments ago were gripping Mum by her neck.

"You'll be alright now," he says before crossing the room and running down the stairs.

We hear the door slam, and even with no windows, hear his boots stamping through the yard. Mum turns to us and Florrie pulls me even tighter to her, shielding me from anything that might come my way. But Mum says nothing. With her cuff, she wipes the spit from her hair, scrubs her eyes dry, straightens her skirts and heads outside.

Chapter 8

December 1906

"Ellen!"

"Shh," I say to Florrie, "Don't let her find me."

Florrie grins and we carry on playing with our stash of fabric we nicked from Mrs Jeffries' bag. I drape a piece of black taffeta over my head and spin round and round until I bump into Florrie and she giggles.

"Shh," I say again.

"Ellen, come here now or there'll be hell to pay."

Mum is downstairs. We should have had far longer to play than this, she's not usually back till six. Maybe they let her out early 'cause of her massive baby belly, but there must still be silk to wind. When she had Maude in her belly, she never got out early. Poor Maude. Poor Mum. I remember Florrie crying when we got back after leaving Maude at the morgue, but not Mum. Mum just carried on with her winding, only taking an hour off to see Maude buried in the ground.

"You'd better go," says Florrie.

We hear heavy footsteps tramping up the stairs and shove the fabric back into its bag.

"Put it under the blanket, quick!" I say and Florrie gets it hidden just as Mum comes into our room.

"What?" I ask her. "I've done my jobs for today, why can't you leave me alone?"

"We're going out. There's someone I want you to meet. You're staying elsewhere for a few days, so pack a few bits in here."

She throws a heavy carpet bag at me. I recognise it, remember Maria clutching it tight as we travelled through the snow. I jump back. Mum picks up the bag and holds it out to me.

"Take it. Now."

I stand pinned to the spot, scared to open the carpetbag for what I might find in there.

"I said, pack your things and while you're at it, stop being ungrateful. Most little girls like adventure, but no, not our Ellen."

Florrie stares from Mum to me, wondering what's going on. I'm wondering the same, but Mum's in one of her moods and I reckon she'd answer my questions with a slap.

"Where are you taking her?" Florrie asks, and I'm grateful, for I couldn't get the words out.

"Oh, don't you worry that pretty head of yours, Florence. Our Ellen is going on an adventure."

Two things now bother me. First, Mum never calls Florrie Florence, and second there's an edge to her voice. It's hard like her scratchy fingers, and too high, like she's playing one of me and Florrie's make-believe games. I shuffle myself behind Florrie and she puts a thin arm across me. Bloody hell, I love my sister.

"Tell us where you're taking her, or I'll not let you pass."

Mum laughs, but not the way we were laughing before she came in. Her mouth is moving but her eyes are hard, like two black stones peeping out of a face as wrinkled as Dad's shoe leather.

"I've found Ellen work, that's all. Just for a few days, but she'll need to stay with her master and mistress."

"Work?" says Florrie. "What work? She's too young to be working."

"Not where she's going. Now stop messing around and do as I say."

Mum pushes the carpet bag between me and Florrie. Bugger, now what should I do? I want to stay behind Florrie's warm arm, but Mum looks mad, and it's not a good idea to mess with her when she's in a lather.

"Come here. Now."

Oh God, she's in a lather, that's certain, but my body won't move. Before I can get my bloody legs to do what my mind is telling them, Mum has pushed Florrie to the floor and is gripping my arm.

"Ow!" I say, but she either don't hear or don't care. My skin is burning beneath her fingers, folds pinched as black grimy nails dig in. She lets go and I rub at the red skin. Tears prick my eyes, but I blink them away. Hardys are tough folk, Dad says, and I should be no different.

Mum is flinging clothes into the carpetbag. Florrie folds my dress at night and leaves everything in a neat pile. Mum don't fold. She shoves, crumples and squashes.

"Put this on," she says, handing me the dress I wore for Sarah's wedding.

"But this is for best."

"You need to look your best today. Don't want to be accused of selling faulty goods."

"Where am I going?" I ask, pinching my hand to rid the shake in my voice.

"I told you, to work."

"But where?"

"It's a surprise."

"I don't like surprises."

Mum stops her packing and stares at me hard. It's a look that tells me to stop talking, a look that tells me I won't find out more, however much I ask. I pull off my old clothes slowly and she taps her foot, sighing big sighs, picking at her nails.

"Hurry up or we'll be late."

Once I've got my posh frock on, Mum attacks my hair with her grimy fingers, yanking out tangles and rubbing spit into my fringe to straighten the kinks. She holds me at arm's length. "You'll do. Let's get going."

I follow Mum to the door, then stop as Florrie rushes across and flings herself at me. She's crying, like she knows something I don't, like she won't see me again. I scrub the tears from her cheeks and look up into her big brown eyes.

"It's alright," I tell her. "I'll be home soon."

She pulls me tighter and by now her body is heaving with big gulping sobs. Mum is shifting from one foot to the other, sighing with impatience.

"Let go of her. Don't you have work to be doing?"

Florrie grabs hold of my hand, but hers is wet from wiping salty tears and slips from mine as Mum drags me from the room. As we pass the kitchen, I notice something on the table. Mum tugs my arm, but not quick enough to stop me seeing what's there. An envelope. A brown envelope with paper notes and shiny coins spilling from it. Where did all that money come from? Mum shoves me out the door before I get a chance to ask.

The yard is heaving with folk about their business, and no one looks up as Mum drags me across the cobbles. She's pulling my arm and I have to run to keep up. My boot catches on the edge of a stone and I stumble, but she don't slow down.

"Mum, you're hurting me."

"Keep walking. We can't be late."

"Late for what?" My words fall on the cobbles and get no reply.

We pass through the dingy alley then Mum stops so suddenly I bump into her arse.

"What time is it?" she asks me. As if I'd know! "Bloody hell, I hope we've not missed her."

"Missed who?"

"Never you mind."

I stick my little finger in my mouth and chew on the nail. It's bitten down so far, I've reached the skin, and the metal taste of blood touches my tongue.

"Stop that will you, we want Julia to think you're a polite girl."

"Who's Julia?"

"Your new boss. It's dirty to eat your fingers. Did you not have porridge this morning?"

"Never you mind," I say, and get a clip round the ear.

Mum bends down to look at me. Her knees crack as she lowers herself, holding her belly like the baby inside might fall out at any moment. I turn my head away from her sickly, stale milk smelling breath. Her few teeth are brown as the river, and the sight and smell of her mouth makes me feel sick.

"Now, Ellen, listen to me. You're to walk to the corner of Oak Street and wait outside the butchers. Understand?" I nod my head. "Julia will meet you there. You be a good girl for her, you hear? I don't want you giving her none of your cheek. She's doing us a great kindness taking you to stay with her."

I nod again and before I know what's happening, Mum's pulled me into her chest, arms holding tight to my back. Her clothes smell horrid, and I try to move my head, but she pulls me closer. As quick as she started, she stops, letting go so fast I nearly fall on my bum. She lifts my chin with her hand. I think she's going to speak, but instead, her button eyes stare into mine then she lets go of my face and turns back to the alley. I stand still, watching her waddling into the darkness.

"Mum," I say, but she don't turn round. "Mum!"

She said I'm going for just a few days, didn't she? I can't remember. Bloody hell, my belly's doing somersaults. I must be mad, for I have a feeling I won't be seeing my mum again.

***

People stare as they walk past. It's not a strange sight, a kiddie on the street alone, so it must be the carpet bag what makes them look. The bag lies beside me on the pavement, for I hate the feel of it in my hands. It's at least fifteen minutes I've been standing here, waiting. I'll give it another five before I head home. We must have been too late, or maybe that Julia lady had no need for a worker after all. My hands knot together, wringing this way and that just like the butterflies in my belly. There's no sign of any ladies, whichever way I turn. One...two...three... I'll give it to one hundred then I'm off.

I've reached eighty when I see her. It must be her, everyone else round here is dressed in grey and brown so she can't be from these parts. The lady rushes towards me, waving. She reaches me and I stare up at her open-mouthed. I've seen no one like her. Bright blond hair hangs in perfect curls, bouncing against her cheekbones as she walks. Her full lips are crimson, thick black lashes frame her turquoise eyes. She smiles and her cheeks become half crescent moons that I want to reach up and kiss. I can't stop staring, I know I should look away, but her face draws me like a moth to a flame. She removes a white silk glove from one hand and reaches it out to me.

"My name's Julia. Pleased to meet you."

I try to speak but have become mute. Long fingers wrap around mine. Her fingernails are painted the same red as her lips. I curl my own bitten stubs, hoping she won't see. My eyes scan her from the waist down. A long purple dress with ruffled hem sits beneath a knee-length green velvet overcoat. I want to stroke it, for it's the finest coat I've seen.

"What's your name?" she asks me, and I mumble a reply.

"It's lovely to meet you, Ellen, I think we'll have a wonderful time together, don't you?"

"I don't know," I say.

"Hmm," says Julia. "Well, we'd best be on our way."

"Where are we going?"

I don't know if she heard me, but she don't answer. Julia takes my hand in hers and I'm surprised by her tight grip. Her palms are rough, but she don't look like no silk winder or machinist, that's for sure. Her nails are hard and leave scratches on my skin as she walks away from Oak Street and down towards the river.

Bloody hell, we're crossing the river, crossing the river! I've never crossed the river in my life, never been much past the yards, except Mousehold, and that time we caught the bus with a dead baby. I've always tried to stay away from the river. It stinks. Full of shit and dead bodies, Arthur says.

***

My feet are sore, for we've been walking for ages. Bloody hell, what's this? We're in some square, enormous buildings peering down on us. Julia drags me through small tents with coloured canvas packed so tight her hand slips from mine and I get shoved along into a crowd of folk.

"Help!" I say, and she turns and chases after me as I'm squished in a bunch of tall bodies. People shout in my ear about fish, apples and beef. The smells, oh the smells, a mix of rotting flesh and stinking fish, sweet and sour all at once.

I look for Julia, but all I can see are people's legs and the hems of their coats. I cover my ears with my hands and scream. People part around me and here's Julia, grabbing my hand and pulling me away. Between sobs, I take big gulps of air as we pass through the tents and onto the street.

"You gave me a right fright, disappearing like that," she says, before yanking me close to her as a horse and cart laden with barrels skims our toes. We wait as a horse-less bus slides past on metal rails.

"This way," she says.

Now she's taking me along Blood and Guts street. This is a street I know, not from having been here but from the stories my brothers have told. The stink of dead animals sticks in my nose and I try to hold my breath, so I don't breathe it in. There's a herd of cattle coming towards us and I wonder if she's going to drag me through the middle of them. But she pulls me into a doorway and waits for them to pass. I could slip between their muddy muscly legs and sneak my way back home, but it's too late for they're passed and we're on the move once more.

"What's that?" I say, stopping to look at an enormous square building, thin slits of windows peering out of pale stone.

"It's the castle. Best keep moving though, you'll see it again, don't worry."

"Does King Edward live there?"

"No, come on."

A castle so near the yards and I never knew. I can't stop staring and Julia presses her knuckles into my back to move me on. We don't stray far from the castle, for she takes me behind it to an area that stretches as far as I can see, covered by a hotchpotch of small brightly painted canvas stalls and finely carved wagons. All the while, the castle looms over us, like an olden day giant, peering through its slit eyes to check no one's up to no good.

Julia pauses for a moment and crouches down to look me in the eye.

"Ellen," she says in a serious voice. "This is your new home. Welcome to the fair."

Chapter 9

December 1906

My head is spinning. The more I look, the more I see. There are people everywhere; men pulling apart wooden frames, women wiping dust from signs with bits of rag, children carrying wooden boards as tall as themselves. One boy is carrying a sack of furry balls.

"Coconuts," says Julia, looking down at my puzzled face.

Even though I'm bloody confused and frightened, I let out a giggle as the coconuts escape the boy's basket and roll away.

"Billy should be more careful with those or his dad will have his guts for garters. Shall we help?"

I nod and we move closer to the boy, stopping the coconuts with our feet and putting them back in his basket. They tickle my hands and I giggle again.

"Who's this then?" the boy asks.

"Ellen. She'll be staying with us a while. You be sure to make her welcome, Billy, she's family now."

"Family?"

"Yes, and don't you forget it."

The boy looks me up and down, then balances his basket between a knee and elbow and reaches out his free hand to shake mine.

"Welcome to the family, Ellen."

"Thanks," I say, though I want to tell him about Florrie, about my family just across the river.

Billy heads off with his basket of coconuts and Julia guides me through the chaos. Curious eyes follow me, and I lower my head, for once not wanting to be the centre of attention.

"Here we go," Julia says, as we reach a long wooden box on wheels. It's the shiniest thing I've ever seen, painted a deep red with gold lettering and leafy designs. The windows gleam and appear to reflect sunlight, even though the day is cloudy. Not a spot of dirt lies on its wood. I go to step inside, but Julia grabs my coat.

"No you don't," she says. "Wait here."

Julia disappears inside and comes out moments later with a round copper tub, like what we do our laundry in. She goes in and out, in and out of her wagon, each time pouring water into the copper from a large kettle.

"Right, first things first. Kneel here and tip your head down."

I do as she says, and she places a large piece of brown paper on the floor in front of me.

"Now, Ellen, this might hurt a little, but it's important we get any stowaways off you before you come into the wagon."

I can't see what she's doing with my head forward and a crown of brown hair around my eyes, but I feel it sure enough. She sections off part of my hair and begins tugging through it with a thin-toothed comb.

"Ow," I squeal as Julia yanks at a tangle, but she ignores me and keeps going. Her tugging and tearing seem to go on forever, but eventually she stops.

"Wait there," she says again.

I stay still, even though my neck is aching, and I want to run away. Now she's back, holding an oil lamp to the paper. She stops several times, then moves the flickering light across once more.

"Good," she says at last. "You can stand up now."

I stand up and stretch my neck to ease the ache.

"Well, your head is free of critters, but I'm not sure the same can be said for your clothes. They'll need burning." I look at her wide-eyed. "Oh, don't worry Ellen, I'm not going to make you run around starkers." She disappears into the wagon, laughing all the while. When she comes back, she has a pile of clothes in one arm and a sheet in the other.

"Here, you get in the tub and I'll hold up this sheet to protect your modesty." I go to step in, but she holds my arm back. "Take your clothes off," she says.

Does she really expect me to stand here, in public, in the nuddy? What if someone comes over? Her sheet will be as useful as a holey bucket then, won't it? Well, this Julia must be a mind reader, for she lifts the sheet higher and says,

"Ellen, if anyone comes near, I'll wrap this sheet around you quicker than you can say coconut shy, and I promise to look away, as long as you promise to scrub yourself good and proper."

I don't have much choice. If I make a run for it, I might not find my way back. Even if I do get back, it don't seem I'm wanted at home. Julia turns her head and I quickly take off my clothes, jumping in the tub before she can catch a glimpse of me. I've never washed so quick or so well, for the last thing I want is her interfering. I grab the bar of soap she's left and scrub it all over my body and in my hair. Then I splash away, making sure every last bit is off again. The water has turned a scummy grey, so I suppose I've done a good enough job.

"Here," says Julia, holding the sheet closer so I can wrap myself in it. She inspects the water in the tub and, satisfied that I've had a good hose down, tips it out beneath the wagon.

"Julia?"

"Yes?"

"My dress... I wore it to my sister's wedding. Me and my sisters were all matching..."

"Ah, so it's a special frock?"

"Yes."

"Alright then, we'll keep it, but it will need a good clean before you can wear it again."

"Thank you," I say.

"Come inside and dress by the fire," she says.

I follow her up the painted wooden steps, and the first thing to hit me is the warmth. Unlike our measly fire back home, here a small coal fire pumps out so much heat I'm not sure I need more than a thin sheet around me. Julia hands me my new clothes. They aren't fancy, just a thick woollen dress, stockings, and cardigan. But they're the first properly new clothes I've ever worn. And I'm sure they weren't made from curtains. I'm almost scared to wear them in case I get them mucky, but Julia is waiting so I hand her the sheet and dress myself.

"How about a cup of sweet tea?" she says. "I'm sure all this has been quite a shock for you."

"Um, Julia, what is all this? I mean, why am I here?"

"Ah, well, I met your mum in the pub last night."

"The pub?"

"Yes, and we got chatting. She told me she's worried about not being able to provide for all her kiddies once the new baby comes. Too many mouths to feed, I think she said. Well, the problem I have is, I've no mouths to feed. Me and Henry aren't blessed with children, so I thought we could help each other out."

"How?"

"I suggested I look after you for a while."

"But why me? There's plenty of us Hardys to choose from,"

"Yes, I know, but all the others are working, aren't they? You're too young to bring in any money, but here with us there's plenty you can do."

"How long will I stay with you?"

Julia ignores my question and pulls cups down from a high cupboard.

"I miss Florrie."

"Is that your sister?" Julia says, turning to look at me. I nod and try not to cry. "I'll keep you so busy you'll not have time to miss her, don't worry."

Busy? I'm still not sure what someone as little as me can do except go up the odd chimney, and Julia don't seem no chimney sweep.

"Would you like to see round the wagon?" Julia asks and I nod. "Well, most of it you can see from here." Julia laughs and points to a cosy armchair. I sit down and she hands me a cup of tea.

What amazes me most is how everything in here sparkles. The walls are dark polished wood, twisting flowers and vines cut into shiny glass. Bloody hell, red and pink flowers even cover the ceiling. It couldn't be more different from my house in the yards. Every shelf and mantel is packed with ornaments, fine china teapots, glass vases, and not a speck of dust on none.

"We sleep through there," says Julia, pointing to a sliding door. "You'll be on this bunk." She pulls back a curtain on the other side of the wagon to reveal a narrow bunk, covered in a

cheerful woollen blanket. A proper bed. Bloody hell, Florrie
will be so jealous when I tell her! A couple of nights in that
and I'll be fresh as a daisy when I go home.

"You sit and finish your tea. I'll get Henry to come and say
hello."

Once she's gone, I sink back into the soft armchair and
with the heat of the fire I could happily doze off. The
strangeness of the day has left me knackered. It's too much
to take in at once, and I miss Florrie.

When Julia returns, it's with a tall, thin man whose face is
covered by an enormous moustache, more like the branch of
a tree than the headmaster's caterpillar. It's hard to see his
mouth beneath all that hair, but his eyes twinkle and I can
tell he's smiling. Before he sits down, he washes his hands in
a little basin and removes his shoes.

"Hello, little gal, you must be Ellen?"

"Yes," I say.

"Well, I'm Henry. It is a pleasure to meet you, princess.
What do you make of your new home?"

"It's clean, sir," I say.

Henry's eyes crease up and a guffaw booms from his chest.
I don't understand how a man so thin can make such a sound.
When he's stopped laughing, he takes my hands in his.

"Now, princess, I'll have none of that sir business. Only the
law calls me that, and not politely. You can call me Henry, or
uncle if you prefer, but if that's strange then plain old Henry
will be grand."

I nod, unsure quite what I should call him. Julia fusses
round us, making up plates of sandwiches which she lays out
on the small table.

"Wash your hands, Ellen," she says. "Then sit back here and have some grub. You must be starving after all your adventures."

I scrub my hands like Henry did, then sit beside him at the small table. The sandwiches are so thick I can barely hold them in my hands. Chunks of ham and fat scoops of butter fill my mouth, and I'm sure I'm gobbling quicker than what's polite.

"You've got a good appetite on you, gal," says Henry, grinning at me.

I can't reply, as my mouth is stuffed with food, and even I know it's rude to talk with your mouth full.

"How does this compare then, to your place in the yard I mean?"

My jaw aches from chewing and trying to push food down so I can talk. "There's no dirt here," I say.

Henry lets out his booming laugh again, and the china ornaments rattle on their shelves. "You can thank Aunt Julia for that. She keeps a tight ship. Also keeps me on the straight and narrow, the books in order and the show on the road. Fine woman I got here," he says, wrapping an arm round Julia's waist and kissing her cheek.

"Away with you, Henry, the gal don't want to see that."

Julia speaks sharply as she pushes Henry away, but her mouth curls in a smile. Henry wolfs down his food and is out of the door as quick as he came.

"Never stops working, that man," says Julia. "Mind you, none of us do really, not till the quiet months and they're few and far between."

"Will I be working too?"

"I'm sure we'll find you something to fill your time. What are you good at?"

"Numbers, 'rithmatic."

"Ah, just what your mum said. Well in that case I reckon we're going to get along fine."

Julia clears away the cups and plates, handing me a cloth to help her dry. Even the dish cloth has flowers sewn onto it, and there's not a tear or rip in sight.

"I'll need your help this afternoon. All these ornaments need to be stored away. Careful mind, any breakages will come straight out of your wages."

"I'll be careful."

"Good."

We spend the next couple of hours taking ornaments and breakables off shelves, wrapping them in newspaper or cloth, and stacking them in boxes. Julia makes me dust each one before it goes away, but my duster's as clean at the end as it was at the start. She won't tell me what the packing is for.

"Right, I think that's us done for the day. I'll see if Henry's ready to move on yet."

"Move on?"

"To the next site. Your mum did explain what working for us would mean, didn't she?"

"She didn't say nothing."

"I see. Well, there's nothing to worry about. I'll be back in a tick."

Julia leaves me alone in the wagon. What's all this talk of moving on? I don't have to wait long to find out. Henry appears with two strong looking horses and attaches them to the front of the wagon. Julia steps up into the wagon, storing the steps and locking the door behind her.

"What's Henry doing?"

"He's staying out there with the horses."

"Why?"

"We're moving on."

"We're leaving Norwich?"

"Yes."

"For how long?"

"We'll be back at Easter."

Easter? But that's months away! Julia tries to get me to sit beside her, but instead I climb up onto her bed and press my face against the back window. The wagon judders and soon we're slowly making our way along the road. I can't tear myself away from the window. Mum never said I'd be leaving the city. She never said I'd be taken from my family. Julia comes over and takes hold of my arm, pulling me away from the window. I whack her hand away and press mine to the glass, trying to catch hold of the city as it disappears from view. The castle grows smaller. As we turn a corner, the light changes and drifts from the castle's slit windows. It's as though it's closed its eyes, blinking its own goodbye.

PART 2

Nellie Westrop

Chapter 10

March 1910

"Nellie?"

"Mmm."

"Come on, time to get on the road."

"Five more minutes."

"Five more minutes and the horses will be moving; you'll tumble from your bed and go flying round the wagon. Come on, get a move on."

I groan and pull my blankets over my head. A pretty face, all sparkly eyes and rosy cheeks, appears beneath a gap in the corner.

"Noooo," I say. But Julia's quicker than me and has the covers whipped off before I can grab them. "Bossy britches," I mumble, as I wrap a shawl around me.

Julia whacks me with a pillow. "Pot and kettle is all I'll say."

"Alright, what time is it? The sun's not even up yet."

"Just gone five. Come on, get out there quick if you need a piss."

I scowl at her and shove my feet in my boots. It's bloody freezing outside, a thin layer of frost covers the wagons and trailers. In the gloom, I squat beside the wagon and relieve myself. This is a god-awful hour to be up, but I should be used to it by now.

"When will we be in Wisbech?" I say, stepping back into the warmth of the wagon.

"By noon, all being well. Would be good to get there with a bit of light left in the sky or setting up will take even longer. The lads won't know what's hit them after months of being idle."

I smile to myself. Julia's idea of idleness differs from most, for the lads have been labouring all winter and their muscles have had no time to grow weak. It's the way of things here though, work away from the fair don't count as proper work, and everyone's keen to get back on the road once more.

I'm bloody delighted we're moving on. Julia makes me go to school in low season and I hate it. The local kids aren't welcoming of us showfolk, the teachers neither. They stick me at the back of the classroom with a book and hope for the best. The locals tried it on with me once, chasing me down the road calling me *gypsy bitch*. Luckily, I've picked up a few tips at the boxing booth and after dishing out a few right hooks, they didn't bother me again.

"Alright, ladies?" says Henry, poking his head through the door. "Ready to go?"

"Two minutes," says Julia. "Just got to pack these last dishes away."

"Give me a shout when you're done then," says Henry, closing the door and perching himself up front, reins in hand.

"See, I could've had another five minutes after all," I say, and Julia sighs.

It only takes her a minute to finish storing the breakables. Out of all of us, Julia's the boss. Not that I'd say so to Henry, for fear of denting his pride.

"Ready," she calls.

The wagon jolts as the horses begin their click clack along the road. We clatter along narrow lanes, a train of brightness among faint morning light. As we pass through villages, kiddies gather at the side of the road to watch us. They wave and cheer, but I stick two fingers up to the window, knowing they'd sooner run a mile than be friends if I wasn't just passing through.

"Stop that, Nell. We don't want them thinking us rogues."

"They think that anyway," I say.

"Well, let's not give them more reason then."

I give up. She can win any row without even raising her voice.

"Sit here and help me with the accounts," she says, and I do as I'm told. Julia pulls out a black book filled with neat lines of writing and even neater columns of numbers. They gave me a book of poems to read in school once, but numbers are my poems. They spell out patterns and stories in a way no words can.

"Reckon we'll match last season this year?"

"Let's hope," Julia says. "But you never know if Mother Nature will throw a spanner in the works and depends who else shows up."

I feel for Julia and Henry, way down the pecking order. There's the top dogs like the Thurstons and Barkers with their latest gadgets and rides, then it gets to us, with our shooting gallery. The shooting gallery's a good earner, but nothing like the bigger rides. Through the back window I see Henry's brother Will, guiding his own horses along. Sophia's most likely sat in their wagon doing the same as us. Their coconut shy's not a bad earner neither.

"Looks like Lynn Mart was our best earner last year. Shame we couldn't get in this time round."

"Yes, let's hope Easter and Whitsun make up for any losses. We've got a good run coming up from Easter onwards."

"It's good to be back on the road again."

"Yes, it is," mutters Julia, distracted by the numbers on her page.

We go through the accounts, which are as orderly and correct as I'd expect from Julia. The roads are so straight, Julia makes us a cuppa without spilling none. I sip my tea and glance out of the window. Land stretches as far as the eye can see. Beside the road, tall grass jiggles in the breeze, and the fields are crisp white, the sun not yet burning through to the green and brown below. The road mostly follows the line of the dykes that criss-cross the ground.

"It's beautiful, isn't it?"

"I suppose it is, in its own way," says Julia.

"You don't like it?"

"Well, where I come from, there's hills and woodland. To me the fens are rather bleak."

"But look at the sun," I say, and Julia gazes out of the window. The sun is rising slowly, a big orange ball filling an enormous blue sky. It turns the fields from silver to gold.

"I like the windmills," Julia says, pointing to a wooden building in the distance. "You don't see those back home."

"Where are you from?" I ask.

"Up north, came south for Henry, but I'll never be a true southerner. I'll take you up there some day if you like?"

"Yes, please," I say, and Julia throws me a smile.

***

By the time we arrive in Wisbech, wagons and trailers are blocking the streets, showmen vying for the best spots in the marketplace. Some of the bigger shows have gone closer to the river; old man Thurston's set his cinematograph up on the North Brink, while Tuby has his cinematograph coliseum over on the South Brink. Tuby's impressive show organ is certain to draw the crowds, and with just the river to separate them, Thurston will be spitting feathers.

"Thurston had a right old time getting here, so I'm told," says Henry. "There's snow further north and his heavy vans struggled. It'll be a race against time for him to get set up."

"How do you know all this, Henry?" I ask.

He laughs. "You get all the news when you're riding up front, princess. Mr Tuby caused a stir too, trying to get his vans over Nene Quay. They thought the old road would collapse under the weight. Lucky for him it didn't!"

Through the window, I see horses, wagons, people milling about, all misty under the smoke of traction engines what pull the heaviest vans along.

Clark's got himself a good spot, setting up his kiddies' roundabout opposite Tuby, and Cheeseman has his shooting gallery beside it. Henry won't be pleased. Cheeseman is competition; Henry would prefer there to be just one shooting gallery in town.

"I've heard talk there's seven shooting galleries here this year," Henry calls through.

Julia frowns, shillings and pennies falling off the hoped-for takings she holds in her head. "Who else is here apart from Cheeseman?"

"Williams, Knight, Parking, Holmes and Marshall."

"Bloody hell," says Julia, and I giggle.

With all the big earning spots gone, we wait our turn and pull the wagon up beside a grand stone building. But the marketplace suits us well, for it's a perfect rectangle and our wagons lie around its edges; shows, stalls and rides in the middle. Our wagons are a barrier, a fortress huddled tight against invaders. It's good to be close to others, for the townsfolk aren't always friendly, in fact, they're often not.

Last year in Yarmouth, a gang of lads started a ruckus after closing. Poor old Henry had a shiner for two weeks; black, purple, then yellow in a moon beneath his eye. William fared worse. He lost his front tooth. Now, when he talks, he whistles. Everyone's taken to calling him Loco, 'cause he sounds like a locomotive pulling into a station.

"I'm off out for some supplies," says Julia, pulling on the velvet coat she wore the first time we met.

I quickly learned that her finery only comes out for associations with flatties, normal folk what live dull lives away from the fair. Within the safety of our fair family, she wears clothes more suited to the endless hours she works. She's still beautiful, though. "A handsome woman," is what Henry calls her, but that makes me think of a man, and Julia's as ladylike as they come. She don't even curse as much as me. Not that she don't know the words. I've heard her curse at flatties what try to rip her off, and they're always surprised by the filthy words coming from a pretty mouth.

"Need some help?"

"Yes, alright, but smarten yourself up a bit, we don't want no trouble."

I want to tell her I'm already smart but looking down I see crumples in my clothes from the journey, and my hair needs a good brush. I've still not grown used to having a fancy mirror to see into. Habit still makes me want to find a window for my reflection.

"Come here," she says, and pulls me in front of the mirror.

I admire my reflection in the perfect circle of the glass. Someone has taken the trouble to carve leaves and vines across it. Whoever did it was smart, for it still leaves plenty of space for my reflection between the leaves. Julia stands behind me and runs a brush through my tangles. She's let me grow my hair long, and I don't look like a boy no more. This is my favourite thing me and Julia do, brush each other's hair. I joke with her about the white that's creeping into her blonde; she teases me about my tangles. I'd love hair like Julia. It flows down her waist, all shiny, golden waves, and the white streaks make her look more glamorous, if that's possible.

"You'll do," she says, turning me round. I reach up, kiss her on her round cheek, and she smiles. "None of your cheek while we're out, alright? We don't want no trouble."

Trouble. It's one of the few clouds what hangs over our fair family. Trouble from locals, trouble from officials in suits, but mostly, trouble from the law. If there's ever a spot of bother, you can guarantee it'll be us what's to blame. The gaff lads, well, they're a slippery bunch, but us true fair folk, we stay the right side of the law. And I'll punch anyone in the nose what says otherwise.

"See you in a while, Henry, we're just nipping out for some supplies," says Julia.

"Don't be too long, there's a lot to do here."

"Well, I've got Nellie with me and if she starts her bartering, we could be awhile."

Henry laughs and walks over to Will, who's wrestling a large piece of iron from his trailer. Julia leads me through the scene of work and excitement. She knows everyone and everyone knows her.

"Alright, Julia, escaping the work, are you?"

"Ah, Bobby, chance would be a fine thing."

Even the great Mr Thompson's crossed the river and doffs his cap as we walk past. His wife gives him an elbow as his eyes follow Julia through the fair.

"All the fellows are looking at you," I say.

"It must be the coat."

"Or it's 'cause you're so pretty."

Julia laughs and puts her arm round my shoulder. "Well, they can look all they want, but Henry's the only one who can touch. When you're older, don't be letting lads near you till you find a good 'un. They're not worth the bother they bring."

I nod, finding it hard to imagine ever wanting to spend much time around stinky boys. I don't mind the fair lads, they're a fun little bunch, but only for getting up to mischief, not for touching.

We turn left out of the market square and onto the high street. Giant brick buildings filled with hundreds of windows tower above the wide road. The fair always brings excitement along with it, and several times I catch titbits of conversations. "What ride will you go on first?" "Have you seen the pigs on the roundabout this year?" "Let's meet at five and grab a bite to eat once we're there."

I hear grumbles too, people complaining we'll fill the pubs, leave a mess behind us, block up the streets. Two of those may well be true, but we always leave a place as we found it. We're not the ruffians they make out.

Julia asks me to wait outside while she heads into the butcher's. From the doorway, I hear the shopkeeper attempting daylight robbery. I step inside and knock him down by a shilling. Julia leaves the shop red-faced and rushes me to the grocer's, telling me she can manage just fine by herself. With her basket full, we head back to the fair.

Henry and Will are standing by our wagon, and they don't look happy.

"Everything alright?" Julia asks, putting her basket down on the front step.

"Bloody cheek of it, you seen what they're charging for rent this year?" Will says.

"No, what is it?"

"Nigh on ten pounds!"

"But that's madness," says Julia. "How can they justify charging that much?"

"Because they hold the power and we don't," says Will.

I don't know who 'they' are, but I don't like the sound of them. Poor old Henry looks like he might cry, and Will's all red in the face, huffing and puffing and clenching his fists.

"You know," says Henry. "Back when dad had the stall, it was £26 5s for the whole fair, each traveller paying no more than a few shillings for their spot. Now us stallholders are each paying through the nose."

"Let's hope we draw the crowds then," says Julia. "Or it will be a very bad start to the year."

Chapter 11

March 1910

We wake early on Saturday. This should be our best trading day. Henry's heard trains have been laid on from Cambridge and between them, the townsfolk, and folk from surrounding villages, it should be a good day of takings. I pull the velvet curtain away from the window and peek outside.

"Rain," I call through to Julia and Henry. I hear them groan from behind their door.

"How heavy?" says Henry, and I check again.

"Not too bad, but the sky don't look promising."

"Bloody hell, that's all we need."

The sliding door opens, and Henry comes out, greying hair sticking up in tufts, pulling on a jumper. He opens the wagon door and a blast of freezing air whips through. I pull my blankets tighter.

"Kneel by your bed and say some prayers, Nell. We're going to need them."

By ten, the rain is hammering on our wagon roof like someone's pelting marbles from the sky. By lunchtime, when Henry leaves to set up, the rain has turned to snow. Julia's face is pinched. If the weather don't improve, we'll be on a knife edge, hanging between failure and success, and that's not somewhere we want to be.

"I'm off to mind the stall," says Julia.

"Want me to help?"

"No, if the weather clears, we'll need you later. Get some rest, and if you can, try to stay warm."

"Alright," I say, gathering up a hat, scarf and gloves so Julia won't be cold.

"Thank you," she says, and heads into the snow.

I turn my hand to a bit of cleaning, then a bit of mending, but it's not long till I'm restless. My head pokes out of the door, and a fat blob of snow lands on my nose. My mind turns to our snowy bus ride to the morgue on Barrack Street, and I shake my head to push the memory away. The new baby must be a proper boy now. Four years old he'll be. I hope I meet him one day. Last time I saw Florrie, she told me he's a darling kiddie, all smiles and cheer. I hope life at the yard don't knock that cheer out of him. My heart twists as I think of Florrie, but I wouldn't swap my life now for my life then if you paid me one hundred pounds.

It does me no good to think of the yard, so I wrap myself up warm and head into the snow. It's a strange sight, bright canvas lying under a blanket of white, wagon windows covered in ice. I shiver and pull my collar up against the freezing March wind. Saturday is market day, but the stall holders are miserable as snow swirls around their stalls. This type of weather is not unusual for March, but we all hope and pray fine days will bless us while the fair is on.

The refreshment stands are tempting; I fancy some gingerbread from Suetts, but they'll make me pay full price. Most of the gaff lads know me, and they'll let me on the rides and stalls for free. May as well make the most of it.

First, I head for Richard's Cake Walk. There's no need to queue, for only a handful of people want a cake walk in the snow. The gaff lad hands me my ticket with a wink;

number six. A large horned gramophone crackles into action and I begin dancing round the squares laid out on the rug. Everyone is grateful for the chance to move and warm up a bit, and we're all disappointed when the music stops.

"Six!" the gaff lad calls.

I check the ticket in my hand, I've won! I go to collect my prize, but the gaff lad shakes his head. Seems my free ticket was as much as I could hope for. Next, I head to Bosworth's bicycle roundabout. Again, the gaff lad lets me on with nothing more than a wink. I climb aboard my bicycle, fixed to a metal frame. How Sam and Jack would laugh if they could see me now. At least there's no chance of me falling off. My legs can just about reach the pedals, though I reckon it will be the chaps what get us moving.

I'm right. Keen to give a show of strength, the fellows stand on their pedals and push as hard as they can. Soon, we're whizzing round like nobody's business and even the wet lumps of snow can't stop my hair flying behind me.

"Time!" calls the gaff lad, and although I'd like another turn, I don't want to push my luck.

I head closer to the river and find myself at Nene Quayside and the forbidden bridge that Tuby mistakenly drove his vans across. Here I find the famous Prince Samonda and his hoopla. I shiver and it's down to excitement rather than cold, for I've never seen a prince, or a black man before.

Prince Samonda is a legend in our fair circles. They say he's an illusionist, so why he's now running a hoopla I can't say. Folk say he was in trouble with the law a while back, for some claimed he was swindling people, making it impossible to win prizes. They reckon over six hundred hoops got pitched, with only twenty prizes won. By all accounts, he gave a right good show at the courthouse, handing out hoops for them to try, and proving that it was skill, and skill alone that could win a man a prize. The judge let him off, which is good, or he wouldn't be here.

Julia said she read a while back that he'd climbed a ladder made of sharp swords in his bare feet. Henry said Prince Samonda is the best illusionist in the country and travelled with Barnum and Bailey in his youth.

I walk over to his stall and a tall man beside it turns round. It's impossible not to stare, for he's the most handsome man I've ever seen. His dark eyes twinkle at me and his mouth spreads into a wide grin, showing a row of perfect white teeth. Mum would kill for teeth like those.

"Hello, miss. You're a tough one, out in this weather. Come to try your luck on the rings?"

"Yes, Your Highness."

Prince Samonda lets out a laugh that booms through the fair and bounces off the stalls around him. "So, you know who I am then?"

"Yes, Your Highness."

He laughs again. "Read about me in the paper, did you?"

I think he's teasing me, but I can't be sure. "No, you're the talk of the fair, that's all."

"Ah, so you're with the fair folk, are you?"

"Yes." I hold my hands behind my back and pinch myself. Why am I feeling like a timid mouse? I'm not usually a bloody scaredy cat.

"Who are your parents? Maybe I know them."

How do I answer this? "Um, well, I live with Julia and Henry Westrop."

"Well, everyone with eyes in their head knows Julia. I didn't think they had children."

"They do now."

"That so? What's your name, love?"

"Nellie."

"Well, Nellie. It sounds like you have a story to tell, and I like people with stories. Come here and try your luck with my hoops."

I reach into my pocket and hold out a shilling. Instead of taking it, his hand reaches up behind my ear and pulls out another shilling.

"You should be more careful with your money, love," he says, and I notice the shilling in my hand is gone.

"Here," he says, handing me back my coin. "On the house. It's not like I'll be making much today anyway."

"Thank you."

He hands over three hoops, and I position myself in front of the stall. It's brightly lit with oil lamps and sparkles against the grey and white day. Wooden blocks sit on a tabletop, each holding a prize. I eye them up. I'd like to nab one with a pile of coins, but the blocks holding toys and sweets look easier. My first two goes are way off. On my third, the hoop wobbles and looks like it will go round the block, but it spins again and misses.

"Have one more go," he says, handing me another hoop.

Success! On my fourth try, the hoop lands neatly round a small box of bonbons.

"Thank you," I say, popping a bonbon in my mouth and offering him the box. He takes one and asks me to call again during the week.

"I will," I promise. But if the weather picks up, I doubt I'll be able to get anywhere near his stall.

It must be a couple of hours I've been out, for the snow has soaked through my coat and I can't stop shivering. I need to get inside, or I'll catch a chill and be no use to anyone. Across the river lies Thurston's cinematograph. I know I should go home, but the lights and sounds from across the river tempt me, and I decide to stay out a little longer.

Well, what a treat lies in wait for me at Thurston's! They're showing a new film, all about a Russian man being arrested and his journey to Siberia. It makes Wisbech seem like the tropics. It takes my mind off the cold. I watch as the man's daughter follows her father, saves the governor's son from a precipice, and gets her dad released. I'm not sure I'd travel all the way to Siberia for my dad.

Despite my gloves, I've lost all feeling in my hands. I rub them together, but it does no good. The wagon's fire is calling to me and I make my way back. There are many temptations on the way; Tuby's show of Richard III, a picture display of two Chinamen with their pigtails tied together, Thurston's motor car roundabout, Mr Westwood with his giant son and daughter.

Darkness is setting in and amid the snow the river looks beautiful. Coloured lights reflect on the water, and the steam from the traction engines makes the place look magic. Rides and stalls hide all the town's buildings, and I could be walking through any town in the country. A few people are milling about, but nothing like what we'd usually get on a Saturday.

Back at the wagon, Julia has a stew bubbling on the stove, and I kneel by the fire to warm my hands.

"Goodness me, what have you been up to? You're near enough frozen to death!"

"I... just... need to... warm... up a bit... then... I'll be fine." Bloody hell, my teeth are chattering that much I'm worried they might fall out.

"Oh, Nellie. What am I going to do with you? You'd better not come down with a cold or I'll have your guts for garters."

"Sorry," I say. "It's just I rarely get time to explore and there's some bloody wonderful sights here."

"You're a fool, Nellie Westrop," says Julia. But she's smiling, and begins peeling my snow-soaked clothes from my frozen skin. She wraps me in a blanket and towels my hair till it's almost dry.

"Tea?" I nod my head. She brings me a fresh cup and sits me in the chair by the fire. "You look just like the poor mite who came into our wagon all those years ago. How you've changed since then."

"All thanks to you," I say. I've taken Julia aback, for although we're loving toward one another, we don't speak it out loud.

"Well, Nellie. You know what? You've changed me too. For the better." She sits on the floor beside me, head in my lap, and I run my fingers through her beautiful hair. "I've never said this to you, but not being able to have children of my own made me both sad and angry. I'm not sure I was a very nice person back then. You've brought a happiness to my life that I never thought I'd have."

I'm not sure what to say to that, so we sit in silence, until the stew bubbles over the pot and the moment passes. Not long after, Henry opens the door, shaking snow off himself and taking off his boots before stepping inside.

"You got time to eat?" Julia asks.

"Sadly, it looks like I have all the time in the world. I'll go out again after, but I think the weather's scared most folks away home. Let's hope it's cleared by morning."

Chapter 12

March 1910

It may be the day God rested, but he's been busy with the weather, for on Sunday morning the skies are clear, and the snow is quickly melting. The ground will be muddy once it thaws, but a bit of mud never put no one off. Things are looking up. We'll not be opening till later, but the local vicar is putting on a special service for us travellers, and Henry says we should go.

We don't normally go to church, and despite Henry's insistence I say my prayers each night, I'm not sure how much store he places in them. But, apart from anything, a gathering, whether religious or not, is a chance to talk business, and no showman will miss that.

The service is being held at Tuby's coliseum. We leave early, to be sure a good position, and it's as well we do, for there must be over eight hundred travellers and hangers-on, all come out for the occasion. Tuby's coliseum is legendary. He was one of the first to take the cinematograph to the fair by all accounts. He's an excellent showman, is Tuby. Even from the far side of the fair we often hear the squeals of laughter as he makes someone in the audience sing a song, while holding a real-life pig. If they don't laugh, they get a prize, but I doubt many manage that.

He's lent his orchestra for the occasion, and it's a fine sound ringing out across the town as the huge crowd belt out the hymns all learnt as children. The Vicar gives a sermon titled 'Travellers Ever'. It's a smart move on the vicar's part, for it goes down very well and makes him friend and ally to all the fair folk. The coliseum's open-sided, but we're all kept warm, crammed together like ants, and all are merry. People linger after, having a welcome chance to share news and do a bit of business, despite it being a holy day.

Both Henry and Julia are in good spirits as we walk back to the wagon, for the service feels like an omen of good days to come.

We head straight to the shooting gallery. I help peel back the canvas and prop up the awning while Henry cleans and readies the rifles. Our shooting gallery is a sight to behold. It stretches up fifteen feet and the panels that make up the front are painted in bright swirling patterns of red, green and gold. At the top letters spell out 'A. Westrop & Sons', a sign not changed since the days of Henry's father. Most of the targets are clay pipes and bottles, but Henry is steadily adding in brightly painted metal animals to liven things up even more.

The crowds trickle in from early afternoon. It's bloody chilly, but folks have wrapped up warm and seem in the mood for a bit of fun. By early afternoon, the fair is jam-packed with bodies.

"Walk up! Walk up!" I yell. "Come to Westrop's, the finest shooting gallery in the east! Only half a crown for five goes, and plenty of prizes to be won."

My patter draws the crowds, and soon they're lining up for their turn. Henry and Julia work on either side of the counter, checking guns are loaded properly, and it's safe as can be. No one wants no accidents. Not just for the sake of the flatties, but for our own. An accident would see us out of business and in the poorhouse quicker than you could say 'load and fire'. Henry will often talk of reports he's heard of accidents. A young lad was killed up in Scotland a few years back after a careless attendant set off a loaded gun while cleaning it. A girl got a shot in the eye after her friend messed around with a loaded gun. We don't want nothing like that happening here.

My job is the takings. It didn't take long for Julia and Henry to realise I was quick with my numbers and trust me enough to be in charge of the money. They trust me far more than any gaff lad. The gaff lads go in for a bit of what we call 'tapping'. They got a sneaky system going, quite clever really; take the money, count out the change, and hold a couple of coins back when they pass it to the flattie. You'd think the flatties would notice, but the gaff lads are smart. They count out the change in one hand, in full view of the customer. Next, they move the coins into their other hand, holding a couple of coins back when they place it in the flattie's palm. With all the excitement around, it's rare they get spotted.

All the showmen know the gaff lad's schemes, but 'cause they're quick and clever, more often than not they get away with it. Since they got me, Julia and Henry don't need no gaff lads helping. Good for them, I say. The gaff lads think they're the bee's knees, prancing round in their wacky clothes, chatting up the poor girls what fall for their charms. When I'm older, if I ever got mixed up with a gaff lad, I reckon Henry would kill me.

Hours pass quickly, and I'm in my element. Here, I'm free to use as much cheek as I like, so long as it don't get too rude.

The flatties love my spiel. They walk up, seeing a sweet little girl, then get the shock of their lives at what comes out my mouth. I also love the coins what come in. For hours on end, I have numbers swirling in my head, 'rithmetic after 'rithmetic as I keep a close eye on the takings. I never give the wrong change. Honesty is an important part of our set-up. If people trust us, they'll come back to us again. If we swindle them, a bad reputation can follow you round the country like a stray dog.

It's ten before we shut up shop for the day. Everyone is tired and happy. It's been a good day's takings and if it carries on like this, we'll soon make up for our awful first day. We've just sat down for a cuppa when we hear a hollering from outside. Henry pulls back the curtains and frowns as a gang of chaps run past our wagon.

"Bloody local lads," he mutters. "Can't handle their ale. They'd better not make trouble for us."

He sits back down but keeps glancing out the window.

"Henry, leave it. Please don't go out there," says Julia.

"Don't you worry, love. I'm not giving the law any ammunition. We'll stay in here until they get fed up and return home."

But the lads don't return home. We watch through the window as they stumble their way round the sleeping fair, throwing bottles at stalls and sneaking under the canvas what protects the rides. A few wagon doors open, and showmen step out. No one wants no trouble, but nor can they sit back as their livelihoods get wrecked.

"Bloody hell, Will's out," says Henry, opening the door and calling his brother over. "Don't get involved, Will, it's not worth the bother."

"You seen them, Henry? How can you stand by while they run amuck? They'll put us all out of business if we do nothing."

"And getting put in jail will put us out of business too."

"The law will understand."

"Really? Don't be such a bloody idiot. It's only a few years back those Scottish showmen fired at the crowd from their shooting gallery after some dispute or other. The law think we're all the same, they won't be taking our side, believe me. Stay well out of it, Will."

But Will shakes his head and disappears off between two rides. A good number of the show folk are out now. Big, burly men hold the flatties back, but the flatties are slippery as fish. They wriggle free from strong arms and continue their rampage through the fair. Suett's gingerbread stall gets hit, the canvas top torn and flapping drunkenly from its pole. Other stalls meet the same fate, and I look on as Will rushes over to a flattie and gives him a good crack on the nose. The flattie's friends come to his aid, and it's not long before the whole thing has descended into an all-out brawl.

It takes the ringing of a bell to break through the madness, and men uncurl themselves from one another, bleeding and clutching their ribs. Two strong horses arrive, dragging a police carriage behind them. There's only two constables, so they can't be too worried about the upset. I can't hear what the law are saying from over here, but they seem to be getting the flatties' story first. The one with a bloody nose points across at Will, and a constable makes a note in his little book.

They let the flatties off lightly, for the law's not been here five minutes before they all skulk away. Now I see them turning their attention to our folk. The men huddle together, putting on a united front. But the law don't seem worried.

They drag Will from the crowd and bundle him into their carriage. I may not have been able to hear the policemen, but there's no trouble hearing our men. Their curses ring out through the air long after the police carriage has left for the jail.

"I have to go and help him," says Henry.

"Are you sure? Do you even know where they've taken him?" says Julia.

"No, but I can find out. I can't leave him to fight this alone. He was only defending himself, and I'm a witness to that."

"And they'll think you're a reliable witness, will they?"

"Who knows, but I'm better than no witness."

Julia sighs, but I stay quiet. I can be gobby at times, but I know when to hold my tongue. This is serious, this is grown-up business. Julia wraps her arms round Henry, kisses him, then he disappears into the night.

After he's gone, we wait up a while. The clock on the dresser chimes midnight and we decide it's silly us all being tired and make our way to bed. Neither of us sleep well. I hear Julia tossing and turning from behind her thin door, and dreams of cops and robbers break my sleep.

At five we get up, and I sit at the table wrapped in a blanket while Julia stokes the fire.

"Tea?"

"Silly question." She manages a smile, but it quickly slips back into a frown.

I fill the kettle from a bucket and wait for it to boil. The sound of bubbling water is better than quiet. I yawn, and my breath pours out like a cloud.

"Bloody hell, it's freezing in here," I say, and Julia fetches me a second blanket.

The kettle whistles and I make us both a warming cup. Steam rises as we warm our hands on the china. It's black as pitch outside, but we both take turns to glance out of the window. The sky has turned from black to grey when we spot two figures crossing the fairground.

"It's them," says Julia, opening the wagon door and letting the warmth out and cold in. She waves and Henry waves back. He looks tired, but happy.

"The wanderers return," says Julia, as Henry and Will step inside. "Everything alright?"

"Yes, nothing to worry about."

"Did they charge you?" Julia asks Will.

"No, but only thanks to my brother here. Talked a good talk, he did. Told them what he'd seen, what the lads had done. I think the bloke I whacked is well known to them, so that helped my cause."

"Yes, and offering them a free shoot whenever they like," laughed Henry.

"So that's the end of the matter, is it?" Julia asks them.

"Yes, darling. It is," says Henry, pulling Julia into his arms.

"Tea, Will?" I ask.

"Ah, thanks, Nellie. That would be grand, but I need to get back to Sophia. She'll be going out of her mind with worry. I'm already in her bad books, and really shouldn't push my luck."

Will steps back into the gloom outside and Henry gives a good yawn.

"Go and get some rest, love," says Julia. "Hopefully it will be a busy day and we'll need you at your best."

Me and Julia wash and dress, as relieved as each other that the matter is settled. We have another five days left in

Wisbech, and if we can all keep our heads down, there'll be good money to be made.

Chapter 13

March 1910

On our final morning in Wisbech, me and Julia sit in the wagon counting coins. Half crowns, farthings, and shillings, lie in tall towers on the table. We record the amounts in Julia's book and scoop the counted piles into a tin. All the cash stays in the wagon, we don't trust no banks with it. Julia's not stupid though, her tin has a lock, and she has a secret hidey hole in a high cupboard, just in case prying eyes come looking.

Wednesday was our best day of takings. No wonder, for the shops shut at lunchtime and all the workers spilled out, their earnings burning a hole in their pockets. Kiddies from the local school were brought down for a treat, all with a few pennies and keen to be rid of them in exchange for a bit of fun. It was so busy; it was hard to find a path among the bodies. The kiddies went home for tea, but the grown-ups stayed long into the night. Some even tried to get us to stay open longer than usual, but we were knackered so there was no chance.

We worked nonstop that day. Didn't get a bite to eat till after dark and even then, it was in shifts and not a hot meal. None of us had time to cook, so it was a case of bread and cheese, and eat on the run.

"How's it looking?" asks Henry.

"Been a fine week by the looks of things. Should make up for us not being at Lynn Mart this year."

"Well done, gals," says Henry, kissing us both on the top of our heads. "You nearly done here? There's a lot of packing up to do."

"Fancy a bite to eat first?" asks Julia. "I can heat some soup? Might be good to get food in our bellies before hours in the cold."

"Good idea," says Henry, joining me at the table while Julia heads to the stove.

Henry's leg jiggles up and down and he flicks his spoon against the table.

"Calm yourself, Henry, we're in no rush. There's a couple of weeks yet till we're in Norwich."

"You're right as usual. I just don't like all that work hanging over me."

"You're as impatient as our Nellie," says Julia, shaking her head.

My leg starts to jiggle too. Not at the thought of work what lies ahead but 'cause we'll soon be headed for Norwich. Norwich means Florrie, and I can't wait to see her. We make it to Norwich twice a year, Easter and Christmas. It's a busy old time, and between the fair and Florrie's work in the factory we don't get many hours together, but what we get, we make the most of.

"You excited for Norwich, Nellie?"

"Do you need to ask?" I grin at Julia.

"I bet Florrie is counting down the days. She can stay with us a night or two if you'd like that?"

"We'd both love that, I'm just not sure she can get away that long. Mum's not been too good the past couple of years."

Julia's face darkens at the thought of my mum. I'd mistakenly thought them friends when we first met, but I get the feeling if Julia never sees her again, it will be too soon.

"Well, it's fine talking about Norwich, but we need to get out of Wisbech first," says Henry. He puts his bowl to his lips and glugs down his soup. "Come out and help as soon as you're done. We need all hands on deck."

It's quite the job getting the shooting gallery down. The sides and roof are heavy, but the canvas comes off with a bit of jiggling. Julia folds it all into neat squares and packs it onto the trailer. Henry takes off the targets and I help him clean them. They're bloody heavy, I can tell you! Thousands of pellets have dented the bright paintwork of the metal animals but they're still beautiful. Will comes over to help Henry lift the big iron plates and load them onto the trailer. In return we'll help them pack up their coconut shy, even though they have a gaff lad helping them.

After hours of lifting, packing, and storing we're ready to get back on the road. I always have mixed feelings at these times. It's sad to see the fair being packed away, brightness and fun draining from a town, leaving only sweet wrappers and toffee apple sticks lying on the ground as a clue we were there. The town that was alive with colour and noise becomes grey and ordinary. The river that dazzled with coloured electric lights is now brown and sad.

But there's also excitement in the air, for we're moving on. We'll have a couple of weeks in Swaffham at our winter quarters, then onto Norwich. All are excited about Norwich, for the cattle market is one of the best spots we get, and the city folk come out in their thousands to welcome us year on year.

I head into the wagon and help Julia pack away the break-ables. I sometimes wonder if it wouldn't be easier if we had fewer ornaments and trinkets, but Julia would never have it. She's as house proud as they come, even though her house isn't a house. For her, the effort of packing and unpacking every few days is worth it to create a home. I'd love to see Mum's face if she ever came to the wagon. She can't even manage to dust a few candlesticks.

Henry hitches the horses to the wagon and trailer and we're off. Not at the speed he'd like, for the roads are jam-packed with others doing the same. Kiddies come out and wave and I wave back, grateful for the coins they've put in our pockets. We're behind Thurston and his long train of wagons and trailers. Steam spews out from his traction engines and it's hard to see out of the windows for all the white smoke. After a few miles, he turns off towards Norwich and the air around us clears. It's a grey day, and I begin to understand why Julia's not so keen on the fens. The scenery beyond the window is the same for miles, fields, dykes, sky. The only interesting thing about it today is the windmills, and even they look gloomy, stood all on their own.

It's a relief when we reach the winding lanes nearer our winter quarters at Swaffham. We pull onto the patch of waste ground that we call home and unhitch the horses. Henry wastes no time heading into town to look for work. If he can get a couple of weeks' casual labour, it will add a helpful dollop to our coffers.

Me and Julia begin the unpacking, carefully taking glass and ceramic ornaments from cupboards and boxes, unwrap-ping them, and polishing them till they're gleaming. Soon the wagon looks just as before. We could still be in Wisbech if you just looked inside. Outside is different though. All the colourful stalls and rides lie on trailers, hidden beneath canvas blankets and secured with rope. Wagons lie in a circle and the kiddies are already out playing while their mums spruce up their homes.

Some of the men are out fixing up rides, mending broken boards on stalls, or just giving their stuff a good clean. It's useful having a couple of weeks back in Swaffham, for a week-long fair means the stalls and rides get plenty of wear and tear.

"You got time to give me a hand?" calls Sophia.

"Good timing, me and Julia have just finished here," I say, and I head over to her wagon. "What do you need doing?"

"Well, all that mud at Wisbech has left my stall in a right old state. I could do with some help cleaning it up."

"Hand me a bucket," I say, and she grins.

Will and Sophia's gaff lad is meeting them in Norwich, so it's just the two of them to get any cleaning and repairs done. I'm glad to help if I can. I like Sophia. She's older than Julia, and not half as pretty, but she's got a filthy cursing mouth and makes me giggle plenty.

"Where's Will off to today?"

"Same as Henry, looking to pick up a bit of work in town."

"Looks like you could have done with him here," I say, as she pulls back the canvas cover to reveal wooden boards, muddy and splintered.

"Yes, I could. Those bloody local lads did a grand job battering the stall. If it wasn't for Will stopping me, I'd have gone out and beat those little buggers black and blue."

I laugh, picturing the scene in my head. Sophia would've done a good job on them, no doubt. She's as strong as any man round here, and built like a steam engine, Henry says. We begin scrubbing the wood free of mud, but as we do, it shows up more patches where holes have been kicked, or broken bottles have scratched the beautiful paintwork.

"Will won't be pleased when he sees this," says Sophia, surveying the damage, hands on her big hips. "Good thing you're helping, or this would take me all day. Julia and Henry are lucky to have you, girl."

"I'm lucky to have them."

"You don't miss your family?"

"No, only my sister. Not the others."

"How many brothers and sisters you got then?"

"Eight now, but I've not met my littlest brother."

"Eight? Bloody hell. Some people have all the luck."

"How come you don't have no children?"

"The Westrop curse, me and Julia call it. We'd both like to have children but it's not happened for neither of us. Our fellas blame us, of course, but we reckon it's too much of a coincidence, two brothers, no kiddies. Maybe they were fed something rotten when they were kids. Who knows? You can't dwell on it, mind, got to make the best of things."

We continue scrubbing, and I feel sorry for Sophia, for she has a faraway look in her eyes. It must be a double blow, no children and being a fair family. The businesses of showfolk are passed down through generations. What will happen to the coconut shy and shooting gallery when they're all gone?

***

Between the mending and cleaning, the two weeks in Swaffham fly by. The morning we're due to leave, I have butterflies in my belly and have to make several trips outside to relieve my nerves. As the horses draw us closer to Norwich, the nerves get worse. Every time we go back, I'm both excited and scared. Excited to be seeing Florrie, nervous I'll be seeing Mum. Not that Mum has come to see me yet, and we've been in Norwich twice a year ever since I've been with the fair.

Our wagon passes through streets that grow more familiar. I peer through the window and see kiddies running in and out of yards, all smiles, dirty faces, and bare feet. We're slowed by a herd of sheep being moved down the road, making their way to the cattle market. The new trams now seem to go all over the city, and I marvel at the sight, crossing my fingers they don't fly off their rails and bash into us.

"You alright?" says Julia. "It must be strange for you each time we come back."

"I'm fine," I lie, my belly churning.

"I can take you to see your mum and dad one day if you'd like?"

"No," I say. "I mean, no thank you. They'll be too busy with work to be bothering with the likes of me."

"Well, if, you're sure. But do say if you change your mind."

"I will," I say, knowing I won't.

Chapter 14

April 1910

We're eating supper when there's a knock on the wagon door. "I'll get it," I say, jumping out of my seat. I fling the door open and there's not time to take a breath before I'm in Florrie's arms.

"Blimey, look at you," she says, pulling away and holding me at arm's length. "You're even prettier than when I saw you at Christmas."

"Bloody hell, don't start that; you'll get me blushing and I'm not one to blush. Come in and have some food. That alright, Julia?"

"Of course it is."

Florrie squeezes round the table that's barely big enough for three. Julia grabs Florrie a plate of food and she tucks into it like nobody's business. She's thin, very thin, like she's not been getting enough good dinners in her.

"Would you like seconds?" Julia asks. Florrie blushes, but Julia ignores her red cheeks and ladles more food onto her plate before Florrie can refuse.

"How are things?" asks Henry through a mouthful of food.

"Not too bad. I'm at the factory all hours, and between that and looking after Mum and Fred there's not much time for anything else."

"Fred's your brother?"

"Yes, a darling little chap he is. Got Ellen's cheek, but at least he's sweet with it."

"Hey," I say, punching her on the arm.

"See what I mean?" she says, and the others laugh. I pretend I'm cross, but I know she's only teasing.

"I thought I'd bring Freddie to meet you tomorrow. If that's alright with you?"

"Yes, that would be grand. Come in the morning, we'll not be too busy then."

"How's your mum?" asks Julia. I'm not sure she really cares, but she's polite enough to ask.

"Oh, so-so. She's not been too well lately, but we muddle through."

"What's wrong with her?" I ask.

"Don't know. She won't go to the doctor and says she's fine. But we all know she's not. They've cut her hours at the factory, so at least she's getting some rest. She seems to be in a lot of pain, but complains about her lack of work more than any pain so it's bloody difficult to know what's going on."

"Think I should go and see her?"

Florrie shuffles in her seat. "I'm not sure about that. Don't know if she's up to visitors."

Julia's eye does that twitchy thing it always does when she's angry. I put my hand in hers and she gives mine a squeeze. I want her to know I'm alright, that I don't care whether I see Mum or not. She won't understand though, how could she, after longing for a child so long.

The fair's not open yet, but after dinner me and Florrie take a walk around the closed-up stalls.

"So, Ellen, what do you recommend when I come back tomorrow?"

"Well, first things first, no one calls me Ellen no more."

"But I've never known you as anything else!"

"Alright, you can call me Ellen, just you mind."

"Alright, alright, *Nellie*. Where should I take Freddie tomorrow?"

"First you must come to our shooting gallery. I'll get you in free, Julia and Henry won't mind."

"Is that safe for a four-year-old?"

"It will be alright with a bit of help. Henry only uses air rifles, too spooked by the accidental shootings on other stalls the past few years."

"You're not selling this very well."

I laugh and punch her again. "Believe me, Florrie, you won't find no shooting gallery safer than Henry's. After that you need to see Will and Sophia at their coconut shy."

"Henry's brother?"

"Yep. Next, I'd go to Thurston's. He's got a fancy cinematograph in the Agricultural Hall this year. Just check what he's showing before you go in. You don't want little Freddie being scared witless and having nightmares. He'd probably enjoy Howden's motor car track, and Richard's cake walk is always good fun."

"Sounds like we'll need the whole day and I've only got a few hours off work."

"Why don't you leave him with me, so long as he likes me?"

"Don't you have work to do?"

"Yes, but Monday is usually quiet, and Julia and Henry love having kiddies around. I'm sure they won't mind."

"Alright, let's see how it goes. He might hate you of course."

I go to punch her again but she's too quick for me and runs back to the wagon laughing.

***

I'm tired, for excitement at meeting Freddie kept me awake through the night. When I did sleep, I dreamt of Maude. I hope she don't haunt me forever. It must be because I'm back in Norwich that she's sneaking into my dreams once more. At nine o'clock, there's a knock at the door and Florrie opens it.

"Morning," she calls, and pokes her head through the opening. "Anybody home?"

"Yep, come in," I say. Julia and Henry are out readying the gallery, and it's fun to pretend the wagon's all mine for a while.

Florrie turns and I hear her whispering to someone behind her. "Fred's feeling a bit shy," she says over her shoulder.

I head over to the mantelpiece and take down one of Julia's china dogs. I poke its head round the door and put on my best version of a doggy voice.

"Woof woof, woof woof. Is there a boy called Fred around here somewhere? I heard he'd like to see inside my wagon." A giggle comes from behind Florrie's legs. "Woof woof, woof woof. Is that Florrie's bum giggling? Really, Florrie, you should have used the privy before you got here." The giggles turn to splutters. "Woof woof, woof woof. Would the giggling bum like to come and see inside my wagon?"

"It's not Florrie's bum, it's me!" cries a little boy, stepping out from behind Florrie.

"A boy? Woof woof. And who might you be?"

"I'm Fred. Pleased to meet you. Who are you?"

"Oh I'm, I'm..." Bloody hell, I need to think quick. "I'm Waggy."

"Waggy? That's a stupid name for a dog."

"Oh, yes, you're right, of course. It was my stupid owner what gave it to me. Would you like to meet her?"

Silence.

"She's very nice, woof woof. Even if she does think of bloody awful doggy names."

Through the crack in the door, I see Fred look up at Florrie. She nods her head to show it's safe to come in, and he climbs the steps and walks through the door.

"Oh, hello, who are you? Have you met my dog Waggy?" I say.

"Can I hold him?" Freddie asks.

Bloody hell, I hadn't bargained for this. Julia will go mad if he breaks one of her precious ornaments.

"Well, I suppose so. But Waggy is a very old dog so you must take care of him. Can you do that? Can you be gentle?"

Freddie nods. I hand him the china dog and he cradles it in his arms.

"Why don't you sit down?" I say and lead him to the chair by the fire. He don't take his eyes off the dog, stroking its cold surface as though it was a real dog with real fur. I crouch down beside him. "Freddie, I have a friend what makes the most wonderful gingerbread. Would you like some?"

He looks at Florrie.

"Gingerbread is like cake, Freddie, only nicer than any you will have tried. Why don't you have a small bit, and if you like it Ellen, I mean Nellie, can give you some more?"

He nods, and I catch him watching me wide-eyed as I pull down a tin and take a chunk of gingerbread from inside. I break off a corner and hand it to him. He holds it to his lips and tickles it with the end of his tongue. Next, he takes a tiny nibble. A smile crosses his face.

"More?"

"Freddie, that's very rude, how do you ask nicely?" says Florrie.

"More please, Nellie."

I hand him the rest of the piece and he gobbles it down in two mouthfuls. "Fancy another?"

"Yes!"

"Yes please," says Florrie.

"Yes please," says Freddie.

"Alright, Freddie, but don't be giving yourself belly ache or I'll be in Mum's bad books."

"Everyone's in Mum's bad books," he says through a mouthful of gingerbread.

I look at him, surprised, and he smiles at me, crumbs falling from his mouth and scattering across the floor. I bend to pick them up and give him a wink. He smiles, and I know I've won him round.

***

Freddie seems torn between excitement and fear as we walk through the fair. His right hand fills mine, and his left hand fills Florrie's. If anyone shouts, he jumps out of his skin and squeezes our hands hard.

"I know, let's see Aunt Sophia and Uncle Will first. I think you'll like them, Freddie, and I'm certain they'll like you."

Sophia is polishing the front of her stall when we walk up. She straightens, hands on her hips, and gives me a smile.

"So, Nellie, is this the mystery brother of yours?"

"Yep, this is Freddie."

"Hello, Freddie," she says.

Freddie twists himself round so he's hiding in Florrie's skirt. I crouch beside him. "It's alright, Freddie, Sophia is very kind. If we ask her nicely, she might let you have a try with her coconuts. Would you like that?"

"What's a coconut?"

I look up at Sophia and she hands me one. "Here, have a feel of this," I say, taking Freddie's hand and running it across the brown skin.

"It's prickly and rough," he says. "What is it?"

"Well, it's a right magical ball. For inside it has a magic potion what looks like milk."

"Can I try some?"

"Not today, only when there's a full moon. You can throw it though, and if you hit a target, you can win a prize."

"I can throw it?"

"Yes."

"Where?"

"How about we let Sophia show you, then you can see if you want a try?"

Freddie nods, and Sophia takes another coconut from her basket, hurling it at a target with a mighty *thwap*.

"Me try! Me try!"

"That alright?" I ask Sophia.

"Course it is. Come stand here, Freddie."

The intrigue of the coconut is too much for him to resist, and he stands beside Sophia as she shows him where to aim. He picks up the coconut and tries to throw it, but it lands at his feet. Sophia hands him another and holds it with him, helping him put some power behind it.

With Freddie distracted, I take the chance to speak to Florrie. "He's a lovely chap."

"Yes, that he is. Sorry he's been so shy; it takes him a while to warm to strangers."

It's stupid, but her words make me sad, for I shouldn't be a stranger to my own brother.

"Why's he so jumpy?"

Florrie stands silent.

"Oh, come on, Florrie. I know what goes on in that yard. You can talk to me."

"Well, I spose it's simple really. With you gone, Mum needed someone to fill your place. And you know what a place that was."

"She's unkind?"

"Sometimes. More often than not she ignores him, but he never knows when the meanness is coming. No wonder he's twitchy, poor fellow."

"At least he's got you."

"I do my best, but I'm at work so often he's left on his own a lot. It won't be long till I up and leave and who knows what will happen to him then."

We stand watching Freddie, giggling away with Sophia, despite none of his coconuts reaching their target. He bends down for another and beneath his shirt collar lies a thick layer of grime. His clothes hang off him, and compared to the well-fed, well-run fair lads, he's all skin and bone. But his bright blue eyes sparkle from his face, and I have a feeling he's a survivor. A tough Hardy, like me.

Chapter 15

April 1910

By lunchtime, Florrie says she has to get back to the factory and asks Freddie if he'd like to stay.

"Stay, stay!" he says, jumping round, full of sugar from the bonbons Sophia gave him.

"Alright, but I'm not sure how to get him home. I'm working till eight tonight."

"I could bring him, if Julia can spare me an hour or so?"

"You sure?"

No, I'm not sure at all. But if spending time with Freddie means going back to the yard, then I don't see I've much choice. "Let me run and check," I say, sprinting over to the shooting gallery. When Julia hears my plan, her face crumples up into a big frown.

"I'm not sure that's such a good idea, Nellie."

"I know, but if I don't, Freddie will have to go home now."

"Alright. Well, the only way I'm letting you do that, is if you let me come with you."

"What about the gallery?"

"It's not like we're run off our feet. If the crowds pick up, someone will lend Henry a gaff lad for an hour or two, I'm sure."

I hug her. "Thank you."

Julia tips my face towards hers. "You're my girl, Nellie. I'm not letting you face that bitch alone."

Her words surprise me, but what surprises me more is the rush of sympathy I feel towards Mum. She was a bitch to me, wasn't she? But maybe her life left her no choice? I push my thoughts away. I'm being a fool, Julia's the one what cares for me, not Mum. I give Julia a smile and run back to find Fred.

Me and Freddie spend a wonderful time wandering round the fair. Business picks up mid-afternoon and I take him with me to help at the shooting gallery.

"Walk up, walk up!" he calls, walking back and forth in front of the stall. He's that sweet, he draws the flatties like moths to a flame, putting my patter to shame. When things quieten down, we head off to explore.

"What would you like to do, Freddie?" I ask. "We could have a go on a ride, or see if we can find some magic?"

"Magic! Magic!" he says.

"Alright, I know just the place."

We weave through the crowds, and I'm careful to keep hold of his hand, for I don't want him wandering off and getting lost. Several of the fair folk ask who my friend is, and I'm proud as punch to tell them he's my brother. It's not long till we're at Madame Yelma's. Freddie's face fills with shock as she steps onto her stage. Her shiny black hair hangs below her waist and rouge covers her lips. She has a string of chains around her neck and jewels covering her clothes that jangle whenever she moves.

She gives the crowd her patter in a deep smooth voice, full of big pauses that keep the audience on the edge of their seats. A young girl appears beside her, carrying ropes, chains, and handcuffs. The poor young thing must be bloody chilly, for her clothes are that skimpy there's little point her wearing none. The young girl wraps Madame Yelma in ropes and chains, cuffing her wrists together. Madame Yelma wriggles about, proving to us that she is stuck fast.

"Count with my beautiful assistant Doreen," wails Madame Yelma. "For I shall break free from my chains in under thirty seconds!"

I cover my mouth as I let out a little snigger. Doreen? Couldn't they have given her a more exotic name? Maybe Madame Yelma don't want Doreen stealing too much attention. Poor thing.

"Ready?" shouts Doreen, arms flung out wide above her head.

"Yes!" scream the crowd.

"Thirty, twenty-nine, twenty-eight, twenty-seven..."

The crowd join in, many of them tripping up over their counting, for they'd struggle to count to thirty forwards never mind backwards. At four, Freddie's doing an impressive job keeping up with Doreen. No doubt he's a brother of mine.

"Ten, nine, eight, seven, six..."

The ropes are off, the chains too. She's got five seconds to get out of those handcuffs. I know it's all a con, but even I'm willing her on.

"Four, three, two, one!"

A roar goes up from the crowd as Madame Yelma lifts her free hands above her head and twirls them in the air like a dancer. She spins around, her gown flapping out around her, then takes a bow. Doreen takes a bow too, though I'm not sure counting back from thirty deserves much of a clap.

"Again, again," says Freddie.

"Sorry, Fred. Don't think I can stretch to another go. How about we find a different ride?"

He don't answer, just grabs my hand and pulls me through the crowd. He stops beside Elliot's school of boxers.

"Hmm, Freddie, I'm not sure Mum will be too happy to find I've taken you to a boxing show."

"I won't tell."

"Neither will I," I say, and we move closer.

From where we're standing, it don't look like a fair match. There's one man, likely six foot, all muscles and brawn. Beside him stands a scrawny creature, not much taller than me, and I'm short for my age.

"That little chap's going to get a battering," I say.

Freddie looks on wide-eyed as the big man throws the first punch. The little one staggers backwards, hand clasped to his eye. Oh, how wrong I was, for the little squirt sure has some fight in him. He charges forward, head butting the big lad in the chest and knocking the wind right out of him. While the big lad tries to catch a breath, the little one's on him, fists flying so fast they blur in front of our eyes. It don't take long before the big lad admits defeat, and roars of laughter fly out from the crowd.

We're about to walk away, when a young woman steps out, dressed in a man's trousers and shirt.

"She's not going to fight, is she?" Freddie asks.

"I think she might," I say, as surprised as he is.

Well, what can I say? That young girl puts her opponent firmly in his place. Her fists fly, throwing punch after punch till the lad curls up in a corner begging for mercy. Now the crowd go wild. They pull the woman off the stage, lifting her high above their heads, parading her round the stalls and shows, hailing her a hero. I wonder how those same chaps will feel, if their own women throw a punch back the next time their husbands go for them?

We have a go on Howden's motor car track, Stock's gallopers, roundabouts, swings, the cake walk. Freddie bounds round the fair, all endless energy and excitement. At five o'clock I buy him a toffee apple and we sit ourselves on the wagon steps.

"I'm tired, Nellie," he says.

"Well, I'm not surprised. I thought I was a lively one but you're full of beans. It's been a job to keep up. Have you had fun?"

Freddie grins, all toffee-covered teeth and dimply cheeks. "It's been the best day of my life," he says.

I put my arm round him and wait for him to finish his apple. Julia walks over, taking off her apron and unpinning her hair.

"You two ready?" she says.

"Yep, we're both done in. Time for home."

"Alright, just give me a minute to freshen myself up."

I'm surprised she's bothering, for no one will be fresh in the yard, but maybe she's as nervous as me. She's got nothing to worry about. Mum wouldn't try to take me back, even if Julia paid her.

"Right, let's go," says Julia. She's got her velvet coat on and has changed her shoes for ones with a higher heel. A silk scarf covers her hair, but blonde waves tumble down her back like gold cloth. I bet Mum hates her.

It's a slow walk across the river to the yard, for Freddie is fading fast. I lift him onto my back and carry him for a while, but he's surprisingly heavy for such a skinny chap, and I can't carry him for long. My pace slows as we walk along Oak Street. What a bloody stupid idea it was to come here. We pass Alice's yard and I'd like to give her a knock, but it would only delay matters. Best get this over with.

After four years of fair life, stepping back into Queen Caroline's is like seeing it for the first time. I nearly puke with the stink, for I've been spoiled with fresh air too long. The only stink that reaches my nose these days is the smoke from engines, and you get used to that pretty quick. Julia's heel catches on a cobble.

"Fucking hell," she says, then seeing my surprise, mutters, "Sorry."

I take hold of her hand and the three of us walk through the yard and up to my old front door.

"See you, Nellie," says Freddie, and reaches up to give me a kiss.

"I'll see you again at Christmas. Don't be forgetting me, will you."

"I'll remember you every day till Christmas comes round. Promise."

"Good chap. Can you let Mum know we're here?"

Freddie gives us one last wave before disappearing into the gloom. "Mum! Mum!" he yells.

There's a shuffle of footsteps on the staircase and an old, bent-backed woman leans against the doorframe. Her hair has lost all colour but grey and is even more straggly than I remember. Her cheeks have sunk lower and deep creases cover her face.

"Mum?"

"Ellen?"

"Actually, it's Nellie now."

Mum huffs. "What do you want?"

"We dropped Freddie back, so thought we'd say hello while we're here."

Thank God Julia's with me, for in front of Mum I feel six again. "Cat got your tongue has it, Ellen? Need your pretend mummy to answer for you?"

"I'm Nellie."

"You'll always be Ellen to me. Don't forget where you come from, girl. You're a Hardy, through and through."

"She's a Westrop now. You saw to that the night we met in that pub."

Mum glares at Julia, and maybe I imagine it, but I'm sure beneath the glare she looks sad.

"Well, you've said hello. Now you can bugger off."

"Let's go," says Julia. "We're not wanted here."

I don't know what I was expecting, but a smile would've been nice. Mum disappears back up the stairs, huffing and hacking away with every step. As we cross the yard, I turn back. A man stands in the doorway of our house. It must be Arthur, but he don't look himself. His clothes are hanging off him, his cheeks sunk back like Mum's. The small bit of hair still left on his head is wispy like a baby. I wave at him. He waves back, but it seems the effort of lifting his arm is too much and he slumps back against the doorway.

"Your mum didn't look too well," says Julia as we step out onto Oak Street.

"No, neither did Arthur. Did you see him?"

"I missed that. How old is he now?"

"Must be about twenty, but he looks like an old man. Maybe there's sickness in that house."

"Was Freddie alright?" I know Julia cares for Freddie's health, but she'll also be worrying he's passed an infection to us. It will spell disaster for the fair if he has.

"Seemed fine to me."

"Well then, it's most likely to be living in a rat-infested hovel and eating scraps that's made them unwell."

It must have pained Julia to see our house. Her face stayed straight while we were there, but she's so house proud. The stink and grime couldn't be further from the tidy warmth of her wagon.

"Come on, let's get you home."

I walk beside her down Oak Street, feeling nothing but relief to be escaping the yard once again.

Chapter 16

June 1910

We're on the road again, this time to Braintree. It's a fair old hike, and we'll be lucky if we do it in less than six hours. We don't usually head this far south, but Henry got wind Thurston will be there with his Electric Vaudeville, and that's guaranteed to draw the crowds.

It's evening before we pull up onto the fairground, though it's close enough to the longest day that we'll have many hours of daylight left for us. It's a smaller set-up than we're sometimes used to, but that means less competition, and hopefully greater earnings.

"What's going on there?" asks Julia, staring out of the window.

"Give us a look," I say, squeezing up to her. "Looks like a row. There's the fair lot, see, but I don't recognise the fellows they're rowing with."

Henry finds us our spot, secures the wagon, and we wander over to see what's wrong.

"Don't get too close, Nell," he says. "It don't look like a friendly meeting to me. We don't want you getting in the way of no flying fists."

Whatever they're talking about must be important, for there's work to do but no one is doing it. It's easy to spot which side is which. The fair folk are dressed down in their work clothes, not expecting to see no one but each other till tomorrow. The men's shirts are worn and oil stained, caps perched on their heads to keep the sun away while they work. The other group don't look like your average flatties. They are dressed up smart; suits, ties and funny round hats what don't quite fit their heads. While the fair folk wave their arms in the air, curse words hurled out everywhere, the flatties keep their arms still, voices quiet, faces serious.

"Oi, Charlie. What's going on?"

Charlie, Will's gaff lad, is stood near the front and moves back to report what's afoot.

"There's trouble brewing, no doubt about it."

"I can see that," says Henry. "What's the trouble about?"

"Well, seems the field has been double booked."

"Double booked? You sure?"

"I don't think those flatties are liars. They're religious nuts, here to preach the word of God and convert sinners like me."

"Good luck to them," says Henry grinning.

I giggle; Charlie's a decent enough chap, but he's a light fingered woo-er of ladies and I can't picture him in church.

"You send for someone right now to sort this out!" Old man Shipley who runs the carousel has a voice like a foghorn. It booms across the group and the flatties take a step back.

I wriggle further into the crowd, slipping between legs till I can hear the conversation. The leader of the flatties is holding something in each hand. I squeeze even further through the crowd. He's got a big old bible in one hand, and a sheet of paper in the other.

"This, sir, is a copy of our lease. I assure you everything is above board."

"You there," says one of the showmen. Bloody hell, he's pointing at me.

"Me?"

"Yes, you. You're Julia's girl, aren't you?"

"Yes, I am."

"Can you read?"

"Yes."

"Well, what are you waiting for?"

He signals to the paper in the flattie's palm. I step forward. The flattie hands over the paper and I try to make out the words on the page. I can read, but I'm not used to fancy words like this. There's unlikely to be anyone else in our group what can do better, so I give it a go.

"All looks above board," I say, and hand the paper back.

"You sure about that, girl?"

"If she says she's sure, she's sure." Julia steps through the crowd and puts an arm around my shoulder. "I can assure you all, that this girl has a bigger brain in her head than all of yours put together. You're best off trusting what she says."

"Sorry, love," says Shipley. "We have to be sure, see?"

"I understand," says Julia.

I expect her to pull me to the back of the crowd, but she stands beside me, as keen to find out what's going on as I am. She keeps her arm on my shoulder, like a real mum.

"Now you have assurances from us, we'd like some from you. Show us your own papers, please," says the flattie.

Oh dear. Our lot don't look best pleased being ordered round by the religious nut. A hum of whispers goes through the group, and a young lad is sent off to find the papers. He returns minutes later and hands them over to the flattie.

"Well, looks like your affairs are in order too. It must be a mix up on the part of the council. As we are all here now,

I don't suppose there's much we can do. Let's try and rub along together the best we can."

The showfolk don't reply. They wander away from the flattie, grumbling under their breath. As we begin to set up our stalls, it becomes clear we're all squished together closer than we'd like. The religious bunch have an enormous tent up to the left of the fairground. It's hard to move the big sheets of iron from the trailer to our spot, for Will's coconut shy is blocking our path.

"Sorry, Henry, there was nowhere else to put mine. I'll give you a hand with the sheets."

It takes all of us to carry the back plate and targets through the tiny gap we've been left.

"This is an accident waiting to happen," says Henry. "Pay close attention to the punters tomorrow, Nell, we don't want no one shooting across the other stalls."

"Don't worry, my beady eyes will keep watch."

"I'm sure they will, knowing you," he says, patting me on the back.

Me and Julia help lift the canvas onto the frame, and Henry locks away the rifles ready for tomorrow. The fairground feels a bit flat, like the religious nuts have stolen our excitement with their mumbo jumbo.

"Maybe you'll discover the meaning of life?" says Julia, but Henry's not impressed.

"Those folk are lucky having time to ponder a higher being. Us ordinary folk just have to get by one day to the next."

"I'm sure they're harmless enough."

"We'll see."

***

I step out into the warm June sunshine to relieve myself, and splutter in disbelief. "Henry, Julia, you got to come see this."

"What is it?"

"You'll see."

They follow me outside and take a moment getting used to the bright sunshine.

"What am I s'posed to be looking at then?" asks Henry.

"I don't know how you could miss it," I say. "Try looking up."

We all look up. Against the bright blue sky, an enormous flag flaps around in the breeze. Henry looks puzzled, unable to read the words painted on it, but Julia claps her hands across her mouth.

"Don't leave me in suspense," says Henry. "What does it say?"

"It says... it says..." I try to be serious, not wanting to make Henry cross, but every time I go to speak another giggle bubbles up. Julia gives me a warning look.

"It says 'Prepare to meet your God'."

"You're joking."

"Sorry, love, I wish I was."

"Prepare to meet your God? Flying high above a fairground? What the bloody hell are they thinking?"

"I think hell is exactly what they're thinking about," I say, spluttering again.

"That's not helpful," says Julia, frowning at me.

"This is a disaster," says Henry.

"No, it's not," says Julia. "Look on the bright side; maybe their punters will come over to us once they've finished whatever is going on in that tent of theirs."

"You think we'll draw the same type of crowd, do you? They're probably rubbing their hands in glee, a captive market of sinners for them to get their hands on. No, it will put our punters off, you mark my words."

Henry storms off to moan with Will, and Sophia appears beside our wagon.

"You seen it then," she says.

"Yes, Henry's not best pleased."

"Will neither. I reckon it's funny. I've bet Will half a crown the novelty factor will draw in more crowds than usual."

"I hope you're right," says Julia. "I prefer living with a happy Henry."

"He'll be happy, don't you worry," says Sophia.

Turns out Sophia's right, and wins her bet, much to Will's annoyance. News of the double-booking spreads like wildfire and it's not just the town folk drawn in. Buses are laid on from surrounding villages and people flood the fair, their pockets jangling with coins. We work day and night to meet their demand for a good time. Flatties with bibles under their arms prowl round the stalls, but the punters mock them and see them as a bit of fun. The religious nuts don't find it fun, and make sure they're back in their big tent before the sun sets.

Our last evening is especially busy, for it's the last chance for folks to have a giggle at the flag flying high above us. Coloured electric lights shine from stalls, and kiddies are allowed to stay up late and join the fun. There's a good bit of liquor been drunk by the punters, and a few are getting rowdy. An older lady dressed in fine clothes draws my eye.

She's stumbling about from stall to stall, a gaggle of young lads following her. She looks respectable, but her mouth isn't. Needs a good clean out, I'd say.

Bloody hell, what's she doing? The crowd what was at the shooting gallery is taken with her, and I follow them to see what the fuss is about. Poor woman, looks like she should be in the loony bin. She lifts her arms wide in the air, and spins round and round till she stumbles into one of the gaff lads. Her hands stroke his jacket, and she tries to give him a smacker on the lips. He pushes her away but not before his friends have had a good laugh at his expense.

Now she starts running round the circle what's formed around her. Oh God, someone needs to stop her. Mums cover their kiddies' eyes as she runs from side to side, lifting her skirt and showing off her knickers. Wild cries are coming from her mouth like she's an animal. Henry walks up beside me.

"Why's she doing that?" I ask him.

"Either drunk or mad is my guess."

"She's making a right bloody fool of herself."

"That she is. I'll try and stop her."

Henry walks into the middle of the circle and tries to grab her arm, but she turns and slaps him. I don't know whether to laugh or scream as she takes off her knickers and begins chasing Henry with them. Bloody hell, poor chap don't know what to do. He runs from her, and the crowd roars with laughter. Of course, this encourages her even more, and she starts chasing other folk, spinning her knickers above her head like a lasso.

Henry makes the most of her attention being elsewhere and runs back to me.

"Come on, into the wagon. I don't like how this is going. Fingers crossed someone's called the law."

Well, that's not a sentence I ever thought I'd hear him speak. He grabs my hand and leads me to the wagon. On the way, we stop and close up the gallery. There's a bigger show in town than ours now, and the way the crowd are riled up, it's better safe than sorry. Julia has already returned to the wagon and is watching the action, face pressed up to the window.

"She gave you a right run for your money," she says as we head inside.

"It's not funny."

"It is a bit."

I can't tell if Henry is mad, but his lip starts to twitch, and before we know it, he's rattling the ornaments with his mighty laugh. "Maybe she was preparing to meet her God by lassoing him with her drawers," he splutters.

"What a strange visit this has been," I say. That sets us off again. We have tears streaming down our cheeks, and my belly hurts from laughing.

The police do come, but the woman puts up a good fight. It takes three of them to cart her off. The crowd boo the law, for they want the show to go on. As I lie in bed, I picture the woman, mad as a hatter, and hope our paths never cross again. Tomorrow we move on. I think we'll all be glad to see the back of Braintree for a while.

Chapter 17

July 1910

Bloody hell, I'm excited. So excited I can't stand still, and skip my way along the street, Julia and Henry huffing and puffing behind me trying to keep up.

"We've got ages yet, Nell, slow yourself down."

"But I don't want to be late."

"We won't be late," says Henry. "But I might have a heart attack before we get there if you keep this pace up."

I stop and wait for them. Henry's the last person going to collapse thanks to a brisk walk. He's thin as a rake and don't stop moving from dawn to dusk. He'll outlive the rest of us, I'm sure.

"Damn these old folks, holding me back," I say, and Henry launches into a sprint, chasing me in mock anger. Of course, I can't outrun him, his legs are lanky as a beanpole while mine are more like a bird's, thin and short and never growing much. He reaches me and scowls, but his face quickly breaks into a grin and he's tickling me so hard, if he don't stop soon, I'll wee myself.

"Oi, you two, we're not among fair folk yet. Don't make a show of yourself on the street, please." Julia is cross, but not so cross she don't give me a sneaky tickle too as she passes. "I thought you were worried about being late?" she calls over her shoulder.

"Alright, boss, coming," says Henry, jogging to catch her. I take a moment to catch my breath and watch them striding off down the road. They must be heading for fifty by now, but they seem like spring chickens to me. It's only their hair what gives them away.

As we get closer to the field, more and more fair folk join us on the path, all chattering, the ladies smoothing down their hair as they walk. Julia has altered my curtain dress, adding a lovely bit of rose cotton to the bottom so it still fits. I must have grown a bit at least, for the hem came above my knees when I tried it on. I'm still small though, short and skinny, not like the other kids who are all strong arms and long legs, even the girls.

We turn a corner and there in front of us lies Thurston's Vaudeville, standing on its own in the middle of a field. It's even more impressive without other stalls crammed round it. They have the electric lights lit up, even though it's daytime, and the sun catches them, spreading a rainbow of red, blue, and green over the grass. The enormous canvas roof lies taut in coloured stripes, waiting to be filled with happy showfolk.

It's bloody kind of Thurston to lend his Theatre Vaudeville to the Showman's Guild for the occasion. Must have been a right pain in the arse putting it up for just one day. Julia takes my hand, and we step inside. They've got tables from somewhere, and they fill the stage, ready and waiting for hungry mouths. Women scuttle round, helping people find their seats.

"Westrop, Henry," he says as an efficient looking woman checks her list.

"Ah yes, here you are. Far side on the left, please," she says, pointing us in the direction we must go.

We find our seats, and Julia spreads a napkin over her skirt. "Best behaviour please, Nellie. It's kind of the Thurstons to allow us to join them."

When everyone is sitting down, I try to do a head count. I reckon there's ninety, maybe a hundred showfolk here. It's hard to count though, 'cause kiddies keep getting up and running round, and men move to other tables, leaning over shoulders, discussing business. An army of women scurry round, serving up cups of tea and sandwiches.

"Don't eat with your mouth open," whispers Julia, as I shove another ham sandwich in my mouth.

"Sorry," I say.

"Don't talk with your mouth full neither," she says, fiddling with her napkin and smoothing her hair. Henry looks across and gives me a wink. Julia is funny on occasions like these. Always polite, always keen to put on a good show. It's like she's trying to prove she deserves her place at the table. She turns to talk with the woman beside her and I shove another sandwich in my mouth before she can tell me off. The sandwiches are followed by cake, big hunks of Victoria sponge filled with fat dollops of jam and cream. I get a splodge on my chin and Julia leans over to wipe it away with her napkin.

"Bloody hell, I didn't know we were in for this," I whisper to her.

She follows my pointing finger to the local vicar taking the stage.

"Bet I fall asleep," I say.

"You'd better not. I'll pinch you if you do."

I bet she would too, anything to keep up appearances. Thurston clinks a glass with his knife and the tent falls silent. The vicar clears his throat and launches into one of the most boring speeches I've ever heard. Reverend Bennett he's called. A young, earnest man, determined to save our souls. Good luck to him I say, stifling a big yawn.

It's bloody hot in the Vaudeville, filled with bodies and the sun beating down on the canvas. I yawn again. Between the heat and my full belly, it's an effort to stay awake. I occupy myself with my napkin, folding and twisting it into different shapes beneath the table. Julia notices but says nothing. She must be pleased my hands are busy and my gob shut.

As soon as the vicar shuts up, Welton stands to thank the Thurstons, the Guild, and the worker ants what served us our tea. Kiddies shuffle in their seats, and as soon as Welton is done, there's a stampede to the door.

"Can I go with them?" I ask Julia.

"Yes. Just don't be getting up to mischief."

Best not make any promises. Instead, I hug her and make a sprint for the door. It's wonderful to be out in the fresh air, for the tent was getting that stuffy I thought I'd stick to my seat. Beside the field is a patch of woodland and that seems to be where the kiddies are headed. It will be nice to play with other kiddies again. Don't get me wrong, I love Julia and Henry to bits, but coming from a house packed with brothers and sisters it's strange being just three. Sometimes I miss my old friends too. It's hard to make friends when you're out on the road so much. The bigger families have no problem, brothers, sisters, cousins all travelling together. But with the Westrops all being childless, it don't give me much options.

"What you doing?" I ask a group of lads.

"Hide and seek, want to play?"

"Yep."

"You're Nellie, yes?"

"Yep, that's right. And you're Simon. I've seen you at some of the fairs."

"These are my brothers, Tom and Ned. These three here are my cousins, Nick, Davey, and Mike."

"Come on, get on with it," says one of the lads.

"Right, Nellie, you can be seeker."

I want to hide, not seek. I'm good at hiding. But as I'm new to their group I don't complain.

"How long shall I count for?"

"How long *can* you count for?"

"As much as you like."

A couple of the boys snigger. I'll show them. "I'll give you to a hundred," I say. I lean against a tree and cover my eyes. I shout the numbers out, so they know I'm a good counter. "Ninety-eight, ninety-nine, one hundred! Ready or not, here I come!"

I run through the woods, not minding the scratches I get on my legs, or the nettles what sting my arms. In five minutes, I've found them all, and they don't look best pleased.

"Who did you find first?" asks Simon.

"That one," I say.

"Right, Tom, you're seeker."

"You need to count to a hundred like I did."

Tom looks worried, and Simon steps in to help his brother. "We'll both be seekers," he says, and they walk over to the tree.

"One, two, three..."

I run round looking for good places to hide. There's plenty of hiding spots, but all can be easily found.

"Fifteen, sixteen, seventeen..."

I look up. A huge oak tree is stretching up into the sky. Is it climbable? I reckon I could give it a go.

"Twenty, twenty-one, twenty-two..."

I grab hold of the trunk and begin shimmying my way up. I slip back down, and bark tears my leg, leaving blood trickling to my shoes.

"Thirty-five, thirty-six, thirty-seven..."

One more try. I grab hold of knots in the wood and push hard with my feet. My hands grip a branch and I yank myself up onto it. It's too close to the ground, I'll be spotted. I need to go higher.

"Fifty-seven, fifty-eight, fifty-nine..."

My hands are sore and my leg stings. Keep going. Have to keep going.

"Eighty-one, eighty-two, eighty-three..."

I slump back against a thick branch. Leaves hide me safely away and those boys will have a job finding me up here.

"Ninety-nine, one hundred. Ready or not, here we come!"

I listen as the boys run through the wood, finding all of the others, one by one.

"Where's Nellie?"

"Maybe she gave up and went back?"

"Too wit, too woo!"

"Did you hear that?"

"Too wit, too woo!"

"Is that Nellie?"

I giggle, high enough up that they won't hear me. Through a gap in the leaves, I see the boys scrabbling around, looking behind every bush and tree trunk.

"Too wit, too woo," I call again.

"Nellie!" calls Simon, his hands cupped to his mouth.

"Simon!" I call back.

"She's round here somewhere," he says. "Keep looking."

It must be another ten minutes that they look for. "Alright, Nellie, we give up," says Simon.

Surely they can't be giving up so soon? It must be a trick. I watch as they walk through the wood. I know their game. They'll pretend they're leaving, then jump out at me when I come down. I sit tight. Another ten minutes pass. Bloody hell, it's boring up here. A twig is poking into my bum and leaves keep going in my mouth. Time to get down.

Getting up the tree was hard, getting down is harder still. The first few branches are easy, a wooden step ladder I can climb down. Closer to the trunk, the branches are fewer. I'll just have to go for it. I shimmy down the trunk, bark and twigs scraping my skin as I go. I'm almost at the bottom when a small branch attaches to the skirt of my dress. I try to pull it off, but I lose my grip on the tree and go slithering to the ground. There's a horrible ripping sound as I go. Bugger.

Safely on the ground, I inspect the damage. That bloody tree has ripped the back of my skirt in two. My cheeks flush, even though there's no one here to see. My leg is stained red with blood, and scratches cover my arm like I've been attacked by an angry cat. I run my fingers through my hair, as if that will make things any better. There's no sign of the lads, so I head back towards the field. At the edge of the wood, I stop. Julia will be mad. Even Henry might be mad.

Bloody hell, I can see them outside the tent, hands up to their eyes, searching for signs of me on the field. I'll have to go. I can't hide forever. With my back to the trees, I edge along the field. When I'm close enough, I wave. Henry beckons me to go to them but I stay put. No chance I'm getting a public bollocking. Henry turns to Julia and says something. I'm too far away to hear what, but he leaves her behind and walks over to me. As he gets closer, the smile drops from his face.

"What the bloody hell happened to you?"

"A tree."

"A tree?"

"Yes, a tree."

"Well, Nell, you're going to have to come up with a better excuse than that before Julia sees you."

"Like what?"

"Oh, I don't know, maybe you were attacked by a bear? Or stolen away by fairies?"

"Really?"

"On second thoughts, maybe telling the truth is best."

He has his arms folded and is doing a good job of looking cross. But he can't stop his eyes twinkling and that gives him away.

"Come over to Julia. Time to face the music, I'm afraid."

I shake my head and fold my arms.

"Nellie, I'm not asking you, I'm telling."

I shake my head again.

"What's wrong with you? This isn't like you. Come on, do as I say."

"I can't."

"What? Why can't you?"

"Promise you won't tell no one?"

"Well, I don't keep secrets from Julia."

"No one except Julia then."

"I promise."

My cheeks go all hot as I turn myself around so he can see my back. He claps his hand over his mouth.

"Stop laughing!"

"I'm not laughing."

"You are!"

"Well, you might not mind me laughing by the time Julia sees you. I doubt she'll find this funny."

We don't have long to find out, for Julia is marching across the field looking cross. How does she know? She must have magic powers.

"Look at the state of you," she says. "You're all cut up and bruised. Are you alright?"

Well, this is better than I'd hoped for.

"I'm fine," I say.

"Same can't be said for her dress though."

I glare at Henry and he covers his mouth again.

"Nellie?"

"It's nothing."

"Nellie?"

"Oh, alright then," I say, turning round and feeling my cheeks heat up again.

Julia claps her hand over her mouth just like Henry did, but she's not laughing. "What have you done to your dress? You look like a vagabond!"

"I'm sure it can be patched up," says Henry.

"Have you seen it? Everyone can see her knickers! She's a disgrace. How can we get her out of here without the Thurstons seeing us?"

"Why do you care what they think anyway? They're nothing special."

"You shut your mouth, girl, and stop your insolence. How ungrateful, after the treat they laid on for us today."

Bloody hell, Julia is proper mad. I shut my gob and look at the ground.

"We can probably get back through the woods. Have you said your goodbyes?"

"Yes, I have."

"Then that looks like our best option."

"Fine," says Julia. "You go in front, Nellie, and I'll protect your modesty."

We tramp through the woods for ages. As soon as we're safely among the trees, Julia grabs my wrist and near enough drags me along. It would have been much quicker on the road, but I'm wise enough to keep my trap shut. And at least this way I don't need to worry about anyone seeing my knickers.

Back at the wagon she makes me strip down to my underwear, and there's no sheet offered to protect my modesty. She warms some water and cleans off my cuts, working in silence. I'm certain she's rubbing my legs harder than she needs to.

"Sorry," I say. "I didn't mean to get mucky, I got stuck in the tree, see, and fell on a branch."

"I know what happened, Nell. What makes me cross... no, what makes me sad, is how careless you have been. I let you wear your special frock, that I spent an age altering for you, and instead of taking care of it you went climbing trees like a savage. I don't know why I bothered."

Now I feel terrible. I'd not thought about the care Julia had put into my dress. I thought she was just mad at being shown up in front of her friends.

"I really am sorry," I say, my eyes welling with tears.

"I can see that, just let this be a lesson. There's a time and place for tomfoolery. A special treat tea is not the place. If you go through life acting how you want when you want, you'll receive nothing but trouble."

"Sorry." How many times will I need to say sorry before she forgives me?

"It's straight to bed with no supper for you tonight. Off you go."

Julia and Henry sit outside to eat, leaving me to stew in my own juices. They're out there for ages, playing cards together under an oil lamp. I'm still awake when they come in for bed. Julia must know I'm awake, but she ignores me, right until she's in her nightdress. Then she squats down beside my bed and whispers, "You awake?"

"Yes."

"You're still in the doghouse, but I have one question for you."

"What?"

"Did the other kiddies find you?"

"You mean when I hid?"

"Yes."

"No, they gave up in the end."

It's dark so I can't be sure, but I think she's smiling. She bends down and kisses my forehead.

"Sleep tight, Nell. Tomorrow's a new day and we'll start afresh."

Chapter 18

December 1910

Blimey, the year has flown. Ilford, Cambridge, Bedford, Thrapston, Aldeburgh, Banbury, you name it, we've been there. Takings have been good, the flatties' appetite for a fair as hungry as ever. The new rides help, steam power making everything faster, brighter, noisier. The flatties lap it up. Ours might not be as fancy as some shows, but the shooting gallery never loses its appeal. Must be the chance to hold a gun what does it. Those office blokes with soft hands like how manly they feel holding metal between their fingers. Have to keep an eye on their macho antics after they've sunk a few pints though.

I'm always excited this time of year, for Norwich is on the horizon. Freddie will have grown big since I saw him at Easter, I hope he remembers me. Before we can get to Norwich, we're in Beccles. It's a pretty little town this, all red brick buildings, and wide river. It would be nicer in summer, mind. As well as the usual stalls and rides, a few folk are selling bits and bobs for Christmas. Homemade wreaths and gingerbread houses. I think it's a bit early, we wait for Christmas Eve to get gifts, but I s'pose there's no harm planning ahead.

We'll only be here for two days, and the first has gone very well. These small-town fairs often turn out well for us, probably 'cause there's not much else for people to do. It's miserable weather, but to be expected this time of year and it don't seem to put people off. The flatties come that wrapped up, they look four times their usual size. Either that, or people are fat around these parts.

"I'll need you to mind the gallery all day today, Nell," says Julia, pulling across her sliding door.

"Everything alright?"

"Henry's not too good."

"What's wrong?"

"Just a touch of cold, I think. Probably from standing in the freezing weather all hours."

"He got a fever?"

"Could be worse, but he's burning up and very snuffly."

An enormous sneeze comes from over in their bed.

"You need anything, Henry?"

"S'alright, Nell, Julia's a fine nurse, got everything under control."

He must be feeling rough, for Henry never stops work for nothing. I've seen him working the gallery with a burning fever and dickie belly and not complain. Strong as an ox, Julia says, and she's right. Best keep our fingers crossed we don't all go down with it, or the Christmas season will be a disaster. And, if it turns out to be something worse than a cold, Julia will have to inform the council, and we'll be out on our own somewhere till no longer infectious.

"You start setting up, and I'll be over as soon as I've made Henry some breakfast."

"I'm not hungry," calls Henry.

"You got to feed a cold, love," Julia calls back.

I wrap myself up nice and warm and head outside. It's a job setting up on my own, for I'm not tall enough to reach the top of the canvas, but I try my best. Will and Sophia notice me struggling and wander over to help. By the time Julia comes out of the wagon, we're all set up.

"Goodness me, Nell, you've done a grand job here."

"Did it all by herself," says Sophia, winking at me.

"That so?" says Julia, giving me a nudge.

"How's Henry?"

"Oh, he'll live. Managed to get a bit of porridge down him and he's perked up a bit. He'll be right as rain soon enough."

***

Me and Julia do a fine job of holding the fort while Henry's laid low, but we're both knackered by the time packing up rolls round.

"You mind me sleeping in with you tonight?" says Julia. "I'd like to avoid Henry's germs if I can."

"Will you fit?"

"I'm not that fat!" says Julia.

"You know I didn't mean that," I say.

"We'll manage if we top and tail. I'll try not to snore."

It's strange having Julia in with me, but nice, too. We chat a while, but when I let out a huge yawn, she tells me it's time for sleep. I don't sleep well. In the night, her feet keep bashing my face, and she wriggles like a worm beneath the covers. In the middle of the night, I give up, and doze in the armchair till morning.

Julia stirs. "Morning," I say.

"Morning."

Bloody hell, she sounds like she's got a peg clipped to her nose. She pulls the blankets tight, shivering, even though I've lit the fire and it's warm in the wagon.

"Oh no, not you as well."

"Seems so," she says, shivering again. "Can you check on Henry for me?"

I slide open the door and find Henry propped up in bed.

"How are you feeling?"

"Better than before, but weak as a baby. Not sure I'll be much use today. Is Julia alright?"

"Seems you've slipped her your ailment. And as she shared with me last night, she's probably slipped it to me too."

"Bloody hell, what are we going to do about the gallery?"

"I'm alright to work."

"I know, Nell, but you can't do it on your own."

"Leave it to me," I say. "I'll make you both a tea, then see if between me, Will and Sophia we can't sort something out."

"I don't know how we managed before you came along," Henry says, slipping back between the blankets and closing his eyes.

Once I'm sure they're comfy, I leave Julia and Henry and seek out Sophia. Somehow, she rallies folk round, and the gallery is covered for the day, folks lending gaff lads and family members in shifts so we're not left short.

The day turns out better than I'd hoped. It's fun working with different folk every couple of hours. I pick up a few new lines for my patter and get a few new curse words under my belt too. In the evening, Sophia relieves me so I can check on the invalids. It's a relief to find them sat up together in bed, chatting away.

"Looks like you're on the mend."

"Getting there," says Henry. "You still feeling alright?"

"Yes, fine. No sign of even a sniffle."

"You're made of strong stuff, Nell."

"That I am. Is there anything you need? I should get back to the gallery, but can make you a cuppa before I go?"

"That would be lovely if you have time," says Julia. She blows her nose on her hanky and gives me a little smile. "A fresh hanky would be nice, too. I reckon I could wring this one out and fill a bucket."

"Yuck."

"Yuck indeed."

I fuss around them, making tea and checking they're comfy. Being the grown-up for a while is fun. I imagine this is how I'll look after my own kiddies. When I'm a mum, I'll be like Julia, not like my mum.

"You alright for me to get back now?"

"Yes, best not keep Sophia too long, she's her own stall to get back to."

"Try to get some rest," I say, sounding all grown up again.

To get back to the shooting gallery I need to walk past Thurston's roundabout, but as I get closer it becomes harder to walk for all the crowds. What are they staring at? The roundabout is turning as it should, organ blaring. Pigs move up and down, up and down, balloons go round and round and round on their poles. All the punters are looking out into the crowd.

I slide myself through the sea of bodies to see what's up. A young lad is stumbling round, out of his mind on drink by the looks of things.

"Stay back please," the gaff lad shouts over at him.

It makes no difference.

"Sir, please stay back."

The drunk man lurches toward the roundabout.

"Fucking hell, stand back, I said," shouts the gaff lad.

The drunk man ignores him, takes a few steps back then sprints forward, jumping toward the roundabout. Bloody hell. Screams fly out from the crowd. He's clinging on to a pole above one of the pigs. Inside the roundabout the engine is working full pelt, causing wheels to squeal as they turn. "Hold on," I say. "Please hold on." Of course, the man will never hear me above the roar of the crowd. The gaff lad runs towards the man as best he can, but the platform is spinning and his progress slow. Before he can reach him, the man loses his grip and slips beneath the platform, down into the working parts of the ride.

"Cut the engine," the gaff lad screams. "Cut the engine."

It takes an age to shut off the engine, though it can only have been a minute or so. The ride revolves round two, maybe three more times, then slows.

"I need some help," the gaff lad yells into the crowd. "Is anyone here a doctor?"

"I'll fetch one," says a woman, turning and running towards the town.

Four burly men climb onto the roundabout and follow the gaff lad down below. The crowd are silent now, all of us sending up prayers for the poor lad trapped beneath. Five minutes pass, and we hold our breath. Some cheer as the men appear, carrying the poor chap. But their cheers turn silent as we catch a glimpse of him. His face is white, shining like a ghost beneath a layer of sweat. His torn trousers turn from grey to red as blood pours from a wound.

"Stand back," shouts a man. I move back with the crowd, pleased to get some distance between me and the broken man. "Lay him flat."

The five rescuers lay the poor chap out on the ground like he's made of china. One of them removes his braces and ties them tight above the leg wound.

"Any sign of a doctor?" calls the gaff lad.

The crowd shake their heads.

Folk are getting jittery. Men hold their women close to shield their eyes from the horrid scene on the ground. I want to tear my eyes away, but I can't. I've seen a dead baby before, but not a grown man, and I hope today won't be the time I do. I pray the blood will stop coming. But beneath the electric lights, I see a pool of red growing across the grass.

"Make way, make way," comes a shout. Horse's hooves pummel against the grass and a carriage pulls up beside us.

"You the doctor?" asks the gaff lad.

"Yes, I am. This man needs to get to the hospital right now. Help me get him into the carriage."

The rescuers do as they're told and carefully lift the bleeding man onto the carriage floor.

"Will he be alright?" the gaff lad asks.

"Only time will tell. Looks like you've done all you can for him. If you'd not bound his leg, he'd have died by now."

As the carriage pulls away, men remove their caps, and women close their eyes in prayer. I stumble away from the roundabout, my legs wobbling beneath me. Sophia is standing beside the shooting gallery, eyes searching for me in the crowd. As I get closer, she rushes toward me.

"What's happened? We got word there was an accident, but I couldn't leave the stall." She bends down so she's looking me in the eye. "Nellie, are you alright? You don't look so good."

I tumble into her, and she wraps her big arms around me. Crying's not something I do much, but right now I make up for that. It's like there's a pump behind my eyes that I can't turn off. Even when the water stops pouring, every few seconds my shoulders shudder, and I can't catch my breath.

"Will," Sophia calls. "Close up the gallery, I'm taking Nell to our wagon."

I try to stand on my own, but my legs are that wobbly, I tumble into Sophia once more. She scoops her arms beneath my legs and lifts me, cuddling me like a baby.

"Lucky you're such a slip of a thing," she says.

Inside her wagon, she lights the fire and sits me down on her bed. Her wagon is smaller than ours, there's no spare bunk, and fewer ornaments. It's clean as a whistle, but she's not so fussed about making a wagon pretty as Julia.

Once I've tea in my hands, I tell her what happened. A few times I think I'll cry again, but I manage to stop myself. I don't want a strong woman like Sophia thinking I'm soft.

"What a thing to see. No wonder it shook you up."

"Will the man be alright?"

"Hard to say, but sounds like they did all the right things, and got the doc over as quick as they could. Let's pray it was quick enough."

We both close our eyes and say a few prayers for the man. I'm not sure Sophia is much of a prayer, but keeping my eyes closed calms me down if nothing else.

"Will the Thurstons get in trouble?"

"I doubt it. Sounds like it was all the fault of the man what climbed on. They're thorough showfolk, the Thurstons. Never get the engine running till all the punters are safely on board. They'll probably have to explain the situation to the law, but there were enough witnesses what will back them up."

I set my tea down on the table and cover a huge yawn with my hand.

"How about you stay here tonight? I doubt you'll get much sleep over at yours with all the snuffling and sneezing going on."

"You're not worried about me giving you the sickness?"

"You look fit as a fiddle to me, girl. I'll head over and let Julia know. You climb into that big bed over there and try to sleep. Me and Will won't be long."

The night's events have knocked all the stuffing out of me, and I do as she says and climb into her big bed. I wake as Sophia and Will return, but lying between them I feel safe, and sleep like a baby.

Chapter 19

January 1914

Nothing feels right, not within our wagon nor the outside world. Everyone's edgy. On the fairgrounds at Christmas people were tighter with their purses than usual, and there were fewer smiles shared around, like something bad is in the air but no one's sure what.

Julia and Henry are late up. I've had two cuppas and a bowl of porridge before Julia pulls back the slide door, carrying a stinking bedpan.

"How is he?" I ask.

"Bad."

Julia's face is grim. She looks like she's aged ten years in a few short months. "Let me get this emptied then we'll have a talk."

"Alright." I sit nursing my tea, warming my hands on the china cup. Henry kept his illness quiet for God knows how long. It was about three months back me and Julia got wind of it. He started getting up in the night to relieve himself, once at first, then as much as five times. Not easy, when you're parked up in the middle of some town or other, I can tell you. He'd been hiding the pain, but once we knew something was up, we kept a closer eye on him. Now we know, even when he's smiling, that if his eye goes all squinty it means he's hurting somewhere.

Julia comes back in the wagon, the bedpan cleaned till it sparkles. She takes it through to Henry then sits by the fire with a big sigh. Bloody hell, she looks awful. Lines have crept all over her skin, and beneath her eyes dark purple skin sags. Her hair is now more white than blonde. She's cut it to her chin, and instead of falling in waves it bounces up in a frizz around her cheeks. I still think she's beautiful, but I'm not sure she'd turn many heads walking through a fairground now.

"Here," I say, handing her a cuppa.

"Thanks, Nell, you're a star."

"What's going on then?" I ask.

"You don't beat about the bush, do you?"

"Come on, spill the beans. We both know there's something going on with Henry."

"I'm worried about him."

"Me too."

"I'm not sure the wagon's the best place for him over winter."

"Really?"

"Hmm."

She stares down at her tea, and I don't press her. Give her time, and she'll tell me those thoughts what are whirring round her head.

"Besides the lack of a privy, he's in no state to take on labouring work, and there's nothing we can do round here."

"What are you thinking?"

"I've been wondering about heading north."

"North?"

"Yes, I've a cousin up there who'd most likely let us stay with her."

"What will we do with the wagon?"

"She lives just outside the town on a farm. We could park up the wagon till Henry's better. Me and you could get work in a mill for a bit, and Henry could help around the farm when he's up to it."

"When will we be back on the road?"

"Who knows, we'll have to see how Henry fares with a bit of country air."

"When will we go?"

"Well, I've written to my cousin, and as soon as I receive her reply, assuming she says yes, we'll get on the road."

"What does Henry make of your plan?"

"Oh, he says it's nonsense. If it were up to him, he'd be out in Swaffham touting for work. But we both know he's not up to it."

***

It's another week before Julia collects her cousin's letter from the post office. Henry has been pottering round the wagon all morning but keeps stopping to sit down. I keep my gob shut, he don't want no mention of his illness and it's a banned topic of conversation. He's too proud for his own good if you ask me.

"What does she say?" I ask as Julia appears through the door.

"I've not read it yet. Give us a chance."

Julia sits down and reads through the letter.

"Well?"

"Read it yourself," she says, handing me the letter. Her cousin's writing is like a child's, all big and round and full of mistakes. I get the gist though. We can stay with her as long as we want, she says. She'll want something towards our room and board but only as much as we can afford. Her kiddies have all grown up now, she says, so there's plenty of room for a few waifs and strays.

"When do we leave?"

"Tomorrow."

"Bloody hell."

"Nell, can you go let Will and Sophia know? I want to talk things through with Henry, get him to see this is for the best."

"Of course," I say, gathering up my coat.

Will and Sophia are that sad they both have tears in their eyes when I tell them. "We'll be back for the summer season," I say. But they stay quiet, and although I don't want to admit it, I know what they're thinking. They won't be seeing Henry after tomorrow. I try and rally us. "Julia reckons the air up there will do him good. A nice long rest and he'll be back on his feet in no time she says."

"I'm sure she's right," says Sophia, patting my hand like I'm still a little girl in need of comfort.

"Well, we can't let you go without a decent send-off. I'll gather up a few folk, and we'll have a proper leaving bash. Not a word to Julia and Henry though." Will taps the side of his nose. I tap the side of mine.

"See you later then," I say, and head over to our wagon. I'm a good five yards away, but I can hear things in the wagon aren't happy. Henry is shouting, Julia is shouting back. I don't want to disturb them, so sit on the wagon step, hands clapped over my ears.

The wagon door flies open, knocking me to the ground. Henry don't even notice me lying in the mud, and storms across the field with more energy than he's had in weeks. I stand myself up and brush off the mud what's clinging to my coat. Julia is sat in the armchair, head buried in her hands.

I sit on the floor beside her and stroke the back of her head. "You alright?"

A sob escapes from between her hands. We sit in silence, the only sound the fire's crackle and the rattle of windows clipped by the wind.

"I don't want to lose him. Why can't he understand that?"

"You're not going to lose him," I say, my voice more confident than I feel.

"I have to do all I can to make him better. I'd swap places with him if I could."

Julia takes her face from her hands and looks at me. Her eyes are red and puffy, there's a drip of water clinging to the end of her pretty nose. She wipes her eyes and nose with a hanky and smooths down her hair.

"There's no point me sitting here blubbing. Let's get packing while we wait for that foolish man and his foolish pride to calm down."

We set to work packing belongings away in cupboards and storing the breakables. Henry don't reappear till the light is fading from the sky.

"Where have you been?" demands Julia.

"Looking for work."

She sighs in frustration and throws herself down on the armchair. "And I suppose you found some, did you? Lied through your teeth that you can heave stone and hammer wood as well as any man?"

"No." Henry's voice is small and wobbly. He sits down at the table and his whole body shrinks as he lets out a long breath.

"I think we need some tea here, Nell," says Julia. "You going to tell us what happened?"

Henry looks broken. "It didn't go to plan."

"Right. And how's that then?"

He speaks so quietly we have to strain to hear him. "I made it into the village, but it took so much of my strength my legs gave way. I collapsed by the side of the road."

"No," says Julia, rushing to him and taking his face in her hands. "Are you alright now? How did you get back?"

"An old boy came along with his cart. Scooped me up and took me to his cottage. His wife took care of me, plied me with so much tea and fruit cake I fell asleep by their fire."

"Oh, my love," says Julia, her eyes shining with tears.

"Julia," he says, his voice cracking. "That old boy had five times the energy I have. What's happening to me?"

"Well, you admitting something is happening is progress in itself. Look, when we get up north, we'll see about getting you to a doctor. Then we can set about fixing you up."

He nods and gives me a smile as I set the tea down in front of him.

"Sorry for how I've been, to both of you," he says. "I know you're just looking out for me and I've been such a stubborn old fool."

"Yes, you have," I say. "But you're our stubborn old fool and we love you."

A tear slides down his tired face, but me and Julia pretend we've not seen and get back to our sorting. Once we're all packed up, Julia makes a warming stew and Henry manages half a bowl.

"Glad you're getting your appetite back, though it means there's no seconds for me," I say. Henry winks at me, but I notice him forcing down the last mouthful, and wonder how long it will stay down.

By six o'clock Henry's napping in the armchair and me and Julia are checking through the accounts. A knock on the wagon door startles us all. I open it and find a grinning Will on the other side.

"Where's that brother of mine?" he asks, looking beyond me to the sleeping figure of Henry. Worry flushes his face, but he slaps his smile back on and steps inside. He shakes Henry's leg gently, not the usual punch he'd have given to wake his brother. "Henry? Henry?"

"That you, Will?"

"Yes, it's me. Look, Henry, I need you to get up if you can manage it?"

"You need my help with something?" mumbles Henry, not opening his eyes.

Will reaches in his pocket and pulls out a small glass bottle. He waves it beneath Henry's nose. Henry's eyes fly open and a grin spreads across his face.

"Just what the doctor ordered," he says, taking a glug of the amber liquid.

"Right, now I've got you back in the land of the living, you'd better come with me. You too, Julia, and you, Nell."

"Will," Julia whispers, "I'm not sure Henry's up to helping you out."

Will grins at her and, saying nothing, opens the door. We follow him outside, and as we turn the corner of our wagon a noisy cheer explodes from the gathered fair folk.

"What's all this?" Henry asks, leaning on Julia as they walk.

"You didn't think we'd send you up north without a proper goodbye bash, did you?"

"What are you like?" says Henry. He's happy, letting go of Julia's arm and walking across to his friends. They've got a huge fire going, and it's so hot we can take off our coats. A bottle of beer is passed Henry's way, and Julia grabs one for me and her. I must look surprised, for she nudges me and says, "I reckon the odd beer is alright at fourteen years of age. Just don't get a taste for the stuff."

I've not had a slug of beer since I left the yard, and it sits bitter on my tongue. It's warming though, and I drink it down quicker than I should. My head feels light, and in the firelight, with all our friends around us, I think maybe, just maybe, everything will be alright.

Chapter 20

January 1914

We've been on the road two days already. Julia is up front taking the reins, while Henry dozes on his bed. We stopped over at an inn last night, and ever since we left this morning I've been glued to the window. For miles and miles it was the dull flatness of the fens, but since yesterday the countryside around us has changed. Flat fields give way to gentle hills, pockets of woodland lining the road, sitting perched below hills. The trees look spooky with all their leaves off, like brown skeletons, watching us as we pass.

We're coming up to a town, and the road's a little busier than before. I poke my head through the front window so I can speak to Julia. "What's that?"

"Lincoln cathedral. Beautiful, isn't it?"

"It looks like Norwich."

"Yes, I suppose it does. It's a smaller city, mind, more of a town really."

"Are we stopping here?"

"No, I think it's best we press on. There's still a long journey ahead of us."

"You alright out there?"

"Not bad, but I could do with an extra blanket if you've got one?"

I fetch her a blanket and pass it through the window to her. "Want a cuppa?"

"Yes please, you're a lifesaver, Nell."

It's a bit tricky, for the roads through the city are that windy, I spill boiling water on my leg and curse so bad Henry stirs from his slumber. I spill more as I pass the cup through the window, and the china's only half full by the time it reaches Julia's hand.

"Where we stopping tonight?"

"I'll get us as far as Sheffield if I can."

"We stopping at another inn?"

"No, not tonight, need to save our pennies. We should find somewhere quiet to pull up easy enough. As long as we're not too close to the city we'll be left in peace."

It takes us another five hours to reach the outskirts of Sheffield. Henry has been up a while, and I can see how much it pains him to have Julia sat out in the cold instead of him. By the time she comes into the wagon her hands and lips are blue and she can't stop shaking. I wrap more blankets around her shoulders, and she sits on Henry's lap, snuggling into his warmth.

"I'm so sorry, love. I'll take a turn out there tomorrow."

"No, you won't. You save your energy. I'll be fine after a good night's sleep."

"Why don't I do some of the driving tomorrow?"

Julia and Henry exchange glances. "Hmm, I'm not sure, Nell. We'll be coming to some tricky roads as soon as we hit the Peak District."

"What's the Peak District?"

"Mountains of sorts, views so beautiful they'll take your breath away, and roads so treacherous they'll take your life if you're not careful."

"Well how about I take the first turn then? I'll drive until we reach the mountains, then you take over from there."

"I suppose there's no harm in trying," says Henry.

Julia's that tired, she don't bother arguing. I cook us up some supper, and as soon as she's eaten her last bite, she yawns and heads for bed. Me and Henry stay up chatting a while longer, before he yawns too, and I pack him off to bed. It takes me a while to get off to sleep. I'm excited to get a chance driving the wagon, but the sound of mountains scare me, and I hope we don't run into no trouble.

***

Snow. There's snow all over the road. The horses aren't happy, neighing and trying to shake it off their manes. Ice covers the inside of the windows and I reckon I've put on all the clothes I have during the night.

"There's no way you can drive in these conditions, Nell," says Julia.

I hate admitting defeat, but I don't want to do nothing stupid neither. "How about I sit up beside you then? You can keep hold of the reins, but I can keep you company and pick up a few tips for once the weather clears."

"Seems silly us both freezing to death."

"Maybe, but I don't want you out there on your own. If you won't let me, I'll just climb out of the window once we're moving." I would too, and Julia knows it.

"Alright, but gather up all the blankets we have, and wrap yourself up warm."

"Yes, boss," I say, and she whips me with the washing rag.

Henry is awake, but stays in his bed, probably too upset we're driving to watch us heading out in the snow. We make sure the horses are fed and watered then attach them to the wagon. Me and Julia snuggle together up front, spreading three blankets across our knees. Julia gets the horses moving, and we follow the road that skirts the edges of the city. We're high up, and to our left see endless rows of houses, and huge buildings with steam pouring from tall chimneys.

"It's enormous," I say.

"Yes, it's a busy old place that's for sure, a lot of industry going on there."

"Is it always this cold up here?"

Julia laughs. "Nell, you'd be cold anywhere sat outside for hours in the middle of January."

After a while the city disappears from view and the road becomes rough and stony. The wheels are sliding around all over the place and the horses' hooves pick their way through the snow.

"We have to get across the hills today. This is no place to spend a night, especially in weather like this." She whips the reins to move the reluctant horses onwards.

It's like we've entered a magical kingdom. Snow-covered mountains tower about frozen valleys, ice clinging to the banks of large streams, smaller streams completely frozen over. The road narrows further and we hug the edge of a hill, a sharp drop down to the valley just to our left.

"Whoa, whoa," Julia calls. She needs the horses to slow now, for one wrong step and we'll be tumbling to our deaths. Her hands are gripping tight to the reins, and my own grip the edge of the wooden seat. I chat away to her, trying to hide how frightened I feel.

"Nell, it's lovely having you up here, but do you think you could shush? Just till we're on safer ground?"

"Sorry."

"I know you mean well, but I need to concentrate. It's difficult to tell where the road even is beneath this snow. If we veer off too far, we'll be in a great deal of trouble."

I stay quiet. My face is burning from cold. Snow whips into my eyes and clings to my lashes. We've been climbing higher and higher, and the wind is worse the further up the mountain we go. We meet no one, for who would be stupid enough to travel these roads in these conditions but us?

"Right, looks like the road starts going down from here. If you thought the way up was bad, you just wait for the downhill stretch."

I cling tighter to the seat. The weight of the wagon pushes us forwards, the horses' hooves slipping and sliding as they go. The snow keeps falling, and as it does, the horses find it harder and harder to walk. They're panting, breath spewing out in a warm cloud through the snowflakes.

"At least the deep snow is slowing us a little. It's hard going for the horses, but a thin layer and we'd be skidding down the hill like we're on an ice rink."

"Will the horses manage alright?"

"So long as there's no accidents, they'll make it to Manchester. But we might need to stop a couple of days there so they can rest up. Don't want to push them too hard for too long."

It takes an age to make it down to the valley. Julia mutters prayers under her breath the whole way, and I have my fingers crossed beneath the seat. When we finally make it to the valley floor, the snow has piled up even thicker, and the horses are struggling to move one leg in front of the other.

"I think it's pointless trying to get further along. The horses need to rest. I need to rest," she says.

It's hard to make out the features of the landscape beneath the snow, but a wide river flows beside the wagon, and the ground we're on is flat.

"We've enough food to last us a couple of days, and plenty of coal to keep us warm. I say we sit tight and wait for the weather to improve."

"Will Henry be alright?"

"Let's hope so. As long as we keep him warm, I can't see he's worse off here than on the road."

Julia places blankets over the horses and lets them out of their harness. They shake their manes in relief, but don't stray too far from the wagon. She nips inside and comes out with grain, which they munch happily beneath the falling snow. A few days' rest seem to have done Henry the world of good, and he even manages to make us our supper.

"You seem a bit brighter, love," says Julia.

"Must be this northern air you keep going on about." She gives him a playful whack on the arm, and he leans down to kiss her cheek.

It's not so bad, being stuck in the snow. It's warm enough with the fire going and there's no shortage of water what with the stream beside us and all the snow. We pass the time playing cards, watching snow fall beyond the window. We've run out of milk, but as long as the tea is warm, it's good enough for us.

I wake in the middle of the night needing a pee. With my feet shoved in my boots, and shawl around my shoulders, I go to open the wagon door. It's stuck fast. Bugger. I try again. Is it jammed? I open the window and poke my head out, trying to see what the problem is. Bloody hell. There's snow piled right up to the handle. No wonder I can't push it open. For a moment I panic; what if we're trapped here forever? But I remind myself snow's not forever. Soon enough the sun will come and melt it away. The bedpan's in Julia's room, and I don't want to disturb them. I grab a bowl from the stove and fill it with wee. With the window fully open, I tip it out, enjoying the slight sizzle it makes as it hits the cold snow. The snow's piled up so high, I can lean down and grab a handful. I rub it round the bowl till I'm sure it's clean and put it back where I found it.

Julia's in a right tizz when she wakes the next morning and finds us snowed in.

"How will we get out? How will I feed the horses? We can't wait for it to thaw; it could be weeks."

"Just push me out the window with a shovel. I'll see to it in no time."

"You sure?"

"Why not? I'm small enough to get through, and strong enough to shovel us free."

"You're an angel," says Julia. Once I'm wrapped up warm and have my boots on, she holds the window open for me to climb out. It's a soft landing, and the snow has come up a good five feet so there's barely any drop.

"Here you go," she says, handing me the shovel.

"Ta da!" I say, opening the door ten minutes later.

"Well done, Nell," Henry calls.

"How you feeling?"

"Bit rough, but not too bad."

"We staying another day?" I ask Julia.

"Reckon it's for the best. The horses are cold, but at least they're resting their legs. If they're strong enough, we might be able to do the final stretch in one push tomorrow."

***

I'm pleased we're making progress once more. The roads are still hilly, but nothing like they were back in the Peak District. The snow has melted a little, and the horses' hooves can feel stone beneath the snow for the first time in days. We pass through Manchester around midday. The roads are clear, most folks staying inside thanks to the weather. Beyond the city, Julia lets me take a turn on the reins.

"You're a natural," she says, as I guide the horses along the road.

"Thanks. I'm not sure I could've managed those mountain roads though. You did a grand job getting us through there safely."

"There wasn't much choice," says Julia. She takes one of the blankets from her legs and wraps it round her shoulders.

"You can go inside for a bit if you're cold," I say.

"No, you're alright. It should only be another hour or two till we're there, and I don't want us getting lost."

"You been to the farm before?"

"Never, but Cousin Chrissy sent me directions, and I know the area enough to find the farm, I hope."

Julia nods off a couple of times, lulled by the rhythmic click clack of hooves and the gentle rocking of the wagon. She wakes when the road becomes rough, jolting the wagon over rocks and potholes. The light is fading, big hills looming up in the distance, the road harder and harder to see in the half light.

"Wait," says Julia, squinting at the land around her. "There should be a track coming up on your left. Keep your eyes peeled."

We move the horses on slowly, glancing around us for signs we're nearing the farm track.

"There it is," says Julia pointing.

We reach the entrance to the track and swap seats so she can turn the horses and wagon sharply to the left.

"What's going on?" calls Henry.

"Nearly there," says Julia. "Best sit down in there, Henry. I reckon this track will likely be a rough ride."

She's right, of course. The track is the roughest we've driven on. Several times the horses stumble, and we all pray they won't fall at the final hurdle. At last, the lights of a building break through the gloom. Julia follows them like a beacon, pulling the wagon up in front of a double-storey stone building.

As soon as the horses still, a door opens and a pack of feral dogs run yapping towards us. I'm used to dogs on the fair, but these ones are wild, jumping up at us and nipping at our ankles. A shrill whistle sounds, and the dogs pause their barking, ears pricked up straight. The whistling comes again, and the dogs run to the woman making the sound.

A short, plump woman is making her way towards us. In the half-light it's hard to make her out properly, but the only resemblance to Julia seems to be her golden hair. Unlike Julia's though, this woman wears hers pinned on top of her head, the odd curl breaking free and framing her pink face.

"Welcome to the farm," she says.

Julia jumps down and hugs her.

"Who's this young thing?"

"This is Nellie. Nellie, this is Chrissy."

I jump down and stretch out my hand. "We'll be having none of that, lass," says the woman. She bats away my outstretched hand and pulls me into her boobies. She smells of animals and sweat, but she's that warm, I reckon I could stay pinned to her all night.

Chapter 21

February 1914

"You'll need your hat on," says Chrissy as she meets me in the hallway. "Damn chilly out there this morning."

I grab my hat from the hook by the door and follow her outside. This is our morning routine; feed the hens and pigs in the freezing cold, then make breakfast for everyone back in the warm. It's pitch black in the yard, but Chrissy holds her lamp up and we spread the feed out evenly enough. It was hard getting out of bed this morning. My room don't have a fire like Julia and Henry's do, and I'm sure there was a layer of ice on the blankets this morning.

"Put the kettle on," says Chrissy once we're back inside.

I do as I'm told. Chrissy is friendly as anything, but not someone to mess with. She's as tough as any showfolk I've met, and that's saying something. She potters about the kitchen, doing three jobs at once. I squeeze past her massive bum to hang the kettle over the fire, and she hands me some bread to butter as I go.

"When d'you start work, lass?"

"Two days' time."

"You and Julia done well to get jobs round here. All the folks are queueing up for jobs at mill. You should bring in a fair old wage if you work hard enough."

"Can't be harder than work on the fair," I say. "I'm sure we'll manage."

"I'm sure you will."

Chrissy chucks a big lump of butter in a pan and throws a handful of sausages on top. They sizzle and spit, making my belly grumble and mouth water. I'm surprised I've not grown as big as a heifer in the two weeks we've been here. Chrissy's a feeder alright. But I s'pose you need plenty of food to keep you going on a busy farm.

"Those sausages I can smell?"

Chrissy's husband Stephen walks in and gives her a peck on the cheek. He's as large as her, but in a strong way. Not fat. His cheeks glow red beneath his beard, and his voice booms out low and gruff, not that he speaks much to me. I'm not sure he was best pleased about us pitching up at his place. He's not unkind, it's more that he pretends we're not there. Happier with sheep than people, Chrissy says.

Julia's next to appear. She looks well rested, and more back to her usual self since we've been here. Even her hair's grown a little and the frizz is turning back to waves.

"How's Henry?"

"Good, slept right through last night. Seems a little stronger too."

Something about this place seems to be helping Henry. It might be that he's getting a rest for the first time in years. It might be the fresh air, not that we were lacking in it before. It could be the lovely room with a big old bed and coal fire. Who knows? I'm only glad he's improving, even if he's not back to the old Henry just yet.

"You want to take his breakfast up to him?" Chrissy asks.

"No, I'll go and wake him when it's ready. It'll do him good to be up and about."

Chrissy chucks eggs and bacon in with the sausages and I butter the hunks of bread while everything cooks.

"You made that tea yet, lass?"

"No, sorry, I'll do it now."

"You're getting her well trained, Chrissy," says Julia.

"Oh, I think you've already done that yourself," she says.

While Chrissy spoons food onto plates, Julia goes upstairs to get Henry.

"Morning, all," he says, finding himself a seat at the table.

Stephen grunts in reply, and Chrissy shoves an enormous plate of food across the table.

"Get that down you, Henry. You'll be right as rain in no time if I get my way."

"Thanks, Chrissy," he says. I watch him as he takes his knife and fork in his hands and begins picking at the food. He's put a napkin on his lap, and when he thinks no one's looking, flicks the odd sausage or piece of bacon into it. Hmm, maybe he's not quite as alright as we'd all like to think. As Julia and Chrissy chat away, he scrunches up the food filled napkin and shoves it in his pocket.

While the others finish up, I sneak outside, and walk round the side of the house till I'm below Henry and Julia's window. I peek behind the bushes and see evidence of what I hoped not to find. A pile of food lies scattered behind the bush directly below their window. So, he hasn't got his appetite back after all then. Julia's too hopeful to notice, so I shall have to keep an eye on him for the both of us.

I head back inside and help Chrissy wash the dishes. Julia appears and they leave me to it, heading off to tend the animals. Henry walks through on his way to the barn. Stephen's set him up in there with some mending jobs and a chair. It's nothing like the work Henry used to do, but at least it keeps him from feeling a burden. I tackle the pile of washing Chrissy's left for me, pulling it through the old mangle, feeling a pang of regret it's not me and Florrie doing it together. It seems an age since we stood in the yard doing Mum's washing together. I suppose it is an age really. Eight years. Bloody hell, how is it already eight years since I left?

I hope to God she's stopped seeing that bloody gaff lad. I've had no word from her since I last saw her and to tell the truth, I'm fearing the worst. It was wonderful to see her and Freddie again at Christmas, but Florrie came along every night and I soon realised it wasn't me she was there for.

Joe, his name is. I'd not seen him before, but I asked around and found out he does the rounds, going from this fair to that, taking what work he can, moving on when he's sacked. He had the spiel down to the ground, no doubt he'd practised it on girls all over the country. Florrie fell for it hook, line and sinker. I caught them one night, kissing behind our wagon. Joe had his hand up her skirt and she went the colour of a tomato when she saw me watching.

Who knows if we'll be back in Norwich at Easter? I hope so, I want to check she's alright and not nursing a broken heart. Worse would be if she's still with him. But there's nothing I can do about it from this far away. The way things are going, I'll be surprised if we make it back to Norwich by Christmas, but you never know. Julia seems to think Henry's on the mend, and she knows him better than anyone.

***

Days pass quickly on the farm, and soon our first morning of work rolls round. I'm nervous. Julia's nervous. All we eat for breakfast is a couple of pieces of toast, our churning bellies can't take no more than that. It's an hour's walk from the farm to the town, so we set off at six in the dark. Julia knows the way, which is lucky, for there's no light to see by. It's hard going walking to town. Up down, up down for miles. My legs aren't used to hills, and I'm worried that after a day on my feet, I won't manage the walk home.

The sun rises as we enter the town. Rows and rows of small houses pack tight together on sloping roads. People are spilling out of them, all headed for the mill. Chrissy told us most of the town work at the mill. India mill it's called, 'cause that's where the cotton comes from, or so they say. We follow the hordes of workers until we find ourselves beside the biggest building I've ever seen. I reckon it could give Norwich Castle a run for its money.

"You two new?" a woman asks.

"Yes, first day today," says Julia.

"Right, let me show you the ropes. I'm Anne by the way."

"Nice to meet you, Anne. I'm Julia, and this is my daughter Nellie."

I can't help smiling when Julia calls me her daughter. It might be a lie, but it feels true to me.

"Nice to meet you, ladies. You done mill work before?"

"No, we've just moved from the east."

That's careful of Julia, not mentioning the fair. Best not give flatties reason to hate us before we've even started. The crowd of workers part to let a horse pulling a loaded trailer of cotton through the gates of the mill.

"I'll show you where t' clock on."

We follow the woman through the entrance and hang our coats on a line of hundreds of hooks nailed into a wall. A man in a worker's coat appears, clipboard in hand. He takes down our names and points us in the direction of our workstations. I had hoped me and Julia would be working together, but despite her insistence I'm not a child, my size goes against me. I see Julia's face drop as I'm classified a child and handed my job. It will mean less earnings, a lot less earnings.

The coated man leads us through to the spinning room. Bloody hell, what is this madness? My hands clap over my ears, but Julia gives me a little shake of the head and I take my hands down. I thought the fair was noisy, but it's nothing compared to this. The room stretches out for miles, machines clanking, clapping, and whirring, all powered by steam engines which make a fair old racket themselves. I doubt I'll be making many friends here; no one will hear me above the noise.

I blow air up at my hair, for we've been here less than five minutes and already it's sticking to my forehead. Why don't someone open a bloody window? I don't reckon I've been this hot since burning summer days back at the yard. Dad would be alright here, what with the time he spent in Africa. Probably hotter than Africa. I'm glad I'm not wearing my coat.

***

At half past six, I meet Julia by the gates. Twelve hours! Twelve hours we've been on our feet, sweating and turning deaf from all that racket. If I'm headed for hell when I die, I reckon the mill will be good training. Julia is red in the face, and her hair has frizzed right up over her ears. She's still bent over, like her body can't straighten itself out just yet.

"Home," she says.

The journey that took an hour this morning now takes two. Our steps are more like shuffles as we make our way along the gloomy roads. We left in the dark and return in the dark. What kind of life is this? Not one I want for much longer; I can tell you. I long for the lights and colour of the fair. I long for fresh air, happy faces. I even long for rain on my skin and rowing with the odd flattie what tries to swindle me. At least we were in charge of ourselves there. Not at the mercy of some damn man in an overcoat barking instructions and checking our every move. No, this isn't the life for me.

Julia barely says a word the whole way home. I'm glad, for I don't think I could summon the energy to reply. It's only as the farm comes into view that she speaks.

"Not a word to Henry about the bad stuff. We've had a wonderful day. Understand?"

I nod and we carry on walking. At the gate, Julia pauses.

"Look, Nell, I know this mill business isn't much fun, but it's only for a time. Only till Henry gets back on his feet and we can get on the road again."

I wrap my arms round her and she sinks into me, like she can't even find the energy to stand.

"It's alright. We'll do what we must do. Summer will soon be here, Henry will be better, and we'll be sticking two fingers up to the mill as we pass by in our wagon."

"I hope you're right," Julia says, brushing away a tear.

"Come on, let's get back. I reckon Chrissy will have a fine supper laid on for us, and as soon as I've shoved some food in my gob, I'm crawling to my bed."

Julia laughs and uses the last of her energy to push on to the farmhouse.

Chapter 22

March 1914

I've been counting the days we've been at the mill and we've crossed the month mark. A whole month in that hellish building. There's been lots of times over the years I've needed to be tough, but I don't reckon nothing's tested me as much as the mill has.

It only took me a week or so to get used to the hours on my feet, but I still can't get used to the boredom. Every day the same thing, over and over and over, until you feel your brain slowly dying inside your head. It's not even like you can chat away the hours. Most of the folk there have got pretty skilled in reading lips, but it's no substitute for a good old chin wag. I miss the music too, the constant chime of an organ, a gramophone blasting out over the cake walk.

I'm beginning to find my way, find ways to soothe the boredom, but I got to be careful the old goat in charge don't catch me. I've made a few friends too, not the type I'd confide in, but those what appreciate a little entertainment in their long day. I've picked up enough over my years with the fair to put on a show. I've invented a new dance. One where only your feet move while your body stays still. Unless the supervisor is walking down my line, he'd never know the jig going on below the machine. The other workers see it though, and I feel bad when they get in trouble for laughing.

I've also learned my voice is good at singing loud and in tune. When the supervisor goes on his break, it's not unusual for me to burst into song, though the other folk are too scared of being caught to join in. Julia's got wind of my antics, and tells me to save them for break times. I make the most of those times too. I'm careful enough that I don't let on we're showfolk, but I tell my new friends stories, that I say were told to me by a showman's wife I met as a child. They lap it up.

The bell goes and we head outside for dinner. Chrissy's packed up thick sandwiches and a hunk of cake what are the envy of every worker at the mill. Most workers trot off home for their dinner, but those that come from round about like we do, hang around me, waiting for my spiel to start.

"So, this old girl told me about an African prince." Gasps go up from my crowd. "Yes," I continue, "a real-life African prince. He was the handsomest man ever to grace the shores of England, and could perform magic like no one had seen before."

"How did he get to England?" someone shouts.

"Well, that's a story in itself right there. Word has it, he sent one of his servants out one night to the local village. The servant snuck into people's homes stealing all the leather shoes he could find."

"They don't have leather shoes in Africa," shouts some clever dick.

"Oh, don't they? You been to Africa, have you?" That shuts the heckler right up.

"Keep going," a young girl shouts.

"Well, I don't know if I want to. Not if you lot won't believe the story I'm telling."

This prompts calls and shouts from the little crowd, and someone digs the heckler in the ribs as a warning to keep his gob shut.

"Alright then. Well, as I was saying. This servant gathered up all the leather shoes he could find, and took them to the prince. The prince then had his best craftsman take them apart till they were flat, and stitch them together into one long sheet. Next, he got his carpenter to cut down trees and nail them together to make a little boat. They covered the wood with the leather and filled the boat with silks and cushions until it was fit for a prince. Now, the prince didn't want his subjects to be sad about him leaving, so one night after dark, his most trusted servants carried the boat down to the sea. The prince dressed himself like a commoner and climbed in..."

The bell goes, signalling it's time for us to return to our drudgery.

"What happened next?" a woman shouts.

"You'll have to wait till tomorrow to find out," I say, gobbling my food as we walk back to the mill.

On our walk home, Julia has a big frown on her face.

"What's the matter, Julia? Spit it out."

"I need you to be careful."

"What d'you mean?" I ask, through the mouthful of cake I'd not had time for earlier.

"Word is getting round that you're quite the clown."

"By clown you mean popular?"

"No, Nell, I mean a clown. It's all well and good to play the fool on our breaks, but the supervisors will be watching you. You'd best be careful you don't land yourself in hot water."

"Don't you worry about me. I know what I'm doing."

"That's what I'm afraid of," says Julia, letting herself into the farmhouse.

Henry is in a big armchair in the sitting room. He tries to get up as we walk in, but slumps back down. You'd be forgiven for thinking that chair had grown since we arrived, but the chair's not changed. Henry has shrunk. He was always a slim chap, but now he looks like the kiddies from Hawke's Yard, all skin and bone. I'm worried for him, but also worried for us, for our chances of getting back to the fair are fast slipping away.

"Good day in the workshop?" asks Julia.

Henry nods. "How was the mill?"

"Oh grand, Nell's been keeping everyone entertained with her tall tales."

"I bet she has." He grins at me. His teeth seem too big for his mouth now.

I go and sit on the floor beside him. "I was telling them about Prince Samonda today. Well, not really about him, I made up a few stories and the flatties loved it."

"You be careful they don't learn you're from the fair. Won't be so popular if they know that."

"Don't worry, I've got myself a good cover story."

"Hopefully we'll see Prince Samonda again this summer."

Me and Julia exchange glances, neither of us wanting to speak our minds.

"Well, there's a while to go till summer. In the meantime, we need food and sleep. You eaten yet?"

Julia's always asking Henry about food. She's obsessed with him getting enough, though we all know he has the appetite of a small bird these days. The doctor came to check Henry over the first week we were here. No one will tell me what he said, but it can't have been good. After he'd gone,

I found Julia at the bottom of a field, leaning on the fence, sobbing her heart out. I've asked her many times what the doc said, but she always replies, "best not think about it."

I'm no fool, I know if he was going to get better it would've happened by now. God knows what will become of Julia once the inevitable happens. What will happen to me? Chrissy and Stephen have been kind putting us up for a while, but it's never been thought of as a permanent arrangement. Our wages from the mill wouldn't cover the rent of a hovel, and that's before you think about needing food and coal.

Everyone else has already eaten, so it's just me and Julia sat at the table eating our stew. Henry's up in bed, and Chrissy and Stephen are out checking on the animals.

"Julia?"

"Yes."

"What's going to happen to us?"

"What you talking about, Nell?"

"I mean... I mean... if Henry... when Henry..."

"When Henry gets better? Well then we'll go back to the fair of course."

She stands up quickly, scraping her chair against the stone floor and tipping the remains of her food into a bucket for the pigs.

"Julia, we got to talk about it."

"No, Nellie. No, we don't. You don't know what it is we're talking about anyway. Don't know what the doc said, do you?"

"No, but I've eyes in my head, as well as a brain."

"I'll hear nothing more on the subject."

Julia is breathing fast, gripping on to the table as if to steady herself. She turns to leave, then grips the table again, afraid to let go. Tears are swimming in her eyes, and she swallows hard to push them away.

"I can't think about it, alright? I mean, I think of nothing else, but I can't say it aloud. I'll let you know when I'm ready to talk."

"Alright," I say to her back as she rushes from the room.

I head to bed, but my thoughts whir and whir and I can't get myself to sleep. Whatever happens, me and Julia must stick together. I won't leave her to deal with this alone. Where would I go anyway? From the other side of the wall, I hear Henry groan. It must be loud to get through these thick walls. The doc left him with some bottles of medicine, but I haven't noticed them helping him at all.

Chapter 23

May 1914

Spring on the farm is a wonder. Daffodils have finished poking their heads around and now the grass is covered in daisies, purple pinks and yellows filling the sheltered spots beside walls and hedgerows. The chickens are laying again, and it's eggs for breakfast every day now. We've hardly seen Chrissy and Stephen while the lambing's been on, but it seems to be settling down now, and they're not out at all hours quite so much.

Our time on the farm should be drawing to a close, but with Henry worse than when we arrived, we're in limbo. Julia's still not spoke to me about what we'll do. Soon she'll have no choice if the look of Henry's anything to go by. I'm terrified of losing him, but I also can't bear to see the shell of him clinging on, in that much pain his face is permanently scrunched.

I've been waiting by the stable door for fifteen minutes. We should've left for the mill by now. It's not like Julia to be late, it's normally her waiting for me. The front door creaks and she walks across the yard. It's nice and light in the mornings now, don't feel so hard dragging yourself out of bed when it's like this.

"You alright?"

"Yes," she says, but she don't look it. She's pale as anything and looks like she could do with a week in bed herself.

"Bad night?"

"It's the pain. I can't bear to see him in so much pain."

Her voice is quiet, like she's saving all the fight she has left for when Henry needs her. How she manages to care for him after a twelve-hour shift and an hour's walk each way I can't say. Most nights I don't even hear his groans I'm that dead to the world. But for Julia, she's lying beside him night after night. Lost sleep has made her irritable and she's prone to temper these days. If she shouts, she then feels awful about it and bursts into tears not long after. I'm careful with what I say, and these past weeks, our walks to and from the mill have been mostly in silence.

We're half a mile in before Julia speaks. "He wants to go back to the fair."

"Well, we both know that won't be happening."

"No, I don't mean back on the road. I mean just one more fair. He wants to be there one last time before..." She turns her head so I can't see her tears.

"You thinking of saying yes?"

"Nell, it's a dying man's last wish, I can't see how I can refuse."

She's said the word. Dying. The word that's been sitting on the tips of our tongue for months now. Death, dying, dead. None of us wants to say those words, but we need to, and she knows it.

"Can we take him to one round here?"

"That's not what he wants. He wants to be around his own people, Will, Sophia, even keeps talking about seeing old Charlie Thurston's Vaudeville one last time."

"Think he'd survive the journey?"

"Not with you and me alone. I'd need to be in the wagon with him, and you can't drive across the country by yourself."

"How can we do it then?"

"I'll write to Will, see if he can catch a train up here and travel with us. I've looked at the schedule and I reckon we could make it to Cambridge for the midsummer fair next month. If we wait any longer it might be too late." Her voice catches as she speaks, and I take her hand in mine.

"What will we do after?"

"Oh, Nellie, I really don't know. Let's get through this next horrid bit first, shall we? Then we can have a proper think."

"Alright," I say. I want answers, I need answers, but I'm wise enough not to ask again.

***

Our talk on the way to the mill changes the air around us. It's like we'd been walking through a thick cloud, and now it's cleared till it's lurking just above our heads. It blocks the sun; people around us laugh and joke, but there's a sadness covering us that's likely to be with us some time. We're certainly in no mood for the bloody jobs worth who clocks us in.

"Five minutes late, ladies. That will be recorded and docked from your wage packet this week."

"Fuck off," mutters Julia. I whip my head round to see if the man heard. He did.

"What did you say to me?" He's snarling, like a wild animal, all curled lip, and squinty eyes.

"I said coat off. You heard me didn't you, Nellie?"

"Yep," I say, unbuttoning my coat. "Coat off, that's right, Julia. Best get to it."

I take her arm and almost drag her through to the spinning room before her mouth shoots off again. "What's that you said about me keeping my head down? Looks like it's you we need to watch out for."

She gives me a small smile. "Sorry. It's just we've got more important things to worry about than five minutes on the clock. Word is, they change the clocks here anyway so they're always running a few minutes early. Stupid bastard's wrong if he thinks I give a damn about time keeping these days."

"Right, gobby, get to your work, and keep out of trouble the rest of the day. See you at dinner. And try not to worry, things will work themselves out one way or another."

"When did you get so grown up?"

"Since you needed looking after. Now shoo!"

Julia heads off between the long lines of machines. I watch her until she's out of sight.

"Stop your daydreaming and get to work, girl," calls the supervisor. I flick him the V's from beneath the machine.

Maybe it's knowing we'll be leaving soon, or maybe it's the sadness that covers me, but the minutes are ticking by slower than I've ever known them go. I click my heels and tap my toes, jigging around, but it don't help. I begin to sing under my breath.

My grandfather's clock was a 'Waterbury' watch,It could live 90 days without food.With a silk 'at on its 'ead and my father's Macintosh,It was dressed up like a Piccadilly dude.

"You singing there, lass? I'd rather see your hands moving than your lips."

"Singing? Me? You sure it's me you saw?"

The supervisor turns his back and I start singing again, this time louder. *It was kept in the hall,'Till the cupboard got too small,And we had no place the food, for to stock. So the butter and the heggs,And the little mutton legs:We kept them in me grandfather's clock.*

Maybe it's the sadness about Henry, maybe it's the thought of leaving, maybe I've just had enough. Whatever it is, I don't care no more.

"Stop singing, lass, or there'll be consequences."

"Oh, and what might those be?"

The supervisor goes red in the face and begins walking towards me. I step back from the Jennie and start singing again;

And the works of the clock,
Through the butter meltin' in it,
Sent the fingers flyin' round,
At a 'undred miles a minute,
And grandad, with a sigh, said
"I haven't time to die,
So I'll put it off until the clock's repaired.

"That's enough. I said, enough!"

Now all the folks on my line have stopped their work, all looking to see what the commotion's about. The supervisor steps towards me. I fling my arms out beside me and let out the longest, loudest note I can. He lurches toward me, and I run, singing all the while;

My grandfather's clock was me mother's p'rambulator,

'Round the park in it we used to ride.
There was me, and Treacle Tummy,
Liza Ann, an' Justice 'Awkins,
Screamin' Jimmy, and the twins all stuck inside.

So grandad, 'oo was dead,
Changed his mind, got up instead,
And the sight that he saw give 'im a shock,
For the man 'oo brought the coal,
Couldn't get it down the 'ole,
So, 'ee slung it in me grandfather's clock.
#
And we didn't need a shovel,
As the pendulum swung 'igher.
For ev'ry time it swung,
It knocked some coal into the fire!
And at nine o'clock, the crank,
Used to chime a double blank,
So Grandad had to knock 'ee wouldn't go!

By now the whole room's in uproar. As I run past, folks join me in singing. I've picked a good 'un. Old Formby's a local lad and people can't resist joining in.

"OUT!" screams the supervisor. "GET OUT AND NEVER COME BACK!"

I run out into the sunlight of the street. The joy of my rebellion only lasts a few minutes. Perched on a wall, I begin to feel a fool. Julia's got enough on her plate without me losing my job. Didn't she say I was grown up? And now I've let her down by behaving like a child. Bugger. I can't decide if she'll be mad, sad, or both. Most likely both. I've got five or six hours till she breaks for her dinner and I have to face her. Not much point sitting waiting all that time. I jump down from the wall and walk through the town. It's pretty enough round here, what with the town being surrounded by hills on all sides.

A tower lies above the town that's always left me curious. One of the workers said it was built for Queen Victoria, but

I can't see her traipsing up to a windy moor and I bet she never came. It should be easy enough to reach, not like I can miss it with it poking all that way in the sky.

It only takes five minutes before I'm out of the town and onto the hills. My legs make short work of the slope thanks to all the walking I've been doing these past months. Higher and higher I climb. It's hot today and I feel the trickle of sweat on my back. The further up the hill I go, the cooler it becomes. There's a welcome breeze up here and I stop for a moment to admire the view. Behind me the town stretches out, smoke pouring out and up from the mill that takes up most of the town. Must have looked a very different place before that mill and its fancy tower were built.

Onwards. I reach the base of the tower and look up. The mill chaps said it's open for climbing. I'm not a scaredy cat, but it looks bloody high. Mind you, I've come this far, may as well give it a go. Through the arches I find the stairway. Twisty turning steps that seem never ending wind round the inside of the tower. I count them as I go, and I've reached one hundred before I see daylight. Bloody hell. I step out onto a platform and fling myself back against the wall. Gives me the willies, this does. Mind you, the view almost makes my wobbly legs worth it.

Ahead of me is the town, but as I edge my way round there's brown and green hills stretching as far as the eye can see, and something's glinting in the distance. In front of me the ground has turned purple with a blanket of heather. Could it be the sea? I've had enough of this. Don't get me wrong, the view's wonderful, but I'm that scared I'll fall, I can't enjoy it. Back down the steps I climb, slower than I came up for my legs have turned to jelly.

Back on firm ground, I find a comfy patch of heather and lie down, waiting for my legs to return to normal. I take out the food Chrissy wrapped for me and nibble on the corner of my fruit cake. The sun has risen higher in the sky, and I reckon there's still two hours till I need to get back. The sun is bright, and I close my eyes for a moment.

When I open my eyes, the sun has risen further and is directly above me. Bloody hell, how long have I been sleeping? If I'm not outside to meet Julia when she comes on her break, I won't be able to say sorry and that will make things so much worse. Standing, I brush broken pieces of heather from my dress and run. My legs fly beneath me and my hair streams out behind. I let out a shriek and tear my way down the hill towards the town.

I'm all out of puff by the time I see the mill. Oh God, there's Julia, waiting at the gates, looking up and down the street for me. I wave and jog over to her. For a moment I can't speak, and bend over, catching my breath. She stands, arms folded, waiting for me to speak.

"You heard what happened?"

"Yes."

"You mad at me?"

"I probably would be, if I had the energy." Julia slumps against the wall until she's on her bum, knees up around her chin.

"I'm sorry," I say, sitting beside her. "I don't know what got into me."

"Well, there's a lot going on, isn't there. Makes us all act out sometimes. I've not exactly been myself either."

I can't believe she's being so kind about it. She really has lost all her puff and fight. It's not like her, and for a moment I wish she would yell at me.

"You may as well go back to the farm."

"I'll wait for you."

"That's another six hours, Nell."

"Why don't you quit too? It's not long till we leave anyway?"

"I might need this job to come back to."

I don't know what to say to that. Where does that leave me now? "You sure you don't want me to wait?"

"No, you get off. Just make sure there's a hot cup of tea waiting for me when I get back." Julia kisses my cheek and heaves herself up to standing. She walks back towards the mill, her steps shuffling, her shoulders bent like she has the weight of the world sitting upon them.

Chapter 24

June 1914

Although no one's said it, I think they were all relieved when I got kicked out of the mill. Being out all day, I hadn't realised how much help Henry needed, and how much time Chrissy spent away from her farm work looking after him. Even washing is a struggle for him these days.

"You ready for a hose down?" I ask. Henry groans as I tip another pan of hot water into the copper beside the fire.

"Do I have to?"

"Yes, you stink."

He laughs, thinking I'm joking. I am, but there's a sad truth to my words. Thankfully, he doesn't notice the smell lurking around him, but the rest of us do. It's a rotting smell, one that makes me want to puke.

Chrissy and Stephen have gone out to the yard, grateful that someone else is seeing to the task at hand. We've long gone past the point of modesty. At first, Henry insisted on keeping his drawers on when I washed him. But he no longer has the energy to care. I help him take off his jumper and shirt, lifting his arms gently, as I know it causes him pain. He has just enough energy to prop himself up while I pull off his trousers and underwear. There's no shoes and socks to fuss with, he's lost the strength to get further than the kitchen these days.

"Lean on me," I say, helping him out of the chair. He's light as a feather and easy enough to move to the tub. With him leaning across my back, I lift his leg and put it in the water.

"Not too hot?"

"A perfect temperature. You've got this down to a fine art now, girl." His mouth is smiling, but his eyes aren't.

The other leg follows, and I lower him down till half his body is covered. It shocked me at first, seeing his wrinkled private parts, but now I take no notice. I don't wash his dangly thing for him, that would be one humiliation too many.

"Lean forward so I can do your hair."

He does as I ask, and I fill the jug, tipping warm water over his head. His hair is the only thing about him that's not changed. It's got even more grey in it, but still sticks up in tufts of all directions across his head. I grab Chrissy's homemade lye and work it into his hair. It leaves a layer of grease from the animal fat, but I rinse it good and proper to get it out.

Next, I sponge down Henry's back. The sight of his spine jutting through skin causes me to choke back tears. This lovely, strong man who's taken care of me so long, is now a bag of bones. He lets out a sigh as the warm water trickles across his skin.

"That alright? Not too hot?"

"It's wonderful," he says. His eyes are closed and his face un-creased for the first time today. "You know, Nellie, this is good training for when you become a mum. Any kiddies you have will be damn lucky to have you."

I laugh. "What you talking about kiddies for, I'm only fourteen!"

"Well, in ten years' time, when you meet a nice fellow is what I mean. No babies before marriage, you hear me?"

"Yes, sir," I say giggling. "Well, if I'd make a fine mum, you'd make a fine grandpa."

Henry looks up at me, eyes filled with tears. "You think so?"

"Well, you've been a fine dad to me, so there's no reason you'd change for the next generation."

Henry grips my hand, and a fat tear falls from his cheek and plops into the water. "You think of me as your dad?"

"Course I do! You've been a better father to me than the one what made me. You may not have done the business with my mum, thank your lucky stars, but you've made me, me. Taught me things I never would've known without you. You've loved me more than I thought anyone could love a kiddie. I'll be grateful to you and Julia as long as I live."

He pulls me into him. Suds and water cover my apron, but I don't care. This is our goodbye. He knows it, I know it. There may be months to go yet, but what needed to be said has been said.

"Come on, you soft old fool. Let's get this finished and get you back to bed."

After drying him down and helping him to his bed in the sitting room I head back to the kitchen. I tip out the soapy tear-filled water in the yard, thinking there'll be many more tears shed before this is finally over.

***

"Will!" I scream, running to the gate and throwing myself in his arms.

"Well, that's a nice welcome if ever I saw one."

Will links his arm through mine and I point out all the animals as we pass them.

"I see now why Julia thought this would be a good place for that brother of mine. How's he doing by the way?"

"Better prepare yourself, Will. He's not good, not good at all. If it weren't for that bird's nest on his head, you might not recognise him."

"That bad?"

I nod, and he takes a deep breath before walking into the farmhouse.

Julia jumps up from the kitchen table and welcomes Will the same way I did.

"Watch out, Sophia will have my guts for garters if she finds out I've had women flinging themselves at me while I've been gone."

Julia gives him a friendly punch on the arm. "How is Sophia? I've missed her chats all these months."

"Same as ever. More importantly, where's Henry?"

"Through there, but he's most likely sleeping."

"Can I see him?"

"Yes. But, Will..."

Will flaps his hand to shush her. "No need, Julia, Nell's told me all I need to know. I'm prepared for seeing him."

"Alright then, I'll take you through."

Julia leads Will to the sitting room and opens the door just a crack. I hover in the hallway behind her. "Henry? Henry, you awake? There's someone here to see you."

"Hmm?" comes a muffled reply from the bed.

Julia leads Will into the room. She opens the curtains and sits on Henry's bed. "Come on, darling, open your eyes. Someone special's come to say hello."

Henry opens his sticky eyelids, and a wide smile grows across his face as he sees Will stood before him. He tries to sit himself up, and Julia fusses around, propping up cushions to make him comfy. All credit to Will, he does a fine job of hiding his true feelings. He takes Julia's place and lifts Henry's hand in a shake.

"Good to see you, Henry."

"Come here," says Henry, lifting his skeleton arms and pulling Will towards him. Will gives Julia a nervous glance. He must be worried Henry will break.

"It's fine," Julia says, and Will lets himself fall into Henry's embrace. "I'll leave you to it," says Julia, closing the door behind her.

Will's in with Henry thirty minutes before he returns to the kitchen. He sits down at the table and puts his head in his hands. Julia moves her chair closer and strokes his back. After a minute or two, Will takes a big breath, scrubs his hands in his hair and squares his shoulders.

"Tea?" I ask.

"Thanks, Nellie."

"You mind if I ask what he said?" asks Julia.

Will's laugh causes me to jump. "Nothing deep and mean-ingful if that's what you're wondering. He made me tell him all the news of the fair, who's got what new stall or ride, what's our schedule for the next twelve months. Even made me talk through my accounts with him!"

"Sounds like you've brought a bit of the old Henry back. I'm so glad you're here." Julia covers Will's hand with her own and only moves it when I hand them their tea.

Will blows the steam from his cup, then looks Julia clear in the eye. "Look, Julia. I don't want to speak out of turn, but do you really think it's a good idea taking him to Cambridge?

I mean, I understand why he wants to go, but it's a long hike over there. All that bouncing around in the wagon will be torture for a man in as much pain as he clearly is."

Julia turns her cup around in her hands. "Sit down, Nellie. You need to hear this too."

I sit beside Will and we both wait for her to speak again. "There's no point beating round the bush now, is there? We can all see what's in front of our eyes. He's not got long left. Thing is, he doesn't want to die here. He wants to pass on surrounded by his own people. Ideally that would be at the fair, but if it happens on the open road, so be it."

"You mean..."

"Yes, Nell, I think he's been hanging on as tight as he can just long enough to make his escape. If I return here, it won't be with Henry. And it's time we face it head on."

"Is there anything we can do to make him more comfortable?"

"I'm going to visit the doc this afternoon. He's agreed to give me enough opium to keep Henry as comfortable as possible for as long as possible. If he survives the journey, we'll need to make sure we're properly set up in Cambridge. I'll write to Sophia and ask her to get all we need."

"What if he clings on beyond midsummer?"

"Then we'll head to Yarmouth to see out his days. When he goes, he wants to be buried beside your father in the cemetery there, Will. Think you can arrange that?"

"Shouldn't be a problem. Dad sorted a family plot so we can all lie together when the time comes."

"Good. Then it's all settled. I'll head off to the doc in an hour or so. Nell, can you make sure you have everything packed and check over the wagon? It probably needs a good old dust and polish. And we'll need enough water and food supplies to last a few days."

"What shall I do?" asks Will.

Julia sighs. "Spend as much time as you can with him Will. Even when he's sleeping, he knows you're there."

"I think I can manage that," says Will, standing and kissing the top of Julia's head.

Before I set about my jobs for the day, I head outside. Stephen is out in the fields somewhere and Chrissy's away at market. Halfway up a hill sits an enormous old oak. I set down my shawl and lie down beneath the leaves. The shade of the tree cools my body and stills my mind. Julia has spoken of her plans, but not how I fit into them. My lids close and I pray Henry will make it to Cambridge. He may not be able to run the gallery, but I reckon dying surrounded by the lights and noise of the fair is as fine a place as any to go. He's a sly old dog really, most men would've given up months ago, but not our Henry. He's working as hard at staying alive as he's worked the fair all his life.

Chapter 25

June 1914

It's a tearful Chrissy what sees us off. Stephen said a gruff goodbye at breakfast, but has left for the fields, keen to avoid the emotion of the day, and probably secretly glad to be getting his house back.

"Let me know how things go," says Chrissy. "You know you're welcome here anytime."

Julia hugs her cousin tight. "Thank you for taking us in. I don't know what we'd have done if you hadn't."

"It's been good to have some company, you might have noticed my Stephen's not much of a talker." Despite the sadness of the day, both women laugh through their tears.

Will heads out of the farmhouse, Henry lying limp in his arms. The contrast between them couldn't be starker. Will's strong arms wrap around Henry's fragile body. The brothers what once stood side by side are now completely unequal in strength and power. It hurts my head to watch them, and I turn to Chrissy and give her a quick hug goodbye.

Once Will has settled Henry in the wagon, he jumps up front and takes the reins.

"Right, ladies, we're ready for the off."

Chrissy waves with one hand and holds a hanky to her eyes with the other.

"I'll sit up with you, Will," I say.

"No need, Nellie, I'll be fine out here. You'll be comfier inside."

"Please," I say, my voice cracking.

"S'alright, Nell, I understand. You sit beside me and grab a bit of fresh air. I'm sure Henry will be glad of the peace." He winks at me and I'm grateful he understands.

Our journey east is a damn sight easier than when we first headed west. There's no snow or ice to slow the horses and with Will at the reins, they trot along happily at quite a pace. The winter wonderland I saw before is now a burst of colour, the grassy verges almost completely covered by blue and purple petals. Every now and then we reach a town, and big plumes of smoke fill the air. I pity the poor buggers trapped inside the mills and factories on such a fine day. Once we're past the latest smoky mist, I fill my lungs deep with the air of the road. Nothing beats travelling, and I've missed it.

By lunchtime we're back in the Peak District. I remember the fear of those mountain tracks, unable to see for snow in our eyes. It's not a restful journey today though, for even though the roads are clear, there's still steep drops and tight bends that put Will's driving skills to the test. Julia bangs on the window and I reach behind and open it.

"You alright in there?"

"Yes, but Henry's asked if we can stop for a moment so he can get a look at the view. He missed it all last time we were up here."

"No problem," says Will, pulling the horses to a stop by the safe side of the road. They're happy with a rest, munching on grass, their long tongues lapping at a stream what flows down the mossy hillside. Julia helps Henry out of the wagon, and he sits himself on the step.

"Anyone for a cuppa?" Julia asks.

"Good idea," says Will, sitting himself on the grass beside Henry.

"How you feeling?"

"Not so bad thanks to your driving. If it was Nell at the reins, my teeth would've fallen out of my head by now."

"Oi! I'm a good driver, aren't I, Julia?"

"Stop teasing her, Henry," says Julia.

I don't mind his teasing, means he must be feeling alright. "You get much sleep?" I ask him.

"All I seem to do these days is sleep."

"You're a lazy bugger, that's for sure." I grin at Henry. He tries to flick me round the ear, but can't quite muster the strength to reach me. Instead, he tips his face toward the sun and lets it soothe his skin. A smile crosses his lips, then he lets out a little snore.

"Wake up, Henry, here's your tea." Julia passes him a cup and sits beside him on the step. He only takes a few sips before handing the cup to her to finish.

"Quite the view you get from up here," he says, shielding his eyes from the sun. Around us lie purple blue hills, below us a tree-filled valley, the sparkle of a river curling along is base.

"Beautiful," says Will. "Never made it this far north myself. I'll have to bring Sophia up here one day. She'd love it."

"Should have seen it in the snow," I say. "It was like when I saw Siberia at Robert's cinematograph."

"You were mad as hatters, making the crossing in those conditions. Sophia was in a tizzy for weeks till your letter arrived letting her know you were safe."

"All's well that ends well," says Julia, tipping the last of her tea onto the grass.

"You alright to keep moving, Henry?"

"Yes, boss. Might need to get a bit of help off this step though."

Julia and Will put themselves under each of his shoulders and carry him back to bed. He's tired as anything, but being back on the road has put the twinkle back in his eyes.

"Should we stop for the night around Derby?" Will asks Julia.

"Let's see how Henry's going. We've got two more days to get to Cambridge, but if he's feeling alright, we may as well press on further."

We reach Derby at five, and Will checks with Julia whether we should stop for the night.

"Henry's fast asleep, so I say keep going. We won't lose the light for another five or six hours. Let's aim for Leicester and camp there if we can."

The light is fading fast when we reach the outskirts of Leicester. Will finds a grassy field with a big enough opening to get the wagon through and we park up for the night. No one will bother us here, and we'll be gone at first light tomorrow.

Will sleeps out beside the wagon, saying he's happiest under the stars. I reckon he just wants to give Henry some privacy. I sleep like a baby after a day out in the fresh air, and Henry sleeps even deeper than me, drugged up to the eyeballs on opium.

***

We've had a good run of it, and by three, we're pulling into the busy streets of Cambridge. People are swarming all around, eager for the fair to open tomorrow. Chrissy would

love it here, so many varieties of sheep and pigs being loaded
out of vans ready for market.

It takes almost as long to drive through the town as it did
to get all the way from Leicester. We get held up by wagons
unloading, people moving machinery into place, and children
running this way and that in front of our horses' hooves. It's
a relief to reach Midsummer Common. Most of the showfolk
have already arrived, but Will tells us Sophia's saved a good
spot for us beside them. He leads the horses to the edge of
the common, and they let out a grateful snort as he uncouples
them from the wagon.

Sophia rushes out of her wagon as soon as she sees us. She
gives Will a good old smacker on the lips before pulling me
into her arms and kissing my hair near a hundred times.

"I've been so worried about you all. Thank God you're all
safe. Henry and Julia inside?"

I want to warn her about Henry, but I don't get the chance,
for she's off and up the steps before I can stop her. I rush to
the door and catch her loud gasp as she sees Henry lying on
the bed.

"Oh, my poor, poor love. What the hell's happened to you?"
Her eyes are full of tears and she's all red in the face.

"You know how to make a man feel good about himself,"
whispers Henry, face screwing up in pain. He sticks out his
tongue and Julia puts a few drops of opium on it. Henry's
eyes glaze over and his head lolls to one side.

"Best leave him to sleep for a bit," says Julia, taking Sophia
by the arm and leading her back outside.

"Fucking hell, Julia, why didn't you let me know things
had got so bad?"

"'Cause I knew you'd be worrying. I could imagine you dropping Will in it to run the stall and rushing up north as soon as you heard the news."

Sophia manages a small smile. "I would have if I'd known. Is there nothing the doctors can do for him?"

"No. By the time he let on something was up, it was too late. Now it's just a waiting game. He's been battling against nature and God these past months, keeping himself going so he can return to the fair."

"And you've been dealing with all this by yourself I suppose?"

Julia pulls me into a hug and speaks over my head. "Not by myself. I've had this one helping me, haven't I. She's been a marvel when it comes to caring for Henry. There's also been cousin Chrissy. She'd never make it as a nurse, but she's a fine cook, and we've needed one of them to keep us all going."

"Good girl, Nell," says Sophia, joining our hug and wrapping her fat cosy arms round the both of us.

"Oh, I nearly forgot. Did you get the things on the list I sent?"

"Course I did. Wait there, I'll fetch them."

Sophia disappears behind her wagon, and comes out pushing what looks like a wicker armchair with wheels.

"What the bloody hell is that?" I ask.

"It's a special chair for Henry, so he can get around the fair without needing to walk."

"He's going to hate it," I say.

"He doesn't have much choice," mutters Julia.

"I got all the other supplies you asked for, but I forgot the bread. Sorry, love."

"Don't worry, I'm sure Nellie will fetch some. That alright?"

"Course. I'll go now."

"Thanks, love."

I head inside for the coin tin and while I'm there I check on Henry. He's fast asleep, little snores coming from his nose every now and then.

"There's a bakery on the corner, two streets that way across the river," says Chrissy.

"Thanks. See you in a bit."

I've never been to Cambridge before, and I'm not sure what to make of all the grand buildings and churches. Don't get me wrong, they're beautiful, but it's all a bit posh for my liking. I walk along the edge of the common till I find a little bridge, the colour of sand. Blokes whizz along the river below, in boats as thin as one of Henry's legs. I can hear them shouting to one another and their voices sound just like King George. Bloody toffs.

The streets are that busy it's hard to follow the directions Sophia gave. I go two streets up from the river but there's just some massive building with stained glass windows and men in suits guarding the entrance. I don't reckon I'll get no bread there. I turn down a side street, maybe this will take me the right way? A bloke in a suit whizzes past on a bicycle. He stops halfway down and pedals back towards me. A leather bag is slung on his shoulder and old musty books poke out the top. He can't be much older than me, for it looks like he's trying to grow a beard without much success.

"You look lost," he says. His voice sounds like he's shoved at least five plums in his mouth.

"I'm looking for the bakery."

"You're not from Cambridge?"

"No, just passing through."

"Ah, you've come to see the fair, have you?"

"Yes."

"A pretty girl like you had better be careful walking round that fair. They're a rum lot over there. I wouldn't trust them as far as I could throw them."

I want to punch this bloke in the nose, but trouble is the last thing I can take back to Julia. The fellow gets off his bicycle and walks beside me.

"If you could just give me directions, I'll be on my way," I say.

"I'll walk with you for a bit. It's no trouble for me."

"No, really, I'll be fine. Thank you."

The fellow drops his bike to the ground, and before I know what's happening, he's pinning me to a wall.

"Get off me," I shout. But there's no one else on the street to hear me.

"Good girls don't walk the streets alone. You must be easy enough. Come here."

I scream as he shoves his hand up my dress and tries to get to my private parts. My legs are trapped beneath his, or I'd knee him in the balls. His mouth is slobbering wet kisses all over my neck. I feel a trickle of drool running down beneath my collar. There's only one weapon I've got, so I'd better use it wisely. I shift my head to the side and bite down as hard as I can on his ear. A taste like metal hits my tongue and the fellow lurches back, screaming like a baby. With my legs free, I whip my knee up and his scream goes even higher as pain rips from his privates. He curls up, dropping to the floor like a slug covered in salt. I don't hang around, sprinting through the streets, heading to the river. I pass the bakery but don't dare stop. It's not till I'm safely back among the fair folk that I catch my breath.

I want to tell Julia, but she'll only worry, so I go to Sophia instead. She listens to my tale in silence, her face growing redder and redder as I describe what the chap did.

"Come here," she says. She holds my shoulders and makes me stand in front of her mirror. "See that?"

"Me?"

"Yes, you. Look at yourself. You're turning into a beauty, Nell. It's time you started being more careful."

"I can take care of myself."

"From the sounds of it, yes you can. But you can never be too careful. What if there'd been two of them? What then?"

"I reckon I could still have got away."

"Maybe, maybe not. Have your monthlies started yet?"

I feel heat rising to my cheeks. There's not much will embarrass me, but only Julia knows about my monthlies and I'd like it to stay that way.

"Well?"

"Yes."

"You know what that means then? What could happen if a chap gets too close?"

"No."

"Right. Sit down."

By the time Sophia finishes her talk and lets me out of the wagon, I'm burning that hot I could boil water on my face.

Chapter 26

June 1914

"All set?"

Henry nods. He's propped up in his wicker chair on wheels with a bunch of cushions. Julia's spread three blankets across his legs, despite the warmth of the evening. Poor old Henry looks utterly ashamed at being pushed about like a baby in a pram, but he's wise enough to know it's the only way. He must still be in his fifties but looks more like an old man of ninety.

"Where to first?" Will asks.

"Everywhere," says Henry.

Will pushes Henry to the centre of the common. It's packed with people hanging around, straining their necks in the direction of the town.

"They're coming," a man shouts. People stand on tiptoes to get a good view. A procession of four shiny black motor cars weaves its way between stalls and rides. The cars stop, and men in fine suits, gold chains and medallions hanging round their necks climb out.

A big-bellied man walks to the front of their group.

"That's the town crier," whispers Sophia.

"Silence for the proclamation, on pain of imprisonment!" His voice booms across the crowd. Children still their fidgeting and the adults hush their chatter.

"Town clerk," whispers Sophia as a tiny little man steps forward.

He produces a scroll and begins to read the fair proclamation. "... the peace should be kept... all idle and evil disposed persons should depart, upon pain of imprisonment or other punishment..."

As soon as he's finished the proclamation, the town crier draws a deep breath and yells, "God save the King!"

"God save the King!" the crowd cry back at him.

Henry crooks his finger and beckons me to put my head close to his. "That town clerk said idle people should depart. Reckon he was talking about me?" He winks at me and I squeeze his hand.

"I think he'll let you off, just this once."

The posh looking men climb back into their motor cars and the crowd scramble in all directions, ready for the fun to begin.

"You want to take a look at the animals?" Will asks.

"I've seen enough animals these past few months to last me a lifetime," Henry says. "What I'd really like, is a go at the shooting gallery."

"Then to the shooting gallery we shall go!"

Me and Julia follow behind the brothers. As his wheels turn, Henry's head moves this way and that, taking in all that's around him.

"Stop," he says, and we pause beside the gallopers. Children climb onto the beautiful horses, giggling and screaming as they move up and down. Henry's smiling, but his eyes are wet. "Remember when we used to sneak a go on the gallopers, Will? Dad would be searching all over the fair for us, and we'd get a right good hiding when he found us."

Will laughs. "I remember us hiding underneath one time. Bloody hell, we got a good walloping for that. He pulled you out by your ear, didn't he?"

Henry smiles. "Those were the days."

"You alright to keep going?"

Henry nods and Will manoeuvres the chair onwards. Plenty of folk do a double take as Henry wheels past. Some remove their caps and look sad, others look confused; is this really the man they knew? Henry greets all with a smile and a wave of his hand. We reach the line of shooting galleries, and Henry points to one.

Will takes out a coin to pay, but the gaff lad waves his hand away and Will puts the change back in his pocket. The gaff lad hands him the rifle, and Will holds it up to Henry's shoulder.

"I've got it, Will," Henry says.

The rifle shakes in Henry's hands and we all take a step back. The gaff lad minding the stall hops from one foot to the other, looking across to his boss for help.

"Right, folks, we got a VIP here," the showman says. "Let's give him a bit of room and he can show you how it's done."

Julia shoots a grateful smile across to the man. The last thing we need is Henry shooting someone by mistake. Henry adjusts the rifle, pushing the butt firmly into his shoulder. He squints, then shoots. Bloody hell, how did he do that? For a man so weak, the shot is a miracle. A bottle shatters into pieces as the bullet hits. A perfect shot. The crowd around the stall clap and cheer. We're all impressed, but you can almost see the sigh of relief coming from folk's mouths that Henry's hit a target and no stray bullet's gone flying.

"I'm ready to go back to the wagon now," says Henry.

"Right you are."

Henry doesn't go straight to bed. We sit outside the wagon with a cup of tea, listening to the sound of an organ ringing out, the screams of folk and the laughter of kiddies.

"I fancy a beer," Henry says.

"You sure, love? That could interfere with your medicine," says Julia.

"Bugger the medicine. I'll take some extra pain for the taste of beer on my tongue."

"I'll get it," says Will, disappearing off to his wagon.

Henry closes his eyes, and I think he's asleep, then his lids snap open, and he looks at me.

"Nell, could you hunt down a small piece of gingerbread for me?"

"Course I can."

When I return, Henry's taking tiny sips of beer. I hand him the gingerbread and he breaks a crumb off the edge and lets it sit on his tongue. "Best taste in the world," he says.

Everyone's playing at being jolly. Anyone walking past would think we're just a family enjoying a picnic in the sun, but there's a last supper feeling about it. Julia has a smile plastered on her face, but her eyes dart back and forth to Henry, and she flinches every time she sees his face crease up in pain.

"I think that's enough fun for one day," Julia says.

"You might be right," says Henry, yawning. "Thank you all for a very special day. It's been just as I hoped. I love you all very much."

Will carries Henry into the wagon, and Julia follows behind. A few moments later, Will comes over and sits beside me on the grass.

"How about we give those two some time on their own today? You can stay with us tonight if you like? You and Sophia take the bed and I'll sleep under the stars."

"Alright," I say. "Can I just go and let Julia know?"

"I've told her, but if you want to go in for a moment you go."

I creep into the wagon. Henry is tucked beneath the blankets of his bed and Julia is lying beside him, his hand in hers.

"I'm off to Sophia's. I'll stay there tonight."

"Good girl," whispers Julia.

"Can I say goodbye to Henry?"

"Come here," she says, shuffling over to make room for me. I lie between them, my adopted mum and dad, the three of us together for what I fear may be the last time. I snuggle into Henry, laying my arm gently across his chest. Julia wraps her arm around the both of us, and we lie in silence. Henry's breaths come fast and light, like airy hiccups.

"Sophia will be waiting for you," says Julia. "It's best you go."

I prop myself up on an elbow and lean down to kiss Henry's cheek. "I'm off," I tell him. "I'll be back in the morning and I'll see you then. Sleep well." I get the last words out with a choke, and close the sliding door quietly behind me as I leave.

***

Rather than bursting in like I normally would, I knock on the wagon door. No answer. The door opens with a quiet click and I let myself inside. All the curtains are drawn, and one thin spear of sunlight breaks through a gap, slicing the air.

"Julia?"

I creep to the sliding door and listen. There's a snuffling sound, like when Chrissy's pigs were rooting around for food.

"Julia?"

"In here."

I slide the door open. Henry is lying on his back, his face more peaceful than it's looked in weeks. Julia is curled like a kitten beside him, arms wrapped round herself, a hanky balled up in her hand.

"Is he..."

"He's gone."

"When?"

"Last night. He waited for the fair to close, must've been listening to its sounds all that time."

"Come with me and sit by the fire."

"I don't want to leave him."

"Julia, he's right there. You'll be no more than three feet away. Come on."

Her hand reaches for mine and I help her off the bed and into the armchair. I uncurl her fingers and replace the sodden hanky with a clean one. She sits staring into space as I set about making tea and lighting the fire. It's a warm day out there, but Julia shivers and shakes in her chair, her body rocked by the ragged breaths and dry sobs that come in waves.

"Are you hungry?"

She shakes her head. The uneaten slice of gingerbread sits wrapped on the table. The sight of it causes tears to burn at my eyes, but I must stay strong for Julia. Perhaps this is my chance to repay all the kindness she's shown me over the years.

All day folks come to the wagon to pay their respects. Julia's in no state to greet them, so I spend much of the day sat on the wagon step, ready to fend off well-meaning folk, accepting their condolences on behalf of the family. The world still turns, and on the fair that means the laughs and screams and jolly organ music sound out across the common all day, at odds with the grief that lingers around our wagon.

I need answers to the questions in my head; what happens now? Where will we go? How long will we stay in Cambridge? But Julia's in no mood for answering them. The only folk she'll allow in the wagon except me are Will and Sophia. Both spend time with Henry, telling him things they wish they'd said before. Their coconut shy stays closed up, partly as a mark of respect, but mainly as they can't face opening. I'm to sleep in with Sophia again tonight. It comes as a relief, for much as I loved Henry, I'm not keen on sharing the wagon with his corpse.

Chapter 27

June 1914

It's been four days since Henry died, and I'm still none the wiser about our plans. Julia had the undertakers in, preparing Henry's body so he can stay with us till he's buried. She's been out collecting wildflowers and they lie strewn around his head. I can't go into the wagon without bursting into a sneezing fit. I've slept with Sophia the past four nights, and I suppose that won't change till Henry's in the ground.

"I'm off into town," says Julia, coming out of the gloomy wagon and squinting in the sun, dressed in black. I wonder how long she's been keeping her mourning clothes ready.

"I can go for you if you like?"

"No thank you, love, there's something I need to see to."

Bloody hell, she's aged since Henry died. It's been four days but may as well be four years. In my mind she's always been the boss, but now he's gone, she's lost without him. She's been struggling even to make a cup of tea. I hope her old self returns soon, or we'll be in a right spot of bother.

It's two hours till she returns and she's looking even worse than before. I'm busy helping Sophia prepare lunch when she walks over.

"Sophia, can I borrow Nellie for a moment?"

"Of course, love, anything you need."

I follow Julia to a patch of grass behind our wagon and she waves her hand for me to sit down. She's barely touched a morsel of food these past days and needs my help getting herself down she's that wobbly.

"I expect you've been worrying what will happen to us now, and it's time I gave you some answers."

"Thank you."

Julia sniffs, and pulls out a letter she's had tucked in her basket. "Before I say anything else, I need you to know that I've thought about our predicament this way and that. I've gone through every which way to make things better for you."

I squeeze her hand, but she pulls it away and looks at the floor. Bloody hell, this don't look good.

"Tell me."

"Alright, well, when I knew Henry was nearing the end, I wrote to Florrie. Asked her to send a reply here. I suspected things would be clearer by the time we reached Cambridge, turns out I was right." She sniffs again. "Thing is, Nell, we can't go on with the fair no more. There's no way we can run the shooting gallery without Henry. Will has agreed to buy it from us, and the wagon too. That leaves me needing to find another way to earn my keep."

"And me."

"Yes, and you."

"Can we head back north? Would Chrissy take us back?"

"That's not so simple though, is it? You've burned your bridges at the mill, and I can see no way they'd let you back."

"Could I work for Chrissy?"

"Nell, they have enough trouble keeping themselves afloat, never mind paying someone else."

"What will we do then?"

"Well, Florrie has put an idea to me. She's engaged to the fellow she met at the fair while we were there."

"Not Joe?"

"Yes, I'm afraid so."

"But he's a no-good gaff lad! I warned her about him. She's got more brains than to fall for his charms, surely?"

"Clearly not, for they're engaged. Seems there's a baby on the way."

No. Not my Florrie. Not that fly by night Joe. Julia must have got it wrong.

"Let me see the letter," I say. Julia clasps it tight.

"There's more," she says. "Seems your mum is pretty sick. Florrie says your mum's finding it hard to look after herself, never mind Freddie."

"Can't Florrie take care of them?"

"That's precisely what she has been doing, but things are changing. Joe won't let her take Freddie in now he's his own kiddie to think of, and he wants them to get their own place."

"What about Dad?"

"Seems your dad did a runner when things started to go bad. They've not seen him these past three months, they've no idea where he's living now. Nell, Florrie needs you to go back."

"No. I want to stay with you."

"I want that too, more than anything, but there's no way I can care for you now."

"I can find work."

"Nell, it's too risky. If we stick together, we could both land up in the poor house. And there's more." She takes a newspaper from her basket and unfolds it on the grass. "Some posh bloke has been shot, and there's talk it could start a war."

I lean across her and read the newspaper for myself. *Archduke and His Wife Shot Dead in the Street... What will the tragedy mean... Far reaching effect... Bombs on the railway.*

"Bloody hell, Julia. What does all this mean?"

"Only time will tell, but it means it's an even worse time to be trawling the country with no home or job. You understand that don't you?"

"Yes. When will I have to go back?"

"There's a train to Norwich tomorrow. I thought you could catch that."

"What about Henry's funeral?"

"Nell, you've said your goodbyes. Funerals are no place for the young."

"But you'll need me there."

"I'll have Sophia and Will. I'm not sure I can face burying Henry and saying goodbye to you all in one go."

"Will I see you again?"

"I'll keep in touch, I promise. As soon as I'm settled, I'll write with my new address. I consider you my daughter, Nellie, I'm not going to forget you that easily."

"Will you be alright?"

Julia picks at the grass, not meeting my eye. "I hope so." She looks up at me. "It might take me a while to get back on my feet. But I've suffered plenty in my life and always bounced back eventually. I don't want you worrying about me. You've your own life to lead."

***

Me and Julia walk away from the fair, the smell of ginger-bread and toffee apples fading into the distance, the noise of the organs and steam engines replaced by sounds of the town. We reach the station all too soon despite me doing my best to drag my feet.

"I won't come in, if that's alright with you. Seeing you get on that train would be too much for me I think."

I wrap my arms around Julia and hold her like I'll never let go. People walking past stare, surprised to see two women locked together, tears streaming like a river between them. Julia holds my face in her hands, rubbing away my tears with her thumbs.

"Don't let your mum get the better of you. You're Nellie Westrop, and don't you forget it. We'll see each other again one day, but until we do, take good care of yourself. Live a good life. Now go, my love."

I stand still, unable to walk away. Julia sighs, kisses my cheek, then turns and walks back towards the fair.

"Julia!"

She turns to face me.

"Thank you for being my mum."

Her hand flies to her mouth and her shoulders shake in a sob. Then, she turns on her heel and disappears among the crowds.

I don't know how I find the ticket office, or the platform but somehow, I do. The guard checks my ticket and I board the train. The carriage is quiet, most folk are coming to the fair, not away from it and I have no trouble finding a seat. The whistle sounds and the train inches forward with a judder. Cambridge disappears in the distance. Have I left Nellie Westrop there too? Am I returning to Ellen Hardy? No. I'll never be Ellen again, too much has happened for me to return to her. Julia named me Nellie, and Nellie I shall remain.

Chapter 28

June 1914

I've never been to Norwich station before. It's bigger than I expected, noisier too. Florrie's not on the platform so I head to the exit and look for her there. She sees me before I see her.

"Ellen!" She's running towards me, her arms waving. When she reaches me, she pulls me into a hug, and I feel her round belly press against my flat one.

"Hello, Florrie."

"Good to see you, Ellen."

I put my bag on the ground and look at her. "Florrie, no one calls me Ellen no more. I'm known as Nellie now, or Nell, I don't mind. Just not Ellen. Please."

"Alright, Nell. Just don't get mad at me if I forget sometimes."

"We heading straight to the yard?"

"How about we find a spot to sit for a minute? Probably best I fill you in on what's been happening before we see Mum."

"Alright."

I follow her to a low wall, and we sit side by side, watching a boat slowly winding its way along the river.

"First things first," I say. "What the bloody hell are you playing at getting mixed up with a gaff lad?"

Florrie checks my face to see if I'm joking. She realises I'm deadly serious and pouts out her lips. "Joe's a good man. I won't have no one saying otherwise, 'specially not you."

"Right, so other folks think he's a wrong 'un too do they?"

"That's not what I said. He takes care of me well if you must know."

"Alright, so what job does he do now the fair's left town?"

"This and that. A bit of labouring, works in the pub sometimes, anything to get by really."

"I see. So, when's the wedding?"

Florrie blushes from her chin to her scalp and her eyes study the floor.

"Well?"

"The wedding happened last week."

"Last week?" I jump off the wall and force her to look at me. "You knew I'd have to come back, yet you got wed without me there?"

"Joe thought it was for the best. What with the baby and all." She cups a hand over her belly. It's only the damned baby what stops me pushing her off the bloody wall.

"You've changed," I say. "The old Florrie would never have got wed without me by her side."

"So what if I have? I'm not the only one who's changed, *Nell*."

I climb back onto the wall and stare out at the river. It'll do no good if the two of us fall out. I'll need all the help I can get if I'm to care for Mum.

"Look, Nell, I'm sorry, I don't want us to fall out. You need to understand though, the world hasn't stopped turning just 'cause you've been gone. We've all had to make the best of what we've got. What I've got is Joe, and this little one what's wriggling inside me."

"I'm sorry too. So, what else happened since I've been gone?"

"Well for starters, we don't live at the yard no more."

"What?"

"Julia's probably told you Dad done a bunk. Well, the lease was in his name, so when he left the landlord chucked us out. Sarah's chap Ted found a place for us to go and put it in his name. It's no palace, but it's a damn sight better than what we had before."

"Where is it?"

"Ely Street. This side of the river."

"Do you live there still?"

"No. It's just Mum, Freddie and Albert living there. You got the news about Arthur?" I nod my head. "Poor chap, far too young to go, but it didn't come as a surprise. He'd not been well for a long time."

I think back to the shrunken man I'd seen in the doorway all those years earlier. "Sorry I didn't make his funeral. We were miles away, and by the time Julia picked up your letter the funeral was long passed."

"Don't worry, I understand."

"Do you live nearby?"

"Me and Joe are a couple of streets away. He wasn't keen on living with Mum."

"I bet he wasn't. So, what's up with Mum then?"

"The doc says it's something to do with her lungs. We thought she'd be dead long since but she's a stubborn old mule and is determined to torment us as long as she can. She'll probably come back to haunt us when she's dead too."

"The illness hasn't softened her then?"

Florrie laughs. "No chance. Look, I know it's awful for you coming back here with her. I'll do my best to help out when

I can. I don't give two hoots what happens to Mum, but Fred needs someone looking out for him, and I can't do that no more."

"I can't wait to see Freddie again."

"He's just as excited as you are. Let's get going."

We jump off the wall and Florrie leads me through streets I've never walked before. I don't take much in as my head is spinning with all what's happened. This morning I was drinking tea with Julia on the fairground. Now I'm heading back to the life I hoped I'd never return to.

Florrie leads me down a street jam-packed with terraced houses. We turn a corner and stop outside number fourteen.

"This it?" I ask.

"Yes, this is it."

The first thing I notice is the windows. They may be covered in grime, but they're a big improvement on no windows at all. Grey bricks make up the whole line of terraces. It looks like they built the lot as one shell, then worked out how many houses they could squeeze inside it. I reckon if I held my arms out either side, I'd be wider than the house. The wooden door is stained brown, and patches of soft rot lie from top to bottom on one side.

Florrie opens the door and yells up the stairs. "Only me, Mum, I've got Ellen with me."

I wince at her using my old name. Footsteps thunder from the back of the house and Freddie runs at me, flinging himself into my arms. I lift him till his face is level with mine and kiss his nose. He giggles then squirms from my grip. "You here forever?" he asks.

"I'm here for a good while, don't you worry," I say, my heart melting and sinking all at once.

"Albert, Albert, Nellie's here."

At least one person in this house knows my name.

A slim man walks through the hallway. "So, I hear you're called Nellie now then."

"Hello, Albert," I say, giving him a quick hug. He stands awkwardly in my arms, hands clasped behind his back. As soon as I release him, he heads back the way he came.

"Let's go up and say hello to Mum," Florrie says.

I follow her up a wooden staircase. Circles of mould cling to the bare walls, and cobwebs hang from the banisters. Julia would have a fit if she saw this place. She'd have her duster out and would spruce the place up in no time. No one else seems bothered by the grime, Florrie leaning her hand against the filthy wall as she huffs and puffs up the steps.

"Mum, here's Nellie."

"Hello, Ellen." I swear Mum snarls the words. I remember Julia's advice. Mum can do her worst, let her try, for it will be water off a duck's back.

"Good to see you again, Mum," I say, hugging her and kissing her wrinkled cheek. "Florrie tells me you've not been well? I'm here now so I'll help take care of you."

"Fat lot of use you'll be."

"Lovely to see you too," I say, leaving the room in search of Freddie.

I check in the parlour but there's no one there, just a dirty mattress on the floor and a pile of clothes I presume belong to Albert. In the room at the back Freddie is rolling marbles across the floor to Albert. I notice the table is the same one we had in the yard, and three chairs sit around it. Looks like it will be the floor for me then.

"You want to play with us?" Freddie asks.

"Yes please. That alright with you, Albert?"

Albert surprises me with a smile. "Course it is. It's good to see you, Nellie, it's been quite some time."

"Eight years. What you doing with yourself these days?"

"Still working at the shoe factory."

"He's courting a girl from St Benedict's Street," pipes up Freddie.

Albert blushes. "You probably know her, it's Maggie, she was two years above you at school all them years ago."

"Isn't she a bit young for you?"

"Only two years' difference. And I treat her well. It's nothing serious, but I like her."

"Well, as long as you don't make her do nothing improper."

"Course I don't."

"Good."

"Albert says there could be war. Says he'll become a soldier if there is."

"That so?" I say.

"It's all everyone at the factory's talking about. They reckon that archduke being shot has stirred up a proper old shit storm."

"Yes, I read about it in the paper." Was that only yesterday? "Anyone for a cuppa while we play?"

"Go on then," says Albert.

"Um, where do I get water from?"

"Pump's out back, next to the privy. We share that with half the street so you should be able to smell it before you see it."

Great. I'll take an open field with a hole in the ground over a shared privy any day. I make the tea only to discover there's no milk. This day just gets better and bloody better.

***

In the three days since I've been home, I've learned to live with the pain in my belly each time I think of Julia and Henry. I save my tears for the night, for they're private. At night I dream of the fair, of the farm. Each morning I wake thinking I'm in the wagon. Each morning the hard floor beneath me reminds me I'm not. I tell myself I'm lucky I had those happy years, but in my bleaker moments I wonder if I'd have been better without them. What you don't know can't hurt you, that's what they say, isn't it? They also say it's better to have loved and lost than never to have loved. Julia taught me that, and I believe it to be true.

I'm finding the hardest thing the house itself. In some ways it's far better than the yard, but it's the dirt and dullness what make me long for the wagon. Here, there's nothing pretty for pretty's sake. There's no care taken to make things look nice, to make a house a home. Yesterday I tried putting one of my lace hankies on the table beneath a jug of flowers. Mum grabbed the hanky out and used it for washing dishes.

The day of Henry's funeral, I took myself off to the nearest church. I didn't dare go in, but sat alone in the graveyard and said a little prayer for them all; Henry, Julia, Sophia and Will. How they must be hurting, how I wish I was there to help them.

"Neeeellllliiiieeeee."

Fred. Darling Fred. I'd jump out of my comfy wagon bed for him, let alone this back-crunching bed on the dirty floor.

"Coming, Fred," I say.

I wrap a shawl around my shoulders, for this house is damn chilly. It's the bloody height of summer, I dread to think what it's like in winter. Fred's sat up at the table, gnawing on an old crust of bread.

"What you got on that?"

"Nothing."

"Nothing?"

"Nothing to put on it."

I can't find a job quick enough. It will have to be something nearby, for I'll need to be able to nip back and check on Mum regular.

"You in school today?"

"Not been to school for ages."

"Well, you need to go, Fred. It's important."

"Why? Mum says I'll be out to work soon."

"Cause if you don't know your three R's you'll be stuck in a place like this forever, that's why."

"Do you know your R's?"

"That I do."

"Well, you're stuck in a place like this, aren't you?"

"Yes, smarty pants, but this is a temporary arrangement."

The poor little chap's face falls. "You leaving again?"

"As soon as I can, Fred, but not without you this time. I'll get us set up somewhere nice, alright?"

"You promise you'll take me with you?"

"I promise."

He smiles at me, and it pushes all the sadness deeper in my belly so I almost can't feel it. Whatever happens with Mum, I'll make sure Freddie gets better than this. We're a team now. I won't leave him behind again.

Chapter 29

August 1914

Mum leans on my arm and holds a grey hanky to her mouth. She's light as a feather, and as she hacks from deep in her lungs, I wonder if she'll blow away. I hope so. Me and Freddie wanted to come out by ourselves, but she insisted on being here to wave Albert off. Took us an age to get to Prince of Wales Road with her sickly arse dragging along behind us.

I hide a yawn behind my hand. It's knackering caring for Mum and trying to work. She's not grateful like Henry was. She seems to think I'm her bloody slave, ordering me around, knowing I can't refuse a sick old woman. Even a sick old bitch like her. The past week's been easier since I left Harmers, but then there's money to worry about. Bloody Harmers. All I was doing was trying to bring a bit of fun to the day. My jokes and songs weren't appreciated. Well fine, I'll just take them elsewhere.

"Can you see him yet?" Fred asks.

"Not yet," I say. Don't help we're all bloody short arses. I stand on my tiptoes and study the sea of khaki bodies marching down the wide road, but thanks to Mum dragging her heels, there's at least five rows of folk in front of us and it's damned near impossible to pick Albert from the crowd.

"Come here, Fred. Climb on my shoulders."

Fred climbs up. We ignore the cursing of people behind us as he cranes his neck this way and that. "I see him! I see him!"

"Alright, Fred, I know you're excited, but could you stop kicking me?"

"Sorry, Nell."

Fred points his finger and I try and follow his direction. There he is, my big brother all smart and proud, his little hat perched on his head, boots shiny as a mirror.

"Albert! Albert!"

Albert glances over, his lips twitch in a brief smile. Then he marches on, following his comrades towards the fight of their lives.

"He didn't wave," says Fred as I lift him off my shoulders.

"That's 'cause he's a proper soldier now. Did you see though? He smiled at us."

"Barely."

I kiss Fred's pouting lips and ruffle his hair. The crowd waves their flags, cheering the men on, proud of the sons and grandsons off to fight for the country.

"When will Albert come home?"

"Let's hope it's soon," I say. "We can have a party for him when he does, for he'll be a hero."

"If he comes home at all," says Mum. I'm thankful her voice is muffled under the crowd's roars and Fred misses her words. I glare at her but soften my gaze when I notice her eyes are blurred by tears. She goes to speak, but launches into another coughing fit. People shuffle away from us, and I gag as a lump of lung slime lands on my sleeve.

"I think we should get Mum home, Fred."

"But I want to stay and watch the soldiers."

"I know, but we've seen Albert now. Mum needs her bed."

"Bloody Mum," he mutters. Mum hears and gives him a clip round the ear. I feel my face burning hot as both women and men around us tut. They probably whack their kiddies too, but they wouldn't do it in public, not on an occasion like this.

I grab Fred's arm, and have to drag him through the crowd. He's cross with me, keeping his head down and refusing to speak. As soon as we're through the masses, he sprints off ahead. Bloody hell, what can I do? I can't leave Mum by herself, nor do I want Fred lost in the city.

"Wait here, Mum," I say, finding a wall for her to perch on. "I need to find Fred; I'll be back in a tick."

I run down towards the river. *Please God, don't let him have crossed the bridge.* If he's made it to the yards, there'll be no finding him. At the bridge I pause; where to? A strange sound, a bit like a cry, is coming from the riverbank. I head down and see Fred, bent double, his face red as anything.

"Fred?" I say. He looks up. Water is streaming from eyes that are bulging out of his skull. I rush over to him and grab his arms. "What's wrong, Fred? What is it?"

"Can't... breathe..."

Oh God, the noise he's making is bloody awful. "Take deep breaths," I say. He tries, but it comes out in that horrid squeal. His body is going limp, and I scoop him up in my arms before he collapses to the ground.

"Help!" I scream. "Help!"

A woman steps out of her shop and sees us. "Come here," she shouts. "I can help."

I run as quick as I can. Fred's not a big lad, but he's heavy enough and I don't want to drop him. "This is my brother. He can't breathe."

"Bring him inside, love."

The woman steps aside to let us in the shop and turns the sign on the door from open to closed. "Through the back," she says. "Get him on a chair."

"Shouldn't he lie down?" I ask, as she pulls out a high-backed wooden chair from beneath a table.

"No, he needs a good clear path for the air. Don't let him bend over."

I hold his shoulders back so he can't bend double again. The woman kneels on the floor in front of him. "What's his name?"

"Fred."

"Right, Fred, you listen to me. Take a really big breath in through your nose and out through your mouth."

Fred wriggles in the chair. "You need to calm him down, love," the woman says to me. I begin stroking his back, rubbing my hand slowly in circles. I feel his shoulders relax a little.

"Come on, Fred, I'll do it with you."

The woman takes a huge breath through her nose and Fred copies her. She breathes out, and he does the same. His eyes have stopped watering, but he's still red in the face. "Keep going, Fred." The woman has his hands in hers and she's looking into his eyes. I feel so helpless just stroking and stroking, but she gives me a smile to let me know it's helping.

It's another five minutes before his breathing sounds better. "How you feeling now, Fred?" she asks.

"Bit better."

"Good. Now let me make you some tea. That should help too."

The woman potters about the small room. "This happened to him before?"

"I don't know," I say. "I've been away for a while and only got back a couple of months ago. I've been out at work most days, so it could've happened without me knowing."

"Fred?" she asks, walking over to him. "Have you had trouble breathing before?"

Fred nods.

"And when does it usually happen, love?"

"It's worse in winter," he says. "Don't happen so much when it's warm, unless I'm in the house and it's been raining a lot."

"I see."

"How did you know what to do?" I ask her.

"My son, Tim. He's had asthma since he was tiny. The doc showed me what to do if he was without his medicine. Saved his life more than once, I can tell you."

"I'll take him to the doctor tomorrow."

"You do that, love. Is your house damp?"

I think of the mould on the walls and peeling plaster. "Yes, a bit."

"Well, I know it's hard, but try and keep him in the best rooms with the most air coming through. Living in bad conditions will only make matters worse."

"I have plans to move us elsewhere, but for the moment our mum's sick so we're stuck where we are for the time being." Bloody hell. Mum. I'd completely forgotten about her sat on that wall. Five minutes I said I'd be.

"Look, I'm so sorry to be rude, but I left my mum on the street while I came to look for Fred. She's not well enough to be on her own, so we really must be getting back."

"That's alright, love. Just let the little lad have a bit of tea before he goes. It will help, I promise."

As soon as he's downed the last dregs, I thank the woman again, and we let ourselves out of her shop. Fred says he's alright to walk, but I can't risk him falling ill again. I crouch down low and make him climb on my back.

Mum's face is like thunder by the time we reach her. "Back in a tick, you said. Bollocks to that. Thought you'd leave a sick woman alone on the street while you had a bit of fun, did you? Well, you're your father's daughter that's for sure. Apple didn't fall far from the tree when we had you."

"I was looking after Freddie. He had trouble breathing, and a lady had to help us."

"Moaning again, was he? Always complaining about his chest that one. He don't know the first thing about what it's like to be proper ill. He should try walking in my shoes for a day, then he'd stop his whinging."

Freddie hides his face in my neck, and I feel the dampness of his tears against my skin. "Come on, Mum, let's get home."

I'm sure Mum would be alright to walk, but she makes a great show of leaning on my arm, and I have the weight of both of them on me. By the time we get home every bone in my body is aching.

"Stick the kettle on," she barks, before pulling herself up the stairs and heading for bed.

The sooner I find myself another job and get out of her way, the better.

Chapter 30

September 1917

"Here, Nell, here, pass."

My toe clips the ball and grass and mud go flying. Olive's right on it, and in a matter of seconds has not only met my pass, but sent the ball flying into the goal. Cheers echo through the crowd. The Canadian soldiers are excited, not just by the quaint English football match, but also by the girls running round in their shorts.

Olive runs over and flings herself at me. The others join in and it's a right old scrum we got going. The riverside team walk over to shake our hands. It's only a friendly, but it's good to win.

"My mother would go mad if she knew I'd been running round a muddy football pitch on my lunchbreak," says Olive. I laugh and link my arm in hers as we head back to get changed.

"She got used to you working yet?"

"No, not really. But there's not much she can say about it, I'm helping with the war effort after all."

"My mum don't give a damn what I do with my day, so long as she has some coins in her palm by the end of the week."

"How is your mum?"

"Same old. Just lies in bed these days doing bugger all. I can't tell if she's getting worse, or just enjoys having me wait on her hand and foot."

"And Fred? How's he getting on?"

"He's an angel. A scrumptious, mischievous angel. Been to school every day so far this year, despite his chest playing him up."

"Still getting the attacks?"

"Yep. The sooner I get him out of that mouldy old house the better."

"You need to find yourself a nice rich man."

"That what you plan to do, is it? I intend to look after myself, not have some old bloke giving me orders."

"Not even Jack?"

"Nah, Jack's just a bit of fun."

"I'm not sure he sees it that way."

It was a nice surprise to find Jack already working at Boulton and Paul's when I first started. A familiar face, one I'd not seen for ten years, mind. Lately his face has become a bit too familiar. When he first asked me out, I thought it was just as friends, but the slobbery kiss he gave me at my front door said otherwise. In moments like these, Henry and Julia sit firm in my mind, giving me advice, and a right old telling-off if I act the fool.

"You seeing him later?" Olive asks, pulling on her coat and wrapping a scarf round her hair.

"Probably. Seems to turn up at my house most nights whether I ask him to or not."

"You could do a lot worse than Jack."

"Maybe. Or maybe I could do a lot better."

Olive laughs and hails a tram to get us back to the factory on time. All the others are already at their seats on the line, but no one minds us being late. They clap as we walk in. Even the supervisor congratulates us on our win, before telling us the fuses won't make themselves and to hurry back to our seats.

I much prefer the factory to the mill and feel for Julia who's been working there ever since she headed back up north. At the factory, it's noisy, but not so much that you can't have a good old chin wag. I sit beside Olive, who despite thinking she's posher than the rest of us, is a right good laugh.

Five o'clock rolls round quickly enough, and me and Olive head up to the canteen.

"Word is Mrs Pim's made beef stew today. Though God knows how she got hold of the beef."

"Probably horse, or dog," I say. Olive looks horrified. "Come on, I'm only joking. I'm sure it will taste good whatever it is."

I'm surprised I'm not fat as a barrel what with all the food we get here. I try to sneak as much into my pockets as I can. Fred's always grateful for my doggy bag at the end of the day. I wish I could be home more for him, but we can't do without my wage coming in, and at least I get one day off a week. It's best when it falls on a weekend, then me and Fred can wander the streets together dreaming of the posh houses we'll one day live in.

I don't like leaving him alone with Mum. She's too weak to hurt him with her fists, but her tongue's as sharp as it's ever been. He's under strict instructions not to go upstairs while I'm out, but I know she gets him running errands for her. Having someone to grumble at is the only thing keeping her going these days.

"What time you on till today?" Olive asks.

"Nine. How about you?"

"Same."

"Best eat up then and get back to it."

***

The house is in darkness by the time I get home. I close the door as quietly as I can and creep through to put the kettle on.

"Bloody hell, you made me jump out of my skin! What you doing sitting there in the dark?"

"Sorry," says Freddie, getting up from beside the fire. "It was too cold upstairs, so I thought I'd come down here and wait for you."

"You scared the living daylights out of me."

Fred laughs and gives me a hug. "Can I sleep in with you tonight?"

"Course you can." I like having Fred in with me, he's almost as tall as me now and I doubt he'll want to be sharing with his sister much longer. "How was school?"

"Good. Mrs Thorpe says I'm a highflyer."

"Ooh, does she now? That's what I like to hear."

"She reckons I'm university material."

"Well then, I'd better keep working my socks off so you can get there. Imagine that, a Hardy at university. That would be a turn up for the books."

Fred starts coughing.

"You alright?"

"Yes, not too bad, my chest's been playing me up again today though."

I watch him struggling for breath. Whatever it takes, I need to get him out of here. I just need a plan, and time to save.

"Sit down," I say. "Remember the deep breathing I taught you."

Fred recovers himself, and I make us both a cuppa. "How's Mum been today?"

"Bad. She's got through five hankies and all were red with blood by the time she'd finished with them."

"I'd best get the doctor in again tomorrow." My heart sinks at the thought, more of my hard-earned coins will be heading down the drain.

We sip our tea slowly, the warmth of the fire more tempting than the cold bedroom.

"Come on," I say, as Fred lets out a big yawn. "Up the wooden hill with you."

Fred heads up and I nip out to the privy, before checking there's enough coal on the fire to keep it warm till morning. On my way to the stairs, I pause by the parlour. Albert's bed lies just as he left it, his civvy clothes folded in a neat pile. I hate seeing them lying there, but with our money so tight, it makes sense to save them for Fred. Poor Albert, we were so proud to be waving him off. What fools we were.

Crouching beside his bed, I lift a shirt to my face. There's no trace of Albert left within the threads and all I smell is damp. War is an ugly, cruel beast. I reckon me and Albert could've become good friends had he returned home. The old familiar pain tugs at my belly as I remember his brief smile as he passed us on Prince of Wales Road. He was so proud to be serving his country. All he got in return was fire, pain and death. What a world we live in.

***

An awful wheezing and screeching wakes me. Fred's body is stiff beside me as he tries desperately to suck in air.

"Here," I say, propping his back against the damp bedroom wall. "Look at me." I take deep breaths in and out. Fred tries to copy, but he can't get the breaths in he needs, and I can see he's starting to panic.

"Where's your medicine?"

"Gone," he squeaks.

"You used it all up?"

"Mum took some."

"Alright, look, Fred, you're going to be fine, but we need to get you to a doctor. Can you walk?"

Fred shakes his head between wheezes. I wrap a blanket round him and make sure his back is firm against the wall.

"I'm going next door. I'll only be a minute."

"Don't leave me," he gasps.

"Fred," I say, holding his cheeks between my palms. "It's only for a minute. I need to find some stronger arms than mine to get you to the clinic. I promise I'll be quick."

I sprint down the stairs, ignoring Mum's shouts about what the bloody hell is going on. She can rot in hell for all I care. How dare she take Fred's medicine for herself? Selfish cow. My fist pummels the Jacobs' front door. No one comes. I hammer harder, shouting loud enough to wake the whole damn street. After an age, Mrs Jacobs opens the door, hair in a net and blanket wrapped round her.

"It's Fred, he needs to get to the clinic. I can't carry him myself."

"Wait there, love."

"John!" she yells up the stairs. "John!"

Mr Jacobs appears at the top of the stairs in his pyjamas. "Nellie needs to get Fred to the clinic. Grab your coat, and wake up James. You may be glad of an extra pair of hands."

Father and son pull on their coats, and still rubbing sleep from their eyes, they follow me up to Fred. John Jacobs must be in his fifties by now, but he's strong as an ox and lifts Fred like he's made of air. Halfway to the clinic they swap over and James takes a turn. All the while Fred is wheezing and crying. Beneath the lamp light I notice his lips turning blue and his eyes rolling back in his skull. "Hurry," I say. "Please, hurry."

We burst through the clinic door and a surprised nurse rushes us to a ward. She scuttles off to get a doctor who appears only moments later with a bottle of medicine in his hand.

"Wait outside please," says the doctor.

"I don't want to leave him."

"I need space to work. Please, go."

Bloody hell, the minutes drag. I send John and James back off home, insisting I can manage. They don't need too much persuasion, happy to be heading back to their beds. A big old clock on the wall taunts me with its tick tock, the hands creeping round like they're half asleep.

It's been sixty-seven minutes when the doctor comes out to see me.

"How is he?"

"Sit down."

No. No. No. Please, God, no. "He's... he's...."

"Oh, good Lord no. Wipe those tears away, there's a good girl."

"He's not dead?"

"No. I've settled his breathing and he's sleeping peacefully now."

"When can he come home?"

"That's what I need to speak to you about."

Chapter 31

September 1917

By the time I get home, there's little point going to bed. It's the early shift tomorrow, a six a.m. start and its four now. The fire is dying so I stoke it and chuck on a few more coals, then sit dozing beside it till it's time for work.

"Bloody hell, what's happened to you? You look terrible!"

"Thanks, Olive," I say, clocking on and hanging up my coat.

"You up late with Jack, were you?"

"No, at the clinic with Fred." I brush my eyes with my sleeve, so Olive don't see the tears. Not like me to be so soft, but I'm in a right fix with Fred.

"You poor thing. Is he alright?"

"They're keeping him in a few days to keep an eye on his chest. The doc don't want him to come home with me."

"What do you mean?"

"Well, he reckons the conditions we're living in are making the asthma worse. Says if Fred stays there much longer, he might have an attack what's fatal." I drop down against the lockers and put my head in my hands. If I wasn't so worried, I'd fall asleep right here and now.

"Is there anywhere else you can go?"

"No. The rest of the family have houses worse than ours, and they've packed them full of their own kiddies. All I can do is save up enough to get us out of there. But that will take time, and I'm not sure I have time on my side."

"You've spoken to Florrie about it?"

"I've not seen her these past few weeks since the latest baby arrived. Joe's got a good enough heart, I know that, but he's so bloody unreliable he's more work than all the kiddies put together. Bloody men."

"Look, you're exhausted. We're only on till four, so how about I come home with you after work, help you see to your mum, then take you back to mine for dinner? Mother would love to meet you."

Olive's a good friend, but I can't have her seeing where I'm living, or meeting Mum. I'd die of shame. "That's really kind of you. How about I nip back and check on Mum, then come over to your house when I'm done? No point us both hanging round mine, and Mum's not the best person to be around at the moment."

"Alright, let's say six o'clock at my place. Does that give you enough time?"

"Yes, that sounds like a plan."

"Do you know how to get to my house?"

Of course I do, it's on the street me and Fred walk when we're dreaming of the future. A street of large brick houses standing all alone, not joined together like ours. They have driveways for motor cars and grass lawns front and back. What I'd give for a house like that.

"I'm not sure," I lie. "Give me directions once we're done for the day. There's no way I'll remember them if you tell me now."

***

Most days, the time at the factory flies by, but not today. Between lack of sleep and worry over Fred, I make that many duff fuses I'm worried I'll be sacked. At lunch I see Olive talking to the supervisor. She must have said something about me for he leaves me alone all afternoon, turning a blind eye to my mistakes. Oh, to have power and influence. The supervisor is a friend of Olive's father, and put a good word in with the boss when she was looking for work, if the rumours are to be believed.

One day, I'll be rich and powerful. People will do as I say, and I won't be at the mercy of others' kindness. Until then, I'll just have to make the best of things. Never mind the future, I need to get through today first. It's all I can do to stay awake over my bench, and I'm that glad when the bell rings at four, I could cry.

Olive gives me directions to her place, and I wave goodbye. I take my time walking home, going the long way beside the river, despite the smell. Most days I rush home to squeeze some time in with Fred, but as it's just Mum, I'm happy to have as little time at home as possible.

"I'm back," I call, hanging my coat on the banister. Nothing. "Mum?" Nothing. Bloody hell, she's not popped her clogs, has she? I creep up the stairs, and as I open the door, two beady eyes stare out from her bed.

"You took your time."

"I've been at work."

"You clocked off at four. It's nearly five now. You're supposed to be caring for me."

"I am caring for you."

"Really? Out all hours while I lie here slowly dying? Florrie should never have left me with you."

I want to scream at her but don't have the energy. If I did, I'd tell her I do all her sweaty, bloody laundry, wipe her arse when she can't make it to the privy, wash her pongy armpits and generally slave for her. All whilst holding down a full-time job and caring for a twelve-year-old boy. Instead, I smile meekly and say, "is there anything I can get you?"

"I'm dying of thirst here, so I'd like a cup of tea if you can be bothered. And something to eat."

"That's no trouble. I'll be back in a tick."

I stand by the fire taking deep breaths. I've managed three years of holding my tongue, and I mustn't break now. I butter the roll I nicked from the canteen and make her tea. She can't even bring herself to say a simple "Thank you" as I set it down beside her.

"I'm off out by the way."

"Off with that no-good fellow of yours are you?"

"Actually, no. I'm going for dinner with a friend what lives on Ipswich Road."

"Ipswich Road? How do you know any of the toffs that live along there?"

"Maybe I'm not destined for a life as God awful as the one you've led. Have a good evening," I say, and run down the stairs before she can talk back.

"I didn't choose this life!"

I close the door on her words and head out into the evening light.

***

"Welcome, welcome. So lovely to meet you. I'm Mrs Barstone."

"Nellie," I say, holding out my hand.

"No need for formalities," the woman says. She ignores my hand and kisses me on each cheek. Lucky I washed my face before coming over. "Shoes off, please, dear."

Please God let my stockings be free of holes. My old leather flats sit beside rows of high heels, polished till they're gleaming. What the bloody hell am I doing? I don't belong here. I'd turn on my heel and run as fast as I could if I still had shoes on my feet.

"You're here!" says Olive, rushing forward for a hug. "I wasn't sure you'd make it what with your mother being so poorly."

"Oh no, is your mother unwell?" Mrs Barstone asks, taking a step back.

"Yes, she's been sick for a while."

"Oh, the poor love. Is there anything we can do?"

I hide my smile at the thought of this posh woman meeting Mum. "Thank you, that's very kind, but I have things under control."

"She's lucky to have you, I'm sure. Now, come through to the sitting room, you must be exhausted after a day at the factory." She leads me through the wide hallway with doors going off in all directions. "Here we are," she says. "Take any chair you like. I'll make us some tea."

My feet sink into thick cream carpet. No wonder she wanted my shoes off. The closest I've come to this is the times I've walked through snow. But the carpet isn't cold, it cuddles my toes like a slipper. I head to an enormous armchair, pale pink with gold trim. This is Julia's kind of place, only I doubt Mrs Barstone keeps it ship-shape without help. I can't help but run my finger across the mantel.

"You won't find any dust there," laughs Olive, throwing herself into a plump settee. "Our lady Mrs Brown is forever dusting."

My face burns at Olive catching me. She must think me so rude. "Sorry," I say. "It's just a treat to be in a room this clean. Haven't been somewhere as nice as this since..." I stop myself from talking about the wagon. I've never got used to trusting flatties with my past. Olive knows I was adopted by Henry and Julia, but she thinks we were up north the whole time. Not out on the road having the time of our lives.

"Since?" asks Olive, curious.

I'm rescued by Mrs Barstone coming in with a silver tray covered in teacups and biscuits.

"I'd hoped Mrs Brown would still be here to serve us, but she had to get back to her family."

"Looks like you've done a grand job without her," I say.

Mrs Barstone smiles and smooths her skirt as she sits down. "So, Nellie, tell me about yourself. Do you have brothers and sisters?"

"I have plenty, but most are married now with their own children. It's just me and Fred at home these days."

"Fred and I," says Mrs Barstone. Olive gives her a glare and winks at me.

"Sorry, Fred and I."

"And how old is Fred?"

"Almost thirteen now."

"And he doesn't mind you leaving him alone this evening?"

"No, ma'am, he's at the clinic. Had a bit of bother with his chest." My bloody eyes go and fill with tears, don't they. I want to curl up with shame. Other than handing me a hanky, Mrs Barstone pretends not to notice.

"And your Fred, is he in school?"

"Yes, he is." Now I smile. "The teacher reckons he's university material. He's a darling, is our Fred."

"Then I should like to meet him too one day."

"He'd love it here," I say. "A place like this would do wonders for his chest."

"And your own home doesn't?"

I colour up again. Bloody hell, why did I go and open my gob? "We've had a few problems with damp and such."

"Can't your father see to that?"

"Dad died a few years back." It's not a complete lie, he could be dead for all I know.

"I see. Well, as soon as your brother is well, you must bring him here for tea and cake."

"That's very kind, thank you."

"Right," she says, setting her cup down on a polished little table. "I'll go and check on dinner. It will just be the three of us tonight. Olive's father has been held up at work. Come through in ten minutes, girls."

I wait till she's out of earshot before turning and whispering to Olive. "What does your dad do? I can't remember if you've said."

"Runs a bookie's. But don't let on to mother you know that. She's all airs and graces, but the truth is neither of them were born into money. They're self-made, and not always through strictly legal means if you catch my drift."

Well, this is a turn-up for the books. I'd never have guessed. 'Self-made', those are two words to give hope if ever I heard them.

The meal is pleasant enough. Conversation flows easily, all of us lying through our teeth in different ways. Mrs Barstone goes on about her husband's work as an office manager, and I talk about Chrissy's farm like I lived there for years.

"Couldn't your brother go to stay at the farm? The fresh air would work wonders for his health."

My belly twists at her words. Not only at the thought of being parted from Fred, but at the hope we had for Henry when we first went there. "I think they've taken in lodgers since we left, so wouldn't have the space for Fred as well."

"I see," says Mrs Barstone. She dabs her mouth with a napkin before folding it neatly on the table beside her.

All through dinner Julia is with me, on my shoulder, reminding me of my manners. Henry's there too, leaning against the doorway, laughing silently at my attempts to cover over our fair life and create an almost entirely fictional life story. God, I miss them.

Chapter 32

November 1917

The fire came as a blessing in disguise. Started in the room next to ours, but all the factory workers escaped with their lives. The company are still paying us an allowance while the rebuilding goes on, and it means I've had the time I need to take care of Fred properly. They reckon we'll be back making our fuses in a couple of weeks or so. Part of me wants to go back, but with both Mum and Fred getting worse by the day, it will be a job to manage it all.

"Only us," I say, letting myself in to Florrie's hovel.

"I'm up here," she says, and me and Fred take the stairs two at a time.

She's sat up on her mattress, a baby to her breast. Fred blushes and looks away at the sight of his sister's chest laid bare for all to see. Florrie don't look too good. Her belly's not shrunk since the baby came along. Childbirth don't seem to suit her like it does some folk. The doc warned her not to have more after the first, but I'm guessing she has a job keeping Joe off her. Bloody men.

"You alright?" I say.

"Getting there." She waves at us to sit beside her. I go over, but Fred lurks beside the door.

"Why don't you see if there's any kiddies outside to play with?" I ask him.

"I'm not a little boy," he says, stretching himself up to look taller.

"Alright then, young man. How about you go and fetch us some bread and milk from the shop? Here," I say, taking a few coins from my pocket.

Fred disappears off outside.

"Why did you do that?" Florrie asks. "I wanted to see him."

"Well, you can see him when you don't have your titties flopping around the place. Poor chap, he looked terrified."

"Fair enough."

"How's the baby getting on?"

"He's doing well, it's just really taken it out of me, taking me ages to get back on my feet."

"Well don't you be having no more. Remember what the doc said. If you can't keep Joe off you there's ways and means."

"Look at you, all knowledgeable in the ways of the world. Anyway, when's it your turn? Jack must be itching to get wed soon."

"That's not going to happen. I gave him the flick."

"What? Why? I thought he wanted to marry you?"

"He said he did, but I reckon he just wanted to do the business. Kept putting his hands in places he shouldn't. I wasn't having any of it. Not before we were wed anyway."

"When did you become such a prude?"

"Henry and Julia taught me well. No good letting yourself be taken so easily, you don't want chaps to think you're easy. When the moment happens, it should be as man and wife."

"You saying I'm easy."

"That's not what I said."

"Yes, it is."

"How is your husband these days?"

Florrie scowls at me and ignores the question. The baby finishes its sucking, and she buttons up her blouse.

"Want to hold him?"

"Yes please."

The baby cuddles into me and gnaws on my shoulder. I breathe in his smell and hold him close. He throws his milk up in a trickle down my back, but I don't care.

"You're a natural."

"Thanks."

"Shouldn't have got rid of Jack so quickly. I reckon you're ready for kiddies of your own."

"Florrie, I'm only seventeen. I want to make a proper life for myself before bringing babies into the world."

"Not like me then."

I sigh. It's hard to have a chat with Florrie these days, she takes everything I say in the wrong way and is snappy and irritable. I love her as much as I ever did, but sometimes I wonder how much I like her.

"Mum alright?"

"She can barely keep her eyes open. The only time she wakes is to spurt blood across the floor. You'd better come round soon if you want to say your goodbyes."

"She could have ages yet for all you know."

I go to speak, but shut my gob. If anyone knows what death looks like it's me. The slow painful change from alive to dead. I hope my ending is quicker, hit by a tram, or knocked on the head by a falling brick would do me. Failing that, falling asleep a very old lady and never waking up would be nice.

***

"Hurry up, Fred." He's panting and his breaths are shallow so I should let up on my nagging. I can't bear the thought of being late for the Barstones though.

"This really where we're going?" he asks, pointing to the big old house.

"Certainly is. You be on your best behaviour. Did you remember to put on clean socks like I said?"

"Yep, no holes, no smells."

"Good boy."

The front door opens as we walk up the drive and a man as broad as he is tall steps out.

"So, you're the famous Nellie, are you? And this must be Fred."

"Nice to meet you, Mr Barstone," I say and shake his hand. I'd be more scared of him if Olive hadn't told me he's a bit of a rogue. His voice is posh, but I can hear the remains of a Norwich accent beneath the plums. I wonder if he grew up at the yards?

"Mrs Barstone's waiting for you in the sitting room, Nellie. I thought I'd steal Fred away, if that's alright? I've something upstairs I think he'd like to see."

Fred looks worried, but I nod to tell him it's alright.

"Good to see you, Nellie," says Mrs Barstone. She walks over and does her strange kissy thing again on my cheeks.

"Stop trying to be so French, Mother," Olive says.

"And you stop speaking to your mother like that, dear. Come and sit down, Nellie. When the boys come down, I'll get out the cake, but we can have tea in the meantime."

We spend half an hour making small talk, before Mr Barstone appears at the door.

"Back in a minute," says Olive's mother, getting up and pulling the door behind her.

"I hope Fred's behaving himself," I say to Olive.

"Oh, he'll be fine. Father has a most impressive train set tucked away upstairs. Fred will most likely be up there for hours. It even interests me, though I don't let on to Daddy."

Mrs Barstone comes into the room and sits back down.

"Fred's not been naughty, has he?" I ask. There's a first time for everything, I just hope this isn't it.

"No, no, my husband is having a wonderful time with him. Says he's the most polite, intelligent boy he's met in quite some time."

"That's a relief."

"Now, Nellie. I have something I wanted to talk to you about. As you may have already guessed from my voice, I come from Wales."

Wales? From her voice I'd have guessed she came from Buckingham Palace.

"No, I hadn't guessed."

"Well, I do. Now, ever since we first met, I have been worrying about that brother of yours and his chest."

"That's very kind of you."

"Thank you. Well, my parents still live in Wales, but are in their seventies now. Myself and my sisters have all moved away, and it's a constant worry for us that they're all alone out there. If they had a fall, or became ill, it would take a while for us to get back to help them."

"I'm sorry to hear that."

"Yes, well. I was thinking, and apologies if you find this suggestion presumptuous, that Fred might be well suited to the Welsh countryside."

"You want Fred to go to Wales?"

"Only with your blessing, of course. It would be a weight off my mind to know my parents had company, and the air there would do wonders for his chest. Their home has all the latest mod cons, and damp would not be an issue."

"What about his schooling?"

"His education would be continued at the local school. If he wanted to go on to further studies neither I nor anyone in my family would stand in his way."

"Sorry, I don't quite understand what you're suggesting. Do you want him to be their servant?"

Mrs Barstone laughs. "Goodness no, nothing as grand as that. My parents' house is a reasonable size, but certainly not big enough for servants' quarters. Besides, they have a local girl going in twice a day to cook and clean the place. No, Fred's role would simply be as a companion. Someone to sound the alarm if anything happens to them and their regular girl isn't there."

"Wales is a long way from Norwich."

"True, but not impossible on the train. I go back to visit several times a year and the journey takes less than a day. You'd be welcome to go and visit him whenever you wish."

"Mrs Barstone, that is such a kind offer, but do you mind if I take a few days to think it over?"

"Of course not, dear. But I really do think it would be in Fred's best interest."

***

I can't sleep. Four bloody hours I've been staring at the grimy ceiling and still sleep won't come. Mrs Barstone's words go round and round in my brain. I feel I know enough of the family now to know I can trust them. Fred wouldn't stop going on about that bloody train set the whole way home and seemed quite at ease in the company of posh folk. A warm house and fresh air would do wonders for him. Really there's no question it would be the right thing to do, but the thought of letting him go terrifies me. What if he gets homesick? What if he's ill and the old folk can't look after him?

"Nellie?"

"Yes."

"Why you still awake?"

"I'm thinking."

"What about?"

"You."

"Oh."

I'd told Fred the idea on the way home. I thought it would upset him, but he seemed excited, not scared.

"What's worrying you?"

"It's just a big decision, sending you all the way to Wales. What if you don't like it?"

"Then I can write to you and you can bring me home, no harm done."

"What if they're cruel?"

"Then I'll do the same. I know you won't leave me there if I'm unhappy. Besides, you went away when you were far younger than I am, and it's not done you any harm."

How can I argue with that? He's right of course. Not only did it do me no harm, it did me a whole lot of good. If I'd never met Henry and Julia, I'd most likely be stuck with a life like Florrie's, miserable and married to a happy-go-lucky liability like Joe.

"I'd miss you," I say.

"I'd miss you too. But you could come visit me. Nell, most days I'm finding it hard to breathe. I want a proper life, one where I can run around with friends without worrying I'll keel over any minute. I want to be well."

"Bloody hell, you're so grown up. Then I guess it's decided. I'll call on Mrs Barstone tomorrow and let her know."

"Thank you, Nell."

Fred turns over and falls asleep in seconds. I'm glad, for it means he don't see the tears I shed at the thought of losing him. With Fred gone, and Mum on her last legs, very soon I shall be all alone.

PART 3

Queenie Read

Chapter 33

February 1924

"Afternoon, Nell."

"Good afternoon, Mrs Waters. Have you had a good day?"

"Not too bad, thank you for asking. You go on up dear, you must be knackered."

"Thank you, I am."

The others in the building hate Mrs Waters. I know the secret to her heart though, paying your rent on time. The odd bit of polite chit-chat goes down well too. I'm glad she didn't keep me long today. I'm so tired I could sleep right here, leaning on the banister, and it's an effort to drag my legs up the two flights of stairs to my room. All I seem to do is work these days. It will be worth it in the end though. My key turns in the lock, and as soon as I walk in, I can tell she's been up here snooping around. The door to the battered old wardrobe is slightly ajar, but when I check, all the boxes are in their place.

It was a shock when I first moved in, to find the landlady taking regular snoops round my room. But I have my systems to stop her finding whatever it is she's looking for. In the base of the wardrobe, I've piled boxes. Most of them hold seconds from the factory that are no good to no one, but she don't know that. At the very bottom is my special box. Best check all's as I left it.

I'm about to take the boxes off the top when there's a knock at the door.

"Hello?"

"Only me."

I open the door to the landlady.

"Sorry, dear, I forgot to say, a letter came for you today."

"Thank you," I say as she hands it over.

Mrs Waters shuffles off downstairs, and I turn the envelope over in my hands. She's bloody done it again. As if snooping in my room weren't bad enough, she also reads my letters. Reckons I can't tell, but I can see where she's held it up to a candle, and that the paper isn't quite folded as it was when the letter arrived. She must be disappointed each time she opens one, for there's never nothing saucy inside, just news from Fred.

I love Fred's letters. He's got a way with words I've never had, describing the hills and valleys of Camarthen like he's painting a picture. Makes me feel I'm there with him. When loneliness hits me, I'm able to remind myself I made the right decision. My darling Fred's thriving in Wales like he never could've here. I wish I had interesting news to send back, but life is a dull blur of work, work, and more work. Olive don't understand why I do it, but she couldn't, could she? Since the end of the war when they kicked us out of Boulton and Paul's, she's not lifted a finger for anything but party planning. She'll be on at me to go to one again in no time and I'm fast running out of excuses.

After checking the door is locked, I return to my boxes. The box I need is right at the bottom. I take care with how I pull it out, for I don't want the contents to go tumbling around. I lift the lid and remind myself of the words I wrote on it all them years ago - *self-made*. If the Barstones can do it, so can I. Good, everything's as it should be. My fingers tap their way along pictures of the king. The rows of neatly stacked coins are still the same height, none taken. God, it must frustrate Mrs Waters that she's not yet found my stash. Bloody fool. I count the coins, even though I know how much is there. Three shillings shy of ten pounds. Ten pounds, blimey. I should pass ten by Friday, if I'm careful.

My bed is calling me, but I'm running low on supplies and will be no good to no one if I don't eat properly. I peel the sodden paper from my bowl of water and take out the half an apple stored there. Julia once told me an apple a day keeps the doctor away. Well, I can't afford an apple a day, but I can stretch to half. I munch through it, pips and all, and chuck the stalk out of the window. There's a bit of dust gathered on the frame and I wipe it with a rag. Having my own place might be lonely, but at least I can keep it the way I like.

A jangling in my pocket reminds me of the treasure that lurks there. I grab the handful of buttons I saved from the rubbish at work and tip them into a cup. It's a wonder how old clothes can look new just with a line of buttons added, or a little bit of lace on the collar. Olive's always admiring my latest outfits. Little does she know they're just old rags dressed up with seconds from the factory. I don't know if she'd be impressed or horrified if she knew, but I'm not about to let her into my secret.

My belly growls. I miss the days at Norwich Components, where food was free and plentiful. The folk at the new factory are far more stingy, everything at the canteen you got to pay for. It's not worth the money they charge, I can eat cheaper and better if I sort myself out. Best get to the market before it shuts.

With Julia on my shoulder, I check myself in the mirror. I think she'd approve, but I give my shoes a quick spit and polish just in case. My coat is that old a stiff breeze could tear it apart, but the satin cuffs and neckerchief I sewed on hide its age well. I pull the beautiful leather bag Olive gave me for Christmas out from its hiding place. Good, I'm ready.

Just before five is the best time to visit the market. It's the last chance the stallholders got to make a sale, and there's some good deals to be done. It takes careful planning, I can tell you, making sure I've enough food to last the week. The factory keep putting me on the late shift as I've no kiddies to get home to, and getting to market at just the right time don't happen often. Florrie says I'm stingy not ever paying full price, but I say more fool her. Maybe if she counted her coins with more care, she'd escape her little hovel. Maybe if she was as careful with her money as I am, she'd even escape that useless bugger Joe.

The market don't scare me like it did that first time Mum brought me here. Now I enjoy being among the coloured canvas and noise. Reminds me of the fair. I like the smells too, though it's dangerous to come here when I'm hungry, and I'll have to be careful I don't get carried away.

I may be small, but folks notice me as I pass. I even get the occasional whistle thrown my way. I keep my eyes straight ahead, not giving them a second glance. If my dalliance with Jack all them years ago taught me anything, it's that chaps can't be trusted. Give them an inch, and they'll try to go the mile.

With enough bread, butter and milk to last the week, I head to the fruit and veg stall. The bloke here is a tricky bugger, and I brace myself. The trader is a big chap, twice the size of me. His jet-black hair seems to grow up, not down, and a carpet's worth of hair pokes out of the top of his shirt. He sees me coming, and I'm sure I hear him groan.

"Yes, madam, how can I help you today?"

"I'd like a pound of apples please."

"A pound of apples coming up."

The apples look tiny in his enormous hands as he weighs them out and puts them in a paper bag for me.

"That'll be thruppence."

"Thruppence?"

"Yes."

"I'll pay you a penny."

"Get on with you," he says, turning his back on me.

"Fine. Two."

"Two? You think I was born yesterday?"

"No, I don't actually. I think you're a scheming so-and-so, trying to sneak the most bruised, oldest apples into my bag in the hope I'm stupid enough to pay full price for them."

"Take your custom elsewhere if you're not happy then."

"Well, sir, I would, but it's five to five and I've no time to get across the market. So, either you let me pay you my tuppence, and hand over that bag, or I'll simply take them."

"Take them? What, you'll steal them?"

"No, not at all. I don't see it would be much of a crime as I've offered you good money and you've refused."

The man laughs. "Think you could outrun me, do you?"

"Judging by the weight on you, yes I do."

"You calling me fat?"

"No, not at all, just making an observation."

"Bugger off back to whatever hole you crawled out of."

"That's no way to talk to a customer. You can be certain I shan't be visiting this stall again."

"Good."

I really need those apples. I can't afford no doctor's bill. In an instant, I'm grabbing the bag of apples from his hand. As I run from his stall, I chuck my coins in the air behind me, for I'm no thief. I can hear the drumming of his steps on the ground, but one advantage of being as short as I am, is you can sneak through small gaps, and it's easy to get lost in a crowd.

I don't stop running till I'm safely behind my front door.

"You alright, dear?" asks Mrs Waters, poking her head from behind her door.

"Yes, fine," I say struggling to get my breath.

"You're not in trouble, are you? I heard you sprinting up the path, and worried you were being chased."

"Oh no, I'm just really hungry," I say.

Mrs Waters looks most perplexed, but I don't give her the chance to ask more questions. I take the stairs two at a time and once I'm safely inside my room, empty my bags onto the bed. That should be enough to last me till my next early, so long as I don't go mad with those bloody apples.

My room is that cold, I can see my breath spewing out as I munch my supper. I wrap a thick blanket around my shoulders to beat the chill. There's no logs for the fire, for I only indulge in them as a Christmas treat. I'd love a good cup of tea, but that's one thing I can get at the factory, and there's no need for me to have one at home. Even a cold-water wash becomes second nature when it has to. My new home, the one I'm saving for, will have a bathtub and a tap. It will be my reward for these years of scrimping. Fred will come and stay, and I'll spoil him with a warm fire and endless cups of tea. I'll have Florrie round too; she can go up to the bedroom for a nap while her kiddies play with mine. What a fine life it will be, I just need to wait a little longer to make it happen.

It's bloody freezing, even with my coat on and a blanket. May as well get into bed, for it's an early start in the morning. I can't face the walk outside to the privy, so wee in a pot and hide it under my bed till morning. It takes a while for sleep to come, for the couple in the room above are yelling at each other again. The sound of glass shattering reaches me through the floorboards. The wall beside mine shudders. Bloody hell, she's at it again. How that trollop Rosemary sneaks her gentleman callers past the sharp-eyed Mrs Waters is beyond me. I bloody wish she wouldn't. The banging and creaking are my lullaby, as my lids become heavy and sleep calls.

Chapter 34

March 1924

Olive's using the whiny voice she brings out when she wants something. It may work on her mum, but it won't work on me.

"But it's your birthday, you have to come!"

"Olive, for years I didn't even know when my birthday was. I don't see why we need to start celebrating it twenty-four years after the event."

"Because it will be fun, and you're no fun these days."

"You know I have to work."

"But you don't, do you? You could marry and live in comfort the rest of your life."

"How many times do I have to say it? I'm not relying on any man, ever."

"Fine, forget marriage, but you're coming to my party. I've told Mother you're coming so you'll have to."

"That was a sly move, Olive. You know I can't be rude to her after all she's done for Fred. Shame on you."

"Oh, for goodness sake, Nell. It's a party. You know? Those occasions young people socialise, make new friends?"

"I don't have time for friends."

"You're telling me."

Now I feel guilty. I've not had much time for Olive lately. I've not even met her chap and they've been courting six months now.

"Fine, I'll come. What time does it start?"

"Now. You're coming home with me. I'll lend you one of my dresses and help you with your hair."

"There's no need for that."

"Think of it as a birthday present."

"Alright, alright."

My favourite presents arrived this morning. Two cards, one from Fred and one from Julia. Fred had filled his card with news, but Julia simply wrote 'much love'. I hope she's alright up there. I wish I'd had the time to go and visit. Maybe this will be the year.

***

"Happy Birthday, darling!"

Mr Barstone mimics a drink being poured down his neck as his wife scoops me up in a cuddle.

"Thank you." I turn my head as she does her kissy thing, and her breath reeks of sherry.

"Always up for a party, this one. Come on, let's get a coffee down you."

Mr Barstone leads his wife through to the kitchen, and me and Olive head upstairs.

"Right," she says, flinging open the doors of her wardrobe. "Choose whatever you want from in here."

"You sure?"

"Of course. Your waist's about the same size as mine even if your legs aren't."

"I don't think my legs are the only thing what's smaller," I say, glancing at Olive's perky chest.

"Well, a nice slip dress will fit all bust sizes. How about this one?"

"I'm not sure green would suit me."

"Why don't you try it on, I think you'll be pleasantly surprised. With your dark hair and pale skin, I think green could be just the ticket."

"Alright, but if it looks God awful, I'm trying another." I quickly change, for no one has seen me in my underwear since Julia, and I've changed a fair bit since then.

"Oh my goodness. Come here."

Olive leads me to a large free-standing mirror. "You're a goddess."

I colour right up at that. I'm no goddess, but I have to admit I could probably pass for a posh lady in Olive's dress. "You don't think it's a bit long?"

"No, not at all. Anyway, longer hemlines are coming back into fashion. What size shoe are you?"

"Five."

"Hmm, mine are a six. Let me check with Mother and see if you can borrow a pair of her heels."

Before I can protest Olive's rushed from the room and down the wide staircase. Below me, I hear muffled voices, then Olive comes thundering back up the stairs.

"Here," she says, holding out a pair of beautiful green pumps. "Try these for size."

I slip my feet into Mrs Barstone's shoes. The heel's not too high and it's nice and wide so walking shouldn't be a problem. The leather feels soft beneath my fingers as I fasten the ankle straps.

"Perfect. Now come here and let me see to your hair."

"What the bloody hell is that?"

"It's an iron. Don't worry, I won't burn you, I'm an expert at doing curls."

Bloody hell, what a palaver. Olive makes me lie my head down on the sideboard and puts the iron down on my hair.

"You sure you know what you're doing?"

"Yes. Stop fretting."

It takes forever, getting my straight hair into waves. Once she's done, Olive starts twisting it up and pinning it to the back of my head.

"Ouch!"

"Sorry. Just stay still, I'm nearly done."

"Right, head up and take a look at that."

"Bloody hell, Olive, you're a marvel. I look like a different person."

"No, you look like you, just with a bit more sparkle. Now, I'll fetch you a gin to relax you, while I get myself ready."

I sit in the armchair in Olive's room, too scared to move. Green silk floats around my legs and jewels lie against my belly. I feel like a princess. Olive takes her time getting ready. She'll be wanting to make an impression on her chap, for word is he's planning to propose any day now.

"Bloody hell, Olive, you look beautiful."

Olive giggles and does a twirl. She looks like she's stepped out of a magazine. Her fashionable wavy hair skims her chin, pink satin clings in all the right places.

"If your chap don't propose soon, I'll marry you myself."

Olive grins and turns this way and that in front of the mirror.

"Let's get downstairs and wait for the guests to arrive. I don't want Mother greeting them, she's far too squiffy."

***

It's lucky they've a big house, for the Barstones are a popular bunch. Me and Olive are forever being called to the door and I'm beginning to wonder if this is how our whole evening will be spent. It's a funny old mix of people. Some old, some young, some what talk with plums in their mouths, some with as broad a Norwich accent as mine. All look like they've got a few bob to spare, the ladies in glamorous dresses, the men in smart suits.

"Right, everyone should be here by now. Let's get ourselves a drink and have some fun."

I follow Olive to the sitting room, where she pours us each a large gin from the glass drinks cabinet. I'm not much of a drinker, but I wouldn't mind one of those in my house. The glass is cut in patterns like we had in our wagon. Funny really, flatties always look down on travelling folk, but then they go and copy the wagon designs in their homes.

"Right, there are a few people here I'd like you to meet."

By 'people' I know she means eligible chaps. God help me.

"Is your chap here yet?"

"No, he's had to work late tonight, should be here in an hour or so."

Olive links her arm in mine and leads me through the house. "Ah there he is," she says, waving. She moves her head close to mine to give me the lowdown on a large man standing with his back to us.

"Now, I'm going to introduce you to Barny. He's more a friend of my father's really, but he's the life and soul of any party. I think you two will get on well."

"Really? Olive, this is the first party I've been to in God knows how long. You really think I'd get on with some socialite?"

"He's not a socialite. His background is not dissimilar to yours actually."

Olive pulls me through the crowd of people crammed into the room. All the rooms in Olive's house are enormous, but the amount of people they've squeezed in makes it feel small and musty. I'd love to escape out into the garden, but Olive's having none of it. She taps the tall man on the shoulder. He spins round and I take a step back. It can't be, can it?

"Barny, I'd like you to meet my friend Nellie. Nellie, this is Barny."

The man holds out his hand and gives me a wide smile. Thank God he doesn't recognise me. It must be the fine clothes what's done it.

"Nice to meet you, Nellie."

He looks different from before. He's smothered his coal hair with that much grease it almost lies flat, and the carpet on his chest is hidden beneath a buttoned-up shirt and tie.

"Nice to meet you too."

"I must apologise," he says.

"Oh?"

"I'd have brought some apples with me if I'd known you'd be here."

I catch my reflection in the mirror behind him. All colour drains from my face, before rushing back and making me look like a bloody red apple myself. Olive's glancing from Barny to me.

"Have you two met before?"

"No," he says. "It's just your friend Nellie here looks like the kind of girl who'd like apples."

"Right, well, I'll leave you to it."

Olive walks off, shaking her head. I'll give her what for later for leaving me with this brute.

"You look a bit hot there, Nellie. How about we get some air for a moment?"

He's teasing me. The bastard. I'm that embarrassed I follow him through the house like a stray bloody cat, when what I should be doing is flouncing off back home.

We step out into the chilly night air and he takes off his jacket and puts it round my shoulders.

"You look cold," he says.

"I'm fine." I hand his jacket back to him, folding my arms to hide the goose pimples that will give me away.

"Aren't you going to apologise?"

"For what?"

"Stealing."

"I didn't steal nothing."

"You did. When I got back to my stall from chasing you, the coins had disappeared. You owe me tuppence."

"Well, if you were stupid enough to leave my hard-earned money lying on the ground, I'd say I owe you nothing."

"Got a right gob on you, don't you."

I fold my arms tighter and stare into the night. I can feel him watching me, and my cheeks colour up again. At least it's too dark for him to see. If we were back at the market, or somewhere less posh, I'd be better at holding my own. But he's caught me at a bad moment. The posh frock, the posh drinks, the posh house, all of it makes me edgy, dulls my brain, muffles my tongue. After five minutes standing there in silence, I can bear it no more.

"So, you're a friend of Olive's dad, are you?"

"Yep. Me and Archie go way back. I help him out with a bit of business now and then."

"I bet you do," I mutter.

"What's that you said?"

"Nothing. I just didn't have Mr Barstone down as a fruit and veg type of man."

Barny smirks and gazes out across the garden. "Olive tells me you're saving for a house of your own."

"Yes, no, I mean sort of. My brother had to move away, I'd like to bring him home one day but for that I need a damp-free house, and they're not cheap."

"How are you getting on?"

"With what?"

"The saving."

"I'm doing the best I can. It would help if stallholders didn't try and swindle me out of my earnings every time I go to the market."

He lets out a laugh and I jump out of my skin. "You know, I might be able to throw a bit of work your way."

"That's a kind offer, and I'm quite sure I'd have no trouble bringing plenty of customers to your stall, but I don't see how I could fit it around my work at the factory."

"I'm not talking about the stall."

He's looking me up and down. I don't like it. Does he think I'm like my neighbour Rosemary?

"Now you look here, mister. I'm not the type of woman you seem to think I am."

"Oh? And what's that? From where I'm standing, I see a woman good at hustling, making a deal, and not averse to unconventional methods when she wants to get her own way."

"So you don't mean..."

"No, Nellie, I bloody don't. What do you take me for?"

Even in the dark I can see his eyes are shining, sparkling you could say.

"Anyway, you think on it. You know where to find me if the thought of a few extra bob appeals."

He disappears inside the house, leaving me to wonder what the bloody hell he's been going on about.

Chapter 35

April 1924

I've left it a month before heading to the market. It helped being on lates these past weeks, meant curiosity couldn't get the better of me. I don't want to appear too keen, too desperate. But the coins in my box aren't piling up as quick as I'd hoped since Mrs Waters put the rent up. Bloody cheek of the woman. The council would tear this place down like they're doing with the yards if they got a peek inside. If I had any sort of power or security, I'd have told her to shove the rent up her arse and found somewhere else. But it's family what's getting places on the new estates, not people like me.

"I thought I'd see you again," says Barny as I walk up to his stall.

"Well, I'll have no one call me a thief." I hold out the tuppence I've brought with me and he laughs.

"Put your money away, Nell. Here, consider this a peace offering." He holds out a paper bag filled with apples.

"I can pay my way."

"Blimey, I'm trying to do something nice here. They're on the turn anyway if that makes you feel better about accepting."

"I can't bear to see good food go to waste," I say, taking the outstretched bag.

"Look, how about you give me ten minutes to pack up, then we'll go somewhere and have a chat?"

"About what?"

"The job opportunity. I'd assumed that's why you're here? Or was it just that you couldn't resist my charms?"

I feel myself flush, which makes me go even redder, this time in anger at myself.

"Don't worry, Nell, I have that effect on the fairer sex."

"Well, not on me you don't. I came here to repay my supposed debt, nothing more. If there's still an opportunity to make a bit extra besides the factory, I'll be willing to discuss that. But don't expect no pleasure from the meeting, I'll talk business with you, that's all."

"You're just like Olive said."

"What's that supposed to mean?"

"Look, the longer you stand there nattering, the longer it will take me to pack up. Why not go for a stroll and come back in a bit?"

"Or I could help you?"

"Pack up the stall? That's not women's work."

I stand with my hands on my hips to show I mean business. "Thank you for your concern, but I helped put up and dismantle a shooting gallery from the age of six years old. I'm sure I can manage a few boxes of apples and tomatoes."

"You were with the fair?"

"It's a long story."

Bugger, how is it I've kept my past from Olive over ten years of friendship, but two conversations with this fellow and I've let it all spill out?

"It's a story I'd not like repeated. Specially not to the Barstones. They know a bit about my background, but flatties can be funny about showfolk and I don't want my past getting in the way of how people see Fred."

"My lips are sealed on one condition."

"What condition might that be?"

"You tell me all about it in the pub."

"Fine. Now I thought you had a stall to pack up. What needs doing?"

***

The King's Head is full of folk what are finished work for the day. I turn a few heads as I walk in, but not so many as Mum would in the days she went to the pub with Dad. There's at least a couple of other girls in here, though they look rough types. I've not thought of Mum in years, and I don't let the image of her drinking among the factory blokes linger in my mind. I'm where I am despite of her, not because. She'll be proved wrong about me in the end, of that I'm sure.

"What you drinking?"

"Just a gin, please."

"Coming right up. How about you get us that table in the corner. I'd rather there were no flapping ears about when we talk business."

I make my way to a dingy corner of the pub. No wonder it's deserted, it stinks and I'm sure there's mould growing on the wall, though it's too dark to be sure.

"So, what's this business proposal then?" I ask, as Barny lays the drinks on the table.

"Oh no you don't. I promised to keep my mouth shut if you told me about life at the fair. We can get to the business later."

I scowl at him and wonder if it would be such a bad thing for the Barstones to find out. Probably not, but I can't risk it, especially now I'm beholden to them thanks to Fred.

"Alright. What do you want to know?"

An hour later and I'm wiping tears away with Barny's handkerchief, having told him not just about the fair, but about life before it. What is it about this man that's made me open up for the first time in years?

"I'm sorry," I say, sniffing again. "I've had no one to talk to about Julia and Henry since I arrived back in Norwich. Fred was too young to understand, and I wouldn't talk to Mum about the weather, never mind matters of the heart."

"You must miss them?"

"Mum and Fred?"

"No, Henry and Julia."

"Yes. Mostly I just get on with things, get by from day to day, then sometimes it hits me. It's mad, but I sometimes think I see Henry walking down the street. And they often talk to me, if I've got a decision to make, or at risk of getting into trouble. You probably think I'm in need of the loony bin."

"Not at all. I'm just sad you've not been able to talk to anyone before me. What about your sister? You said you were close?"

"Oh, I love Florrie as much as ever, but our lives have gone in different directions since I left Norwich. I thought coming home would bring us back together, but it seems the fair changed me, while she stayed the same."

"You still see her?"

"I go over there once a week. Her chap's a good laugh but not very skilled at being a good husband. She has a hard old time of it, trying to raise all those kiddies while keeping her husband on the straight and narrow. You'd like Florrie, everyone does. I do. She's just got so many problems of her own, I'd never burden her with mine, even if I thought she'd understand."

"You're quite something, Nellie."

"A blubbering mess? I never cry, I can't believe I've just filled your hanky with snot, you're practically a complete stranger."

"This is our third meeting, so I'm no stranger."

"No, I suppose not. Anyway, I've told you everything there is to tell about me. Now, what's this business you got in mind?"

Barny leans forward across the table. What's he doing? He'd better not try and kiss me, for I'll bash him in the nose.

"Nell," he whispers.

I move my head back. He beckons me forward. "I'm not trying anything; I just need to make sure I'm not overheard."

I move my head closer, and he whispers again. "What do you know about off course betting?"

I sit back in my seat. Truth is, I know bugger all about betting of any kind. "Not much," I say.

"Right, well lesson number one. It's illegal."

"I see."

"Lesson number two, there's a fortune to be made in it, if you go about it the right way."

"And is that what you do?"

"Let's just say, the fruit and veg don't account for all my income."

"I see, and how would I fit into all this then?"

"Olive says you're good with numbers?"

"That's true."

"Well, there might be opportunities to move up in the company, but you'd start off as a runner."

"A runner?"

"Yes, a bookie's runner. My runner."

"Do I look like an athlete to you? I'm faster than you but that's not saying much, my legs are as short as a child's."

"I don't mean...oh you're pulling my leg."

"I'm not sure what a bookie's runner does Barny, but I'm quite certain it don't involve running no marathons. Unless it's me folks are betting on?"

"For a start, you wouldn't be on foot. I'd sort you out with a bicycle. All you need to do is go around town collecting bets, putting them in the clock bag and bringing them back to me. Once the results come in, you then go back to the chaps what won, and hand them their winnings."

"Sounds simple enough, but why me?"

"The coppers are always on the lookout. Often they turn a blind eye, but sometimes they get a bee in their bonnet and try to catch us out. We mostly use young lads for the job, but I don't reckon any police officer would suspect a pretty young thing like you."

"Could I go to prison if I'm caught?"

"No, it would most likely be a slap on the wrist. I'll understand though if you'd rather not be involved or need a bit of time to think it over."

"I must admit, I'm not keen on the idea of being on the wrong side of the law."

"Hasn't done the Barstones any harm, nor me."

"That's true..."

"And, Nellie, it's not like I'm asking you to kill nobody. My guess would be most of the city folk place bets now and then. It's only the politicians what frown upon it. Want to keep ordinary folk's hard-earned cash for themselves in taxes, and us off-course chaps aren't paying no tax."

"I'm in."

Barny looks surprised. "You sure you don't want longer to think it over?"

"No. So long as you can fit the work around my hours at the factory, it's fine by me. It'll be years till I've got my own place at this rate, and I don't have a moral problem with what you're doing."

"That's settled then. How about you come over tomorrow evening and I'll show you the ropes."

He gives me the address and I stand and offer my hand. The touch of his skin sends a little shiver through me, but I brush it away. It's excitement about the cash that's getting to me. I'd never be so stupid as to involve myself romantically with a ruffian like Barny.

Chapter 36

May 1924

I can't help but smile as I whizz along Newmarket Road, for I checked my stash of coins before I came out, and the coins have turned to paper notes. In two months, I've doubled my savings, and if I can prove myself, I stand a chance of making a damn sight more. The guilt at breaking the law faded fast, for it turns out every man and his dog in Norwich is keen to place the odd bet, and don't get me started on the women. In the past couple of months, my bike has seen me round the yards, up to big, detached houses like Olive's and even to the odd solicitor's office.

Folk are getting to know my face, and I'm even getting girls coming up to me with their slips at the factory. I don't accept them, of course. My two worlds are kept separate, and I plan on keeping it that way. I still can't afford to leave the factory, and if the blokes in charge get wind of my second occupation, they'll kick me out of there fast as anything.

A bloke waves to me as I cycle past. I pull up onto the pavement.

"You're Barny's girl, right?"

"I'm his runner if that's what you mean."

He hands me his slip and I add it to the collection in my clock bag. We got a good system, me and Barny. Depending on my shift, I either cycle round before or after work with the clock bag hidden inside my wicker basket. Once there's enough slips inside, I head down to Lakenham and hand it over. He's the only one with a key. It's bloody knackering working two jobs, but the thrill of my growing savings is better than sleep for keeping my energy up.

Newmarket Road's my last stop today. I've done the market, St Benedict's Street, Magdalen Street and the yards all around. The aching in my legs tells me I've cycled miles today, not bad after a ten-hour shift. The house on Newmarket Road's a special one. Barny won't tell me who the chap is what lives there, but it's a maid what greets me at the door, and since I started, I'm the only runner Barny's let come up here. It's always a large bet too. Last week the chap placed twenty pounds on a horse, just 'cause he liked the name. I can't imagine a time I'll ever have twenty pounds to throw around willy-nilly. He lost his twenty pounds, but it don't seem to have dampened his appetite for a roll of the dice.

It's a quick run from Newmarket Road to Lakenham. Funny really, rich and poor living almost side by side, their worlds only colliding when there's money to be spent on the horses.

I pull my bike up behind the grotty house. The windows are boarded, and it looks ready for demolition.

"I'm back."

"Come through."

Barny's sat at a table counting money by the light of five naphtha lamps. It seems an extravagance but fitting electric lights would draw attention and no one wants that. He's counting and recounting piles of coins, his breath coming out in sighs. A muscle in his face is twitching. All us workers know the meaning of that twitch. He's angry. An angry

Barny's enough to scare off the bravest of men, but I realised early on his bark's worse than his bite.

"Something wrong?"

"We're short two pounds."

"You sure about that?"

"Of course I'm bloody sure!" His shout sends a couple of the younger chaps running, but I stand my ground.

"What are you saying?"

"I'm saying that someone's broken my trust."

His stare burns out of his skull, eyes black against his red face. I fold my arms and stare back.

"You better not be accusing me of nothing." I keep my voice quiet, but strong enough for him to know I'll not be wrongly accused.

"Well, someone's taken it. If it's not you, it must be another runner." Now he's pacing this way and that across the room.

"They're all decent chaps. I think you should count again."

Barny's face goes redder. He's not used to having folk talk back to him, and he's as angry as a bull ready to charge. His fists clench up by his sides. Instead of shouting, he whips his arm across the table, sending coins tumbling in all directions.

"Count it yourself," he yells, stamping out of the room and slamming the door so hard it near enough falls from its hinges.

When he returns an hour later, he brings the smell of beer with him. I've collected all the coins from the floor, and they lie in neat rows across his desk.

"It's all there. You'd counted wrong."

He goes to speak, then sits beside me in the chair, staring at the piles of money.

"I think the word you're looking for is 'sorry'."

Barny stares at me, shakes his head, then smiles. "Sorry. You know I didn't really think you'd swindle me?"

"I bloody well hope not."

"Anyway, how d'you get on tonight? You got the box?"

I hand over the clock bag and he unlocks the safe and pulls out a key. The clock stops as the lock opens and he lays the slips out on the table.

"Our Newmarket chap's betting big again. Thought he might have learned his lesson after last week's mistake," I say.

"Money's like water to people like him. His house alone cost him more than I'll earn in a lifetime."

"And you won't tell me how he comes by all that cash?"

"Can't risk the trust of the punters over a titbit of gossip."

"You still don't trust me?"

Barny eyes me up and runs a hand through his hair, leaving it even more messy than usual. "You've proved I can, and I do, but that worries me. I'm not the trusting type."

"Well, if you can't give me the lowdown on the Newmarket chap, will you finally tell me who owns this house? I'm guessing you don't live here, you're too smart for that."

"I live next door."

"At the pub?"

"Yep. Dad's the landlord. This place was my grandmother's, but both her and mum are long since dead. She'd turn in her grave if she knew what it was being used for now."

"Isn't it a bit too close to home? I mean, surely the police would expect you to have seen something?"

"If they ever come knocking, I'll tell them I keep myself to myself. It's not like anyone uses the front door."

"But what about your name?"

Barny laughs. "You didn't think Barny was my real name, did you?"

Now I feel foolish. Of course I thought it was his real name, but I of all people should've guessed. "What is your name then? Come on, you say you trust me."

"Ernest."

I can't help but laugh, and he looks cross. "You don't like my name?"

"Ernest is a perfectly good name. No, it's just you don't look like an Ernest to me."

"Well lucky for you you'll never have to call me it. If the police come sniffing round and someone shoots their gob off, it will be Barny they go looking for, not Ernest."

"Clever."

"Thank you. You got time to deliver yesterday's winnings, or is your bed calling?"

My bed isn't calling, it's screaming. "Yes, no problem."

"Give me a hand counting it out then."

We sit side by side, counting coins and notes. I'm much quicker than he is. He double checks my piles to make sure I've made no mistakes, even though it's me should be doing the checking after the earlier fiasco. Of course, he don't find none.

"Be careful, won't you? That's a lot of cash to be carrying round, and it's getting dark out there."

"You worried about me or the money?"

"Both."

"You remembered I'm off tomorrow?"

"Seeing Florrie, aren't you?"

"Yes. You'll manage alright without me?"

He chucks his pen at me and chuckles as I leave the room. I load the wads of cash into my basket and head out in the fading light. I understand why trust is important in this business, for there's over a hundred pounds stuck on the front of my bike. Must be a fair few runners what keep a little for themselves. I'd never break Barny's trust like that. Partly 'cause I'm no thief, and partly 'cause I've seen enough of his temper to know he'd not spare me his wrath just 'cause I'm a woman.

**

"You didn't have to do that," says Florrie, as I struggle to fit through her door with all the bags I'm carrying.

"I did. Can't visit my nieces and nephews without bringing a few treats, can I?"

"It's more than a few treats, there's a week's worth of shopping in them bags."

"Just take it, Florrie, and stop complaining."

She hugs me a good while, but winces at the sight of the bags.

"You alright?"

"Yes, just wish I could fend for myself."

"Don't be daft."

She fixes a smile and begins storing the food I've brought in the larder. It's plain as day she's struggling, and I wish Joe would grow up and start helping out more. All my fears have been confirmed, the flighty gaff lad has never taken to settled family life and I can't see him changing now. I like the man, but I'd like him a lot more if he weren't married to my sister. I've gone as far as suggesting she leave him, but every time I do it ends in a row, and I don't want her stopping me from coming round. All I can do is try to help any way I can. I used to bring her a few shillings when I saw her, but I realised soon enough they were heading to Joe, not her and the kiddies. A few loaves of bread and a bag of veg aren't so handy when he heads to the pub.

"How've you been? I've hardly seen you these past couple of months."

"Sorry, it's just with taking on a second job, there's no hours left in the day."

"And how is the new job going?"

I decided to trust Florrie with my news just after Barny offered me the job as runner, on the condition she kept it to herself. I doubt she's told Joe; she's as soppy about him as ever, but has learned the hard way she can't trust him as far as she can throw him.

"Apart from the tiredness, it's going well. The punters trust me, and Barny's already started giving me a bit more responsibility."

"Hmm, don't be getting too close to that Barny. Sounds like a wrong 'un to me."

She's a fine one to talk. "He's actually a good man, so long as you don't get on the wrong side of him."

"Oh, how's that?"

"You got to be tough in that line of work. There's always someone looking to make a bit on the side at his expense. It's right there's consequences, he has to protect all he's built."

"Listen to you, defending him. You're not keen on him, are you?"

"Don't be daft. He's got to be a good fifteen years older than me. I'm a child in his eyes."

"And what's he in yours?"

"My boss. Now, can we drop it, please?"

I'm saved by little Alice running into the room and flinging herself on my lap. She sticks a dirty thumb in her mouth and nuzzles into my neck.

"How's school, Alice? You've been going, I hope?"

"She has, that's why she's so bloody knackered all the time. Don't feel right, sending her off there every day when she's still so little."

"You know it's the right thing to do."

"But is it though? She'll end up in the factory like we did, and what use is an education then?"

"You don't know that. Look at Fred, he's near enough finished his degree."

"Only 'cause you sent him away."

Bloody hell, not this again. Florrie's always been mad at me for sending him to Wales, despite all the good it's done him. "I'm just saying, because her parents have led one sort of life, don't mean she has to."

"There's nothing wrong with the life her parents lead. Anyway, you're not exactly setting a good example, unmarried, childless and working for a crook."

I bite my tongue. I can't be having this argument again. Why is Florrie always so argumentative? I love her to bits, but it's been quite the relief not having to watch my tongue constantly these past weeks.

"I'm sure Alice will be fine, whatever path her life takes. Fancy doing some skipping?"

Alice yawns and smiles. "I'll fetch my rope," she says.

"You joining in?" I ask Florrie.

"We're not children anymore."

"No, but grown-ups are allowed a bit of fun sometimes too. Alice, you want Mum to play with us?"

"Yes, come on, Mum, come, come."

"Alright then, but only five minutes. Dinner won't cook itself."

It's a fine sight, seeing Florrie jumping and giggling out in the yard. It takes me back to when we were kiddies ourselves. Her face is all flushed and Alice beams at her mum. She's probably never seen her like this before. I'm distracted by the rope, and only know Joe's home by his shout.

"Playing without me? We can't have that!" He scampers over to us and jumps into the rope. Alice giggles, but Florrie's face is set in weary resignation.

"Any luck on the job front?" Florrie asks.

"I've got a few leads from a chap in the pub."

"The pub? You think that's the place to find work do you?"

"Oh no, Alice, Mummy's cross with me." Joe pulls a worried face at his daughter and she giggles again. Florrie crosses her arms. Joe wanders over to Florrie and plants a big smacker on her lips. She pushes him away and storms back towards the house.

"Alice, love. I think your mum's tired. I'd best get off back home now."

"No, stay," says Alice, clinging to my skirt.

"Look, how about I promise to come back round next week?"

Alice pouts at me, and follows Joe inside. What rotten luck Florrie's had. Seeing her struggle with Joe is enough to put anyone off marriage for life.

Chapter 37

June 1924

"How do I look?" Olive asks, turning to catch her reflection in the mirror.

"Like a princess."

"You like the dress?"

"It's a masterpiece. What did your mum say about the length?"

"She looked a little shocked when I first tried it on, but she likes to think she's up with the latest fashion so couldn't say too much." Olive laughs and adjusts the lace cap veil covering her bobbed hair.

The Barstones have gone all out on their only child's wedding day. I've been sneezing ever since I arrived, there's that many flowers in the house. I don't know why they bothered, for most people will be in the garden when we return from the church.

"You know, you'd suit a bob."

"Not likely, Mum always made me wear my hair short when I was at the yard. It was Julia what let me grow it. I don't care what the fashion magazines say, I'm sticking to what I like."

"You are a one. Now, whatever you do, don't make me laugh, this stuff goes everywhere if you're not careful."

"What is it?"

"Petroleum jelly mixed with charcoal. Makes your eyes look huge if you put it on right."

"Bloody hell, charcoal?"

"Just wait till you see it on."

Olive sits in front of the mirror dabbing black gunk onto her eyes. I have to admit it looks pretty, but I'm not sure I could be bothered to go to that much trouble. My eyes are big enough without it. Next, she covers her lips in red and turns to me for an opinion.

"Too much?"

"No, you look very glamorous. Cecil won't know what's hit him."

From the moment I met Olive's chap, I knew what had attracted her to him. Money. Can't have been anything else, for he's an ugly bugger and boring as hell.

"You're sure you don't want me to do your eyes for you?"

"No thanks, but I'll take some of that on my lips if you can spare it?"

"Yes, but let me do it. I don't want you looking like a clown."

Olive gets that close, I can smell booze on her breath.

"You been drinking already?"

"Champagne, if you must know. Mother insisted on opening a bottle at breakfast."

"I bet she did."

"Stop talking or you'll end up with red teeth not lips."

It's a proper treat being a bridesmaid. Got myself a new dress and shoes out of it without paying a penny.

"Hurry up, girls, the car will be here soon."

"Mother's been saying that for the past few hours. She's more excited about getting me married off than I am." Olive stands up and smooths down her dress. "You don't think anyone will be able to tell, do you?"

"Tell what?"

"About the baby, of course."

"Oh, that."

"For goodness sake, Nellie, stop being so old-fashioned. Everyone's doing it before marriage these days."

"Not me."

"No, well, don't expect to find a chap with that attitude."

"If a fellow isn't prepared to wait, then they're not good enough to have me at all."

"Oh, I despair of you, I really do. Just don't expect me to look after you when you're an old spinster."

I laugh, and straighten out the veil what trails down her back. At least the low waist and loose fit of the dress hides any scandal. The thought of going to bed with Cecil makes me feel sick. Olive must be keen to get her hands on his cash, for she surely can't enjoy getting her hands on anything else.

"The car's here," yells Mrs Barstone.

"Ready?" I ask Olive.

"As I'll ever be."

I don't let on to Olive, but the most exciting thing about the whole day is the chance to ride in a motor car. I let out a little squeal as I sit myself down on the deep red leather seats.

"It's only a motor car, Nell."

"It may be nothing to you, but I thought my bicycle was the poshest thing I'd ever ride."

The driver weaves us through the centre of the city. Folk stop to stare, for the flowers tied to the car suggest royalty sits inside. I reckon Mr Barstone would've booked the cathedral for the wedding if he'd been able. We pull up outside

Saint Augustine's and I wait beside the car for Olive to get out. A photographer appears by my shoulder.

"Make sure to get a mother and daughter snap," says Mrs Barstone, posing beside Olive. She's a little unsteady on her feet, and her lipstick has smudged in the corner of her mouth.

"Wait a moment," I tell the photographer and lean across to tackle the offending smudge with my hanky.

"Thank you, dear."

I resume my position on the side-lines and as the organ strikes up, follow several paces behind the bride. Mr Barstone puffs his chest in pride as Olive takes his arm at the door. Mrs Barstone scuttles past us to take up position at the front of the church.

"Wait a moment," I say as we're about to go inside.

"Whatever's the matter?"

"Nothing... it's just...just..." I let out an enormous sneeze which I hope to God was drowned out by the organ. "Sorry, it's the bouquet, there's so many flowers in there they keep tickling my nose."

"Goodness me, is that all? I thought you were about to stop the wedding and claim Cecil for yourself."

I shudder at the thought. We begin walking again, and it's bloody terrifying, I can tell you, walking up the aisle past so many staring faces. I know they're not watching me, but still, I'm quaking in my boots. I try to keep my eyes ahead, but as I pass one of the pews someone taps my leg and I turn to see Barny, grinning at me. He gives me a wink and I colour right up.

Bloody hell, the vicar don't half drone on, and there's that many hymns I'll be hoarse by the time we make it out of here.

I wish I'd had a wee before we left the house, for I'm bursting by the time the service draws to a close.

***

A clinking of glass signals it's time to take our seats. The band finish up their song and there's a rush to tables laid out at the end of the lawn. I'm sat at the top table beside Olive's mother. I've been given strict instructions to top up her wine glass with water at every chance I get.

If I thought the vicar was dull, he comes up like a show-man beside Cecil. On and on he goes, in that reedy voice of his. I've no idea what he says, for it's all I can do to keep my eyes open. Mr Barstone's not all that brief neither. Goes on and on about his wonderful daughter. Don't get me wrong, I'm bloody fond of Olive, but I don't recognise the high-achieving woman he's describing. At least he throws a few well-timed jokes in among the boasts and lies.

Young lads in sharp suits bring out plate after plate of food. It's all posh stuff that looks better than it tastes. I reck-on some folk only made it through the speeches by guzzling champagne, for many seem half cut already, and it's only two in the afternoon.

"Fancy escaping for a bit?" Barny asks, strolling up to the top table.

"You're a lifesaver. Think they'd mind me leaving the top table?"

"No, all the speeches are done, now it's time for people to get pissed and the couple to escape off to their honeymoon."

We find a quiet corner of the garden and Barny rolls a ciggie. He offers me one, but the smell alone is enough to put me off.

"That dress suits you. You can really hold your own among this crowd, you know."

"Thank you. It was kind of the Barstones giving me the dress and shoes. Will save me buying a new pair this year. You know what they say? Look after the pennies..."

"And the pounds will take care of themselves."

I smile at him. He looks handsome in his suit, not that I'd tell him that.

"You've never thought of marrying into money rather than scrimping and saving?"

"Bloody hell, you sound just like Olive. No. Never. If I do ever wed, it will be as a man's equal, not as some skivvy relying on his wage packet, cooking and cleaning all day."

"Don't you want children?"

"Of course I do. I've always wanted a family of my own, just not at any cost."

"You're quite something. You know that don't you?"

I don't know what to say to that, so I look out over the garden instead. The band have started up again and squiffy folk bump into tables and each other as they make their way to the dancefloor.

"Fancy a dance?" Barny asks.

"With you?"

"Yes, with me. I'm not suggesting you go up there by yourself."

"You sure you can dance?"

"Why don't you come with me and find out?"

He holds out his hand and I let him lead me back to the party. The dance floor is packed. It's just a load of old boards laid on the grass, but Mr Barstone's had them polished till they gleam like the floor of a London club. As it turns out, Barny's dancing isn't half bad for a man as large as he is. He puts his arm round my waist and takes my hand in his. It feels bloody uncomfortable at first, being held in my boss's arms. But as I grow used to it, it's not too bad.

"Why don't you ever talk about your family?" I ask.

"Not much to tell. My dad's a drunk and my mum's been dead years."

"Got any brothers or sisters?"

"Two brothers. One runs the pub with Dad, the other died in the war."

"Did you fight?"

"Yes. I was one of the lucky ones who came back. I think Dad has always felt the wrong son came home. Can't blame him really, Charlie was a true gentlemen, everyone loved him. I'm just a ruffian with a temper who folk steer well clear of."

"You don't seem like that to me."

"That's 'cause you've not known me long enough."

"Why have you never married?"

"I had a sweetheart before the war, but after I came back she decided she'd be better off with my brother Bertie."

"Do they live at the pub too?"

"Yes."

"That must be strange for you."

"No, not really. I was a mess after the war, didn't want to be around no one, least of all her. She gives Bertie a real hard time these days, so I think I had a lucky escape."

"But the war ended six years ago. There's been no one since then?"

"Truth be told, I like my own company. From what I've seen, all wives do is nag at you and take your money. There's not much about marriage that appeals."

"Yet everyone seems to do it."

"Except us." He laughs and spins me round before pulling me close again.

"Ladies and gents, your attention please." Mr Barstone stands on a chair. "The bride and groom are about to depart for their honeymoon. If you'd like to wave them off, I suggest you hurry across to the front of the house."

"Quick," I say, grabbing Barny's hand and pulling him towards the house.

"They're not going this second," he says, struggling to keep up.

"No, but I want to say goodbye, and if we don't beat that lot, I won't get a chance."

Olive is looking out of the car window when I sprint through the front door. She winds down the window and calls me over.

"Have a wonderful time in...where is it you're going?"

"Italy."

"Have a wonderful time in Italy. I'll miss you. Let me know as soon as you're home. You take good care of her, Cecil."

He nods, and Olive reaches through the window to hug me. With a cheer from the motley crew on the drive, Cecil beeps his horn, and the car pulls away.

Chapter 38

September 1924

Me and Barny sit side by side. I'm counting out a fellow's winnings ready to hand to the runner, and he's checking the slips that have just come in.

"What do you make of the new lad?" he asks.

"Seems trustworthy to me. He's a bright chap, knows which side his bread's buttered. I don't think he'd risk ripping you off."

"Trouble is he's slow on his bike, not like you, whizzing here there and everywhere at the speed of a motor car. The punters keep asking for you back."

"I can go running any time you like. Just say the word and I'll hop back on my bike."

"No, you're more use here with the money."

Not since Henry and Julia has anyone trusted me the way Barny does. Even at the factory, they check all my piecework, convinced there's no way I could work as fast as I do and still do a good job. They never find nothing wrong with my work, and I love how much it sends them in a lather. I'm on my third and final warning for joking around. They tell me I distract the other workers. It's not my fault if they're too slow to enjoy a joke or song and keep working at the same time. At least now Barny's promoted me the fear of being given the boot isn't so great. If I wasn't saving so hard, I could easily get by on what he pays me.

Little Johnny comes in ready to collect the money. He's a scrap of a thing, not more than twelve. But I see the way his eyes dart around, taking everything in, learning all the time. He'll go far.

"Here you are," I say, handing him the wad of notes and coins. "Watch out now won't you, it's getting dark out there."

"I'm always careful, Missus."

"I know you are, you're a good chap. But please, please stop calling me Missus."

He nods and retreats out the back to find his bicycle.

"Why does he always call me Missus?" I ask Barny once he's gone.

"The new chaps all think you're my wife."

"Bloody hell."

"Charming."

"No, it just makes me cross they don't think I can manage on my own."

"I don't think it's that."

Barny stops counting his slips and turns to me. He's looking at me all funny, like I've got something on my face.

"Would it be such a bad thing?"

"What?"

"If you were my wife."

"I don't understand... Are you?..."

"I'm making a business proposal. I've been thinking about it for a while now."

"A business proposal?"

"Yes. If we were married, we could be proper business partners, a fifty-fifty split."

"You're asking me to marry you so I can be your business partner?"

"Well... not just that, but I know your views on marriage."

"I'm not sure I understand. Do you love me?" How I'm able to be so bold, I can't say, for my legs are shaking beneath the table.

"What a question. Well, to answer it, I think you're a looker, I think you're very clever, I think you can hold your own in a man's world, I think we'd make a good team."

"Is that love?"

"I honestly don't know, Nell. I've not felt much beside anger since the war. I'm not sure I'm capable of love in the way you're meaning."

I sit back in my chair, trying to wrap my tired mind around all he's said.

"What about you?" he asks. "Would being married to me be such a bad thing?"

I look at him, trying to piece words together in an answer. I've never loved a man before, not like he's meaning anyway. Julia, Henry, Fred, Florrie; I've loved them as deeply as it's possible to love. But Barny? Does racing to work to be with him count as love? Do the flutters I feel when I'm with him count as love, or are they because he can turn from happy to angry in seconds? Is it just the excitement of the work, of spending all my free time on numbers and counting, of being needed what make me want to be around him?

"What would happen to my savings if I said yes?"

He lets out a loud laugh and bangs his hands down on the table. Coins topple from their towers and notes flutter to the ground. "That's such a Nellie thing to say. I propose, and the thing you're most worried about is your savings." He laughs again, then takes my hands in his.

"Your savings would be safe. We could put yours with mine and buy a nice place together. Fifty-fifty, like I said."

"Would I take an allowance from you? Would you expect me to keep a home, stop working?"

"There'd be no allowance. You'd get a fair wage for the work you do, plus a fifty-fifty split on any profits we make. I've spent enough time with you to know you'd keep a nice home, but I'm not the kind of chap to think that's all you do. I don't want a wife what spends her days in a pinny dusting. I'd go mad with boredom."

"You want children?"

"It's not something I've given much thought, but if that's part of the deal, it's fine by me."

I take my hands from his and put them in my lap.

"Is it a no then?"

"It's a yes." I hold out my hand to shake his, and he takes it, laughing.

"Can I give my future wife a kiss?"

Colour floods to my cheeks and I sit very still as he leans towards me. His lips scuff mine and he pulls away.

"Barny, I'm a prude, as Olive would say, but not that much of a prude."

It's a mystery where my confidence comes from, but I lean towards him and kiss him properly. Not the way Jack used to kiss me, for I don't like slobber, but firm and like I mean it. The kiss sends tingles all through me. Barny must feel the same, for his hands clasp my face like he don't want to let go. The backdoor latch clicks, and we pull away from each other.

"Sorry," says Johnny, walking into the room. "I took the money but forgot the list. Bloody hell, what's happened here?" he asks, seeing the fallen coins and notes. "You two been scrapping?"

"Watch how you talk to Nell," says Barny. "You're speaking to the future Mrs Read."

Johnny looks confused, of course he would, he thinks we're already married.

"Spread the word round town, lad, we'll be in the Trafford Arms later to celebrate."

Johnny nods and rushes off with his list and instructions.

"If you're going to spread the word round town, you could've told me first. I can't have Florrie finding out through hearsay. That was bloody inconsiderate of you."

"Bloody hell, we're not going to have our first kiss and our first row all in the space of five minutes, are we?" He grins at me. "I got carried away, sorry."

"Apology accepted. Now are you going to give me a couple of hours off to see Florrie and Olive?"

"Yes, boss."

***

"You're what?"

"I'm getting married."

"To whom? Oh God, please tell me it's not that old bloke you work for."

"If you mean Barny, then yes. Yes, it is."

"But he's old enough to be your dad!"

"Hardly. Anyway, it was you told me to get wed."

"Yes, but I meant to a normal chap, not to him."

"Florrie, you're being unfair. You've never even met him."

"I don't like the sound of him."

I sigh. There's no point trying to persuade her. "Will you come to the wedding? I'd like you to be my maid of honour."

Finally, she smiles. "You would?"

"I wouldn't have asked you if I didn't."

"What about that posh friend of yours, Olivia?"

"Olive."

"That's the one."

"Olive's a great friend, but she's not my sister. It's you I want beside me as I take my vows."

"When's the wedding? Will I have to get a new dress?"

"It's next month, and I'll be getting the dress for you. Barny's insisted on paying for everything seeing I've no dad around to help out."

"Maybe he's not such a wrong 'un after all. Why are you getting married so quick, there's nothing you need to tell me is there?"

"You mean a baby?"

"Yes."

"Florrie, all we've done is kiss, and from the little I know, that's not how babies are made. There just didn't seem any point waiting once we'd decided."

"No, I s'pose there isn't. Alice will be thrilled to have a wedding to go to."

"So, you're happy for me?"

"Yes, yes I am. Good for you, Nellie. Now you can set about making some cousins for my kiddies. They'll have great fun getting up to mischief together."

"Let's get the wedding out of the way first, shall we?"

Chapter 39

September 1924

"Bloody hell, you've been hard at work," I say, as Olive shows me through to her sitting room.

"Yes, it's not quite what I would've chosen, but Cecil said it's better to go for a classic look than something that will be in fashion one day and out the next."

Olive's house certainly isn't in danger of being too fashionable. It looks like someone let their Nan loose with a roll of wallpaper and a paint brush. It's all sludge greens and browns, and swirly patterns what make my head ache.

"It's certainly a classic look."

"You hate it."

"I didn't say that."

"You didn't need to."

"It's just not very you."

"Well, I'm a wife now, so I'm bound to change somewhat."

"How's the baby getting on in there?"

"Oh, I wish he'd come out soon. I have such terrible heartburn, and don't get me started on the piles."

"Urgh, sounds wonderful."

Olive laughs. "Don't let me put you off. As soon as you've found yourself a nice young man, I bet you'll sail through pregnancy."

"Actually, that's what I've come to talk to you about."

"You're having a baby?"

I smooth down my dress, so it lies flat on my belly. "Olive, do I look like I'm having a baby? No, I meant the finding a nice man part."

Olive leans forward in her seat. "Tell me everything. Who is he? Do I know him? It's not Gerald Fleckson, is it? Or Jeoffrey Beaumont?"

"No, and I'm not even sure who those chaps are."

"Nellie, you've met them at least three times now at various parties and dinners."

"Then they must be very dull. Anyway, it's not Gerald, or Jeoffrey. It's Barny."

"Barny?"

"Yes."

"Barny? Are you sure?"

"Sure whether he proposed, or sure I want to marry him?"

"You're engaged? I thought you were here to tell me you've started courting. When did this start?"

"Today."

"Today? You mean you started courting and got engaged all in one morning?"

I laugh. "Yes, and when you put it that way, I can see why you're surprised. It surprised me too."

"But why Barny? He's not much younger than Father."

"Because he asked me, and his terms suited what I'm after."

"You discussed terms and conditions as part of a marriage proposal?"

"Of course we did."

"And what are these terms then?"

I explain the agreement I reached with Barny earlier.

"So, it's not a romantic match then?"

"I wouldn't say that. I've had worse kisses."

"He kissed you?"

"Yes."

"Wasn't it a bit scratchy and hairy?"

"Oh, Olive, you have such a way with words. No, it was... it was... surprising."

"In a good way?"

"Yes, in a very good way."

"Well, you're a pair of dark horses that's for sure. When's the wedding?"

"Next month."

"Are you sure you're not expecting?"

"Bloody hell, why does everyone assume I must have a baby in my belly? No, we just don't see the point in waiting."

"Can't you wait? I'll look awful in my maid of honour dress with this huge bump."

Looks like I'll be having two maids of honour. I hope Barny don't mind the extra expense.

"You'll look beautiful as ever. How are things with Cecil?"

"Oh, you don't want to hear about that. Why don't we go through to the dining room and have tea and cake to celebrate your news?"

However much I try to prise it out of her, Olive don't seem keen on talking about Cecil. Perhaps how me and Barny have gone about marriage is a little odd, but neither Florrie nor Olive are great adverts for going about things the normal way.

***

As soon as I'm out of view from Olive's front window I stop and take big gulps of fresh air. Her house might be big, but it's that old and stuffy it feels more like prison than luxury. Olive's the same as she always was on the surface. But I know her well enough to tell she's very quickly moved past the honeymoon stage. If she even had one of those. Hopefully the baby will give her a bit of purpose. I tried asking how she spends her days, but she struggled to think of anything except cooking and needlework.

The air is still warm, and the city is looking lovely in the autumn sunshine. Life feels charmed for most people compared to the dark days of war. It's a treat to have an afternoon off, so I walk the long way home, giving myself time to think. Any doubts about my decision to marry Barny have been laid to rest since meeting Florrie and Olive. One look at their lives told me all I needed to know about the way I want mine to turn out. Me and Barny might not be madly in love, but I reckon our partnership will be strong. I'll be his equal, of that I'm sure.

Mrs Waters is waiting for me when I eventually make it home.

"You alright, dear? I don't usually see you home during daylight hours."

"Yes, I'm very well thank you, Mrs Waters. Actually, I have some news. I am to marry next month, so shan't be needing my room for much longer."

Mrs Waters' face falls. "But you're the only one what pays their rent on time. Couldn't you move your fellow in here with you?"

"No, I'm sorry. We'll be wanting to start a family soon, and the one room isn't big enough for two adults and a child."

"I see. So, what's he like, this fellow of yours? I've not noticed you sneaking anyone in like that Rosemary tries to do. Where've you been hiding him?"

"We met at work. He's a supervisor."

It's not strictly lying; he is a supervisor of sorts.

"Well, isn't that lovely. Congratulations, dear, though I'll be sorry to see you go."

"I'll pay up this month and next months' rent, as I'm not sure how quickly we'll find a place of our own."

"Very well. Thank you for letting me know, dear."

Inside my room, I pull out my writing paper and pen. It's short notice, but I hope to God Julia will be able to make the journey to Norwich next month. And I'll need to let Fred know too. It may be unconventional, but I want them either side of me as I walk up the aisle.

***

"Here she is," yells Barny as I walk through the pub doors. He lurches over and kisses me, right there in the pub, in front of everyone. All the chaps around us cheer. I pull away and glare at him, my cheeks as red as a berry.

"Been here a while, have you?"

"Since lunchtime. Turns out there's plenty of folk wanting to wish us well. I've closed up shop for the day, and Billy's manning the stall anyway, so I'm a free man."

"Won't be a free man much longer," says one bloke, and the others cheer again.

A man walks up to me. He's that squiffy he can't see straight and looks over my shoulder the whole time he's talking. "How d'you do it?" he slurs.

"Do what?"

"Convince Barny to settle down. We never thought we'd see the day. You must have some right good tricks up your sleeve... or skirt."

He grabs me and tries to shove his hand up my dress. In a matter of seconds Barny's on him, grabbing him by the scruff of his neck and smashing him into a wall.

"That's my fiancée and you'll show her some respect."

"Sorry," says the man, writhing round trying to get out of Barny's grip.

"It's not me you got to apologise to. Go and say sorry to Nell."

Barny loosens his grip, and the chap comes over, rubbing his neck and looking very sheepish. He stands in front of me. My hand whips up and slaps him round the face.

"Don't you ever, ever touch me, or any other woman like that again. Understand?"

"Yes, miss."

"Now bugger off, you're not welcome here."

All the fellows in the bar stare at me.

"Is someone going to buy the good lady a drink?" Barny calls, and a handful of men scramble to their feet.

"Thank you for stepping in, but I can take care of myself."

"I can see that," says Barny, laughing. "Someone taught you well. You've got a fine slap on you. I hope I'm never on the receiving end."

"Treat me proper and you won't be. I was brought up to know my worth, and I'll not be taken advantage of by anyone."

"And the chaps wonder how you nabbed me. You're one of a kind, Nellie Westrop, one of a kind."

Chapter 40

October 1924

"I hope Julia got her train alright."

"That's what's going through your mind right now, is it? Julia? Clearly I've gone wrong somewhere."

Barny pulls me closer, and I lie my head against his broad chest. His hands stroke my naked back. No one's touched my bare skin since I was a child and Julia would give me a good hose down outside the wagon.

"She liked you."

"I liked her."

"I didn't recognise her when she stepped off the train. She looked like an old woman."

"She is an old woman."

"You should have seen her years ago, a real beauty she was, turned heads everywhere we went."

"She's still a beauty if you ask me, just an older one."

"And sadder. Even when she was smiling, I could see a sadness in her eyes. I don't reckon she's ever got over losing Henry."

"We're not that different to them, are we? We'll be living and working together. Let's hope we don't fall out or life will be unbearable."

I prop myself up on my elbow and lean in for a kiss. Turns out I do know how to love a man after all.

"Was it worth the wait?" Barny asks between kisses.

"What?"

"You know what."

"Yes. Yes, it was."

Barny pulls a strand of hair away from my eyes and tucks it behind my ear. "We should probably unpack."

"Five minutes longer."

"Nell, this floor's doing nothing for my back. I'm an old man, remember. Need my creature comforts."

"Less of the old. You're a spring chicken. Anyway, the floor's not too bad."

Barny wriggles around to find a more comfy spot. "It's a shame Julia couldn't stay longer."

"I know. She could only afford a few days off. At least Fred's here for a while yet. Don't have to go back till the weekend."

"I'm not sure he approves of me."

"Oh, don't pay any attention to him, he's picked up a few airs and graces at university, that's all. He'll love you as much as I do once he gets to know you."

"Oh, so you love me, do you? I thought this marriage was purely business."

"I think we both know that's not the case."

He wraps me up in his big arms and we lie on the floor of our empty house, each as content as the other. Our first place together. We're only renting, but still, it's clean and modern, there's even a tap and an oil stove for cooking. We've got our own privy in the yard, no bathtub, but one step at a time. I'd thought of inviting Fred to stay here, but I'm glad I didn't in the end. Apart from having no furniture to speak of, it's been good to have a bit of privacy on our first evening as man and wife.

***

"Where do you want this, Nell?" Fred asks.

"By the fire, thanks."

He dumps the armchair down and flops into it. "Please tell me we're done for the day."

"Yes, that's everything. There's still a few boxes of Barny's left to sort, but all my stuff fit in one suitcase."

"You're a miracle worker. How many days have you been here?"

"Four."

"Four? Blimey, you've got this place shipshape in no time. It looks like a proper grown-up home."

"Thanks, Fred."

He's right, it does look nice. I've painted the walls cream, and there's a matching cream rug covering most of the floor. It feels like fairy floss when you step on it. Julia gave me a few ornaments from the wagon as a wedding present, and they're in pride of place on the mantel above the fire. I wish she could've stayed long enough to see me put them up. Barny's present to me was letting me get his old armchairs recovered in dusky pink velvet. Must have cost him a fortune. He reckons they're not very manly, but I bet he don't complain when his bum hits the soft cushions.

"Fancy a tour?"

"Go on then."

The tour won't take long, for the house is tiny, more of a cottage really. We head through to the kitchen.

"That looks like the table we had in the old house."

"The very same. When Mum died, I got Florrie to store it in her yard for me. Pissed Joe right off, he kept walking into it on his way home from the pub and I can't count the number of times he threatened to burn it. It was covered in moss by the time I was ready to take it back, but a good old sand and a few coats of oil and it's good as new."

"It doesn't bring back too many memories?"

"No, the sanding was a tonic, like rubbing out the past. They'll be many new memories made around that table. What do you make of the oil stove?"

"Very fancy. Now you just need to learn to cook."

I give him a whack on the arm. "I can stretch to making tea, want one?"

"Yes please. I'm gasping after lugging round those bloody chairs for you."

With the kettle filled and on the stove, I continue with our tour. Our savings are too precious to spend on carpet, but I've sanded down the wooden stairs and they'll do for now. At the top there's two doors, one on the left, one on the right.

"This is our room."

"Blimey, this is fancy."

"Yes, I suppose it is."

The bed is just an old one Barny had in the pub, but I've layered it up with cushions, and draped pieces of silk from the ceiling to the headboard. After making the bed nice, I couldn't afford to do much more. Barny found a few scraps of timber and built a wardrobe for us, not that either of us have many clothes to fill it. My shoe box sits at the bottom, same as in my last place. Barny don't trust banks, so we've agreed to keep a box each, and put them together when we're ready to buy.

"What's that other room?"

"I'll show you, but there's not much to see."

I lead him across the hallway to the second bedroom. The walls are bare, and other than a dustsheet, the room is empty.

"Will this be a spare room?"

"I'm hoping it will be a kiddie's bedroom. Seems like tempting fate to be painting it yet. We'll wait till it's time, then get it ready for the arrival."

"Well, I for one can't wait for that day. I'll be the favourite uncle, spoiling my niece or nephew with sweets and toys."

"Only if they see you more than once a year. You planning on coming back to Norwich when you're finished with your studies?"

"I don't think so. I love it in Wales. The air there does me good, and the people too."

"You got anyone special?"

"No, I'm too busy studying, but I'd like to meet someone and settle down one day."

"Fred?"

"Yes?"

"You've never resented me, have you? For sending you away, I mean."

Fred walks over and wraps me in a hug. "You saved my life, Nell."

"Well, that's going a bit far. Come on, you soft idiot, I can hear the kettle whistling downstairs."

***

"I'm back."

"Through here."

"Oh, has Fred left already?"

"Yes, didn't want to miss his train."

"You alright?"

"Yes, I just miss him, that's all. I wish he lived closer."

"Nell, being away from here has done wonders for him. Don't be regretting it now."

"I don't, it's just he's the only person who really understands me, knows what it's like to leave and start again somewhere else, as someone else."

"Well, there's no running needed no more. You're here with me, I'm your family now."

I stand up on my tiptoes and give him a kiss. "Come and see the chairs. Fred brought them in for me."

Barny walks through to the sitting room and shakes his head. "I'm still not sure it's the done thing for a chap to have pink chairs in his front room."

"Well, you did say fifty-fifty. You picked the house, so it's only fair I get to pick what goes inside it."

"You drive a hard bargain, Mrs Read, and not for the first time. How does it feel to be a lady of leisure?"

"Lady of leisure? So, you don't need me down the shop no more then? Or doing the books? Or counting the winnings?"

"I meant the factory."

"It's a bloody relief, I can tell you. I just can't believe I left of my own free will, rather than with a supervisor's boot up my arse."

"Well, there's plenty I need you for. You alright to mind the shop tomorrow? I need to meet a man about a dog."

"So long as you tell me what man and what breed of dog you're meeting."

Barny sighs and sinks into pink velvet. "I've been thinking about our money. We can't use a bank and keeping it in a shoebox seems risky as hell. I've been thinking about us getting into the property game, putting our money into bricks and mortar. From what I've heard, there's good money to be made. And you'd have no trouble fixing the books to adjust for our earnings without drawing suspicion."

"Fine, but don't go promising nothing without talking it through with me first. Fifty-fifty."

"Fifty-fifty."

Chapter 41

November 1924

"You bloody bastard," I scream, moving my head as a dusky pink vase flies past me and smashes into the wall.

"If you shut your gob for one minute and listened to me, you'd know I've done the right thing!" Barny's voice is so loud, the windows are rattling.

In the mirror behind him I see a few folk have gathered on the street outside, eager for the entertainment of our row. Seeing them gawping stops me in my tracks and I move so close to him, his breath teases my hair.

"You're a bloody liar. I should never have trusted you. Fifty-fifty?" I laugh, though I'm finding none of this funny. "What a fool I was believing your claptrap." My hands push into his broad chest. "Get out." He stands still. "Get out!" I know I sound hysterical, but I can't stop myself. "GET OUT!" I scream, pushing him hard enough that he takes a few steps backwards.

Barny stares at me, his face red, his breath coming fast. Will he hit me? I doubt it, I've seen his fists fly with ease at chaps what have crossed him, but I doubt he'd use them on me. He shakes his head, grabs his coat from the back of the chair and marches outside. He bangs the door so hard, I have to run to the mantelpiece and steady Julia's ornaments to stop them tumbling. I hear him yell at the onlookers on the street, and they scuttle off in all directions, probably disappointed the show's over.

After leaning against the mantel and catching my breath, I climb the bare floorboards to our bedroom. Our row has knocked the wind out of me, and I must look like Mum, huffing and puffing my way to the top. I cross to the wardrobe and take out my precious shoe box. My back slides against the wall and I slump against it, box open at my feet. Empty. Bloody empty. The bastard has taken all my savings and all that remains are the faded letters spelling out 'self-made'. What a bloody joke. Tears come, but they're not sad tears. They're hot, burning my cheeks as the shame of my misplaced trust hits me. All these years I've struggled by alone, all those hours to save the coins. What was I thinking, placing my trust in an old rogue like Barny? Through the blur of my tears, I see Henry leaning against the doorframe, shaking his head. "I thought I taught you better," he says, though I know his words are only in my head. Mum appears beside him, I expect her to laugh, but instead she folds her arms and gives me a sad smile. Maybe she wanted better for me after all.

I rub my eyes to clear them and give my head a brisk shake to rid the nonsense of ghosts. There aren't such things as ghosts, just the here and now, and the mess I've made of things. I feel the tears threatening once more, and slap my cheek hard to push them back. I replace the lid of the shoebox and make my way downstairs. Tea. Tea makes things better. While I wait for the kettle to bubble on the stove, I pour myself a good measure of Barny's special whisky, and chuck it down my throat in one go. That will teach him. The liquid burns my throat, and it's a relief when the kettle boils and I can wash the taste away.

I take my half-drunk cup back up the stairs and pull out Barny's box. I don't know why I didn't do it earlier. Maybe he just put my money in with his? The lid rattles as it lands beside the box. His is empty too. Where's it all gone? What has he done? I won't get no answers from staring at two empty boxes, so I head back downstairs and begin clearing the mess we've made. One of my lovely chairs lies on its side, and a small wooden table lies top down. As I right it, I notice one of the legs wobbling. I'll need to fix that.

This wasn't our first row, but it was definitely the worst. It was the first time Barny had taken his anger out on the furniture anyway. Mind you, it's better to have things out in the open than be like Olive and Cecil, mouths pinned shut while anger and sadness eat them up from the inside. Or I could be married to a man like Joe. Florrie admitted he's restless, misses his travelling days and feels trapped by marriage and children. He don't have the words to say how he feels so drowns those feelings in beer. That's the coward's way if you ask me. And bloody unfair on Florrie, who don't get the chance to drown sorrows of her own.

I've calmed down and am sweeping the last few shards of vase when Barny reappears. I stay quiet as I hear the front door close, and wait for him to come to me. He fills the doorway of the sitting room, making it look like something from a dolls' house. It's clear he's not going to speak, so I'll have to go first.

"What you got there?"

He holds out a brown paper bag and I take it, not looking him in the eye.

"Peace offering."

I uncurl the folded top and see four shiny red apples lying inside. With the bag flung on the armchair, I return to my sweeping.

"Cost me five pence," he says, smiling.

"You were barmy paying that much. Don't think this lets you off the hook."

"Nell, can you stop that and sit down? I need to explain myself."

"I'd rather an apology than an explanation."

"Sit down and I'll give you both."

With my broom propped up against the wall, I plonk myself down in the armchair. All this rowing's left me tired, and I'm grateful for the squishy velvet that cuddles me. Barny fusses round, lighting the fire. I expect him to sit down, but instead he wanders over to the drinks cabinet and makes me up a gin.

"You think you can win me round with gin?"

"No, but if you've a drink on the go, it might give me a few seconds to get a word in."

I smile at him, despite myself. "Alright then, tell me why my savings box is empty."

Barny flops into the armchair beside mine. "Firstly, I'm really sorry. Taking it without asking was a bloody stupid thing to do. I suppose I'm still getting used to this partnership business. I'm used to working on my own, acting on my own decisions as and when I please."

"Yes, but our agreement was equal partners. You promised me that."

"I know. I'm sorry."

"So, what have you done with my money then?"

"I've invested it."

"Into what?"

"Bricks and mortar. Like we talked about."

"You mean that chat where you promised to run everything by me first?"

Barny sighs. "Yes, that's the one. Anyway, an opportunity came up, one that was too good to miss. I had to act quickly."

"But, Barny, we're together all day every day. Are you really saying you couldn't talk to me first?"

"I wasn't sure you'd say yes. Anyway, I think we're onto a sure thing."

"We'd better be. Tell me everything."

"I met this chap down the pub. He's brought some land that came up after the council's clearance scheme. Got a good deal, on the understanding he builds new homes. But he needed an investor for the building side of things. We've come to an agreement. I'll work on the site as a labourer, then once the flats are sold, we get a fifty-fifty split of the profits."

"And what do I get out of this arrangement?"

"Like I said before, it's a good way to hide any extra earnings what come our way, and my half of the profits will be shared with you."

"Right. And what about the fruit and veg stall?"

"I've given it up."

"You've given it up, without asking me?"

"It's not like I've been working there much anyway."

"True, but it all sounds very risky to me."

"Nellie, with the yards being knocked down, there's a real shortage of housing in the city. If ever there was a time to get into property, it's now."

I sit quietly, thinking over all he's said. I can't fault his logic, but the fact he didn't consult me first still stings.

"Alright, I can see you have a point. But I need to make one thing clear."

"What's that?"

"You broke the terms of our agreement. I'll let that slide just this once, but I promise you, Barny, if you ever do it again, I will walk away from this marriage quicker than you can say fifty-fifty. Understood?"

"Understood."

"Good, now how about I finish up in here, and you can cook us dinner?"

"Yes, boss."

Chapter 42

December 1924

I rub my eyes to push away the sleepiness that's hanging over me. It's been nonstop since Barny got involved in property. He's been labouring as well as ploughing money into investments and is out all hours on the site. At least he trusts me enough to step away from the bookies, otherwise he'd have no time to sleep. It does mean long days for me though, for the horses keep racing and slips keep flooding in. Walk round Norwich at midday and you'll find many fellows with their heads in a newspaper, picking out the right horse to try their luck on. You can be sure a good amount of those bets will be headed our way.

Little Johnny walks in through the back and we all shush him as he says hello. Quiet is needed as we sit round listening to the Newmarket race on the wireless. It's a right motley crew we got gathered in the shop. There's five runners now. Four of them are just out of school, but one chap must be heading for sixty. Barny took pity on him when he couldn't find work and brought him into the fold. He's not as quick as the young fellows, but knows half the betting men in the city, and don't look out of place in the pubs. Then there's my assistant Stephen. He don't much like having a woman for a boss, but he'll have to get used to it for I'm here to stay.

Stephen's face goes all shiny and pinched as the horses race round the track. He'll be praying as much as the rest of us for Misty Hill to win. There's good odds on her, for us, at any rate. Plenty of slips have come in for Indian Prince. If that one wins it will be a bad day for us for the odds are four to one. It's that tense in the shop, we all jump out of our skin at the banging on the door.

"Coppers are on their way!"

Bugger. I can't be found here with the slips and cash. *Think, think, think.*

"Stephen, help me load the cash from the safe into my bag."

"Leave it, we need to get out of here."

"Just do as I bloody say."

Stephen stands rooted to the spot, bubbles of sweat popping from his face. He wrings his hands, looks this way and that, and jumps each time another fist bangs. I slap his face so hard he doubles up.

"Sorry, but we got to get going. Help me with this. Quick."

The slap did the trick, and he follows my lead. We pile notes and coins into the clock bag as quick as we can. A few fall to the floor, but there's no time to pick them up. A hammering comes on both the front and back doors.

"You sure they're locked?"

"Certain, but it won't take the police long to get through."

"I'm taking the cash with me. You distract them in here so I can get away."

"I need to get out too."

"Look, with the money and slips gone, there's not much they can charge you with. If they come in heavy handed, I'll make sure you and the others are well compensated. Alright?"

Without waiting for Stephen to answer, I nip across the hallway into the side room. I close the door behind me, turning the key and slipping it in my pocket. There's an old dresser on one wall, and I shove my shoulder behind it till it's wedged behind the door. It won't keep the coppers out long, just enough for me to make a hasty exit. Banging fists turn to thuds of a battering ram. They'll be through in a minute. There's a chair in the corner and I drag it to the window. It's only got three legs, but I send up a prayer it will be strong enough to hold my weight. It wobbles as I climb up, but the legs hold, and I reach the window. Lucky I'm small, for only me or a child would fit through.

"This is a police raid. Remain where you are, nobody is to leave the premises."

Bloody hell, I reckon I've got a minute at most. The escape must be well timed; go too soon and there'll be coppers outside, go too late and they'll break the door and catch me in the act. One second, two seconds, three seconds, four seconds. Go.

My arms take my weight as I heave myself up on the frame. What a bloody stupid idea, putting a window so high up. I throw the clock bag out before me and pause just a second. No feet come running so I squeeze through the frame. I land in a heap at the bottom, and it takes everything I got not to cry out at the pain in my ankle. I hobble away in the opposite direction to the house.

"Hey! You! Stop right there!"

My ankle is screaming at me to stop, but I push on faster. Thank God I left my bike in the pub yard today. I lock the garden gate behind me, grab my bike, push off down the alleyway and in under a minute I'm flying away from the shop. I don't dare turn my head in case I'm recognised, but

I hear footsteps pounding the pavement close behind. Lucky I'm on a downhill stretch and my short legs are strong. As I put more distance between me and the shop, the angry shouts from the police officers are carried off on the wind.

***

Barny's home earlier than usual. He must've got wind of the raid, and comes running through to the kitchen, where I've been sat with my ankle on a chair since I arrived home.

"You alright? What happened?"

"You heard about the raid?"

"Yes. Did you get much warning?"

"Five minutes. One of the local kiddies gave us a shout, but we didn't have much time to clear out. Any idea how many got caught?"

"All but you."

"Bugger. We'll need to make sure they're well paid off, or tongues will become loose."

"I'll see to it. How are you? You hurt yourself?"

"Twisted my ankle when I went through the window. Apart from that I'm alright. I got away with as much as I could."

I nod my head to where the clock bag lies discarded on the floor.

"I don't suppose you got the key, did you?"

I pull the key from my pocket, and Barny kisses my head. He smiles as he opens it.

"You can't have left much behind for them to find. Well done, Nell."

"What will we do about the shop?"

"Oh, don't worry about that. We can do the house up, sell it on and make a profit. It shouldn't be too hard finding someone with a room to rent for the business. No one round here will see us go under, they rely on us too much. I'll start looking tomorrow. If you're up to it, I reckon we should start going through these slips. I'll take the winnings round myself. Raid or no raid, folk will expect us to pay up on time."

***

"Nell! Nell!"

"What is it?"

"Come down here, there's something I want to show you."

I burrow back under the blankets and pull a pillow over my head. It was midnight before Barny finished delivering the takings last night. I waited up for him to come home, for the coppers were bound to be on the lookout after the raid.

"Nell, get down here."

"Alright, alright, I'm coming."

I check the clock beside the bed. Eight. Eight in the bloody morning. What's he even doing up at this time? I force myself out of the warm bed and wrap one of the blankets round my shoulders. Barny's sat at the table, a cup of tea and plate of toast untouched in front of him.

"You're in the paper."

"What d'you mean? How am I in the paper?"

Barny clears his throat and begins to read. "Police raid betting shop in Lakenham. Five arrested but Queen Bee escapes."

"Let me see," I say, grabbing the paper from him.

The whole thing is there in black and white. 'The five suspects have been released awaiting trial...betting slips and cash found at the property... no clues as to the proprietor... off course betting a scourge on our city.'

"They don't like us much, do they."

"At least they don't know who we are, *Queenie*."

"Oi, enough of that."

"Actually, I think it suits you, Queenie Read. Got a nice ring to it that does. Also means the coppers would have a right old time tracking you down if anyone ever passes on your name."

"If I take on another new name, I might forget who I am! Anyway, do you think any of the others blabbed to the coppers?"

"No, they'd have been round here by now if they had. They know what side their bread's buttered. I'll see them right, don't you worry."

"What are you up to today?"

"I'm on the site this morning, then I've got a few leads to follow up on for some new premises."

"Want me to come with you?"

"If you like. How about we meet at the market around one o'clock?"

"Works for me. I need to get Christmas presents for Julia, Fred, Florrie and the kids so I could do that first."

I'm slow getting going this morning. It don't help that as well as my ankle, both my head and belly ache thanks to the monthly what's arrived. I'd got my hopes up this might be the month a baby filled my belly, and shed a little tear when I got to the privy and saw the blood. It's early days though, me and Barny have plenty of time. Soon we'll be in a bigger place, full of kiddies, I'm certain of it.

As I hobble my way down St Giles, a peculiar thing happens. Folk must've read the morning paper for they wave at me and shouts of "Morning, Queenie" follow me down the street. It's the same at the market. Everyone's heard about the raid and all want to know more. Several chaps bow to me, and one woman even gives me a curtsey and calls me 'Your Majesty'. Bloody hell, I didn't know there were so many folk around what can read.

It takes an age to buy my presents, for every stall I stop at fellows want to hear about the raid. I manage to find a smart navy tie for Fred, and a dancing lady made from china for Julia. I buy some fabric to make a dress for Florrie, and new winter coats for the children. I don't bother getting something for Joe. The silly bugger deserves a lump of coal and nothing more.

Barny's waiting for me by his old stall. I smile as I remember how we met.

"Fancy some apples?"

"You seen the prices they're charging now? And I thought you were bad."

"Take no notice of my missus," Barny says to the stall holder. "She's a bloody skinflint."

"Come on," I say. "Where are we headed first?"

"Magdalen Street."

"Let's get going then."

***

The room on Magdalen Street is just what we're after. An old widow owns the house and she's desperate to earn a few bob on the side. She shows us to the front room and tells us this is the one available. It looks straight out onto the street. So long as we keep the curtains closed, it shouldn't be a problem. There's no electric in the house, but we didn't expect there to be and are used to working by lamp light. The room smells musty, like it's been shut up for decades.

"Well, Mrs Sharp, I think this is just what we're after. You understand we'd need a key, and would require access to the property till fairly late at night."

"Oh, I know what you're up to. I wasn't born yesterday. So long as you keep me out of it, you're welcome to the room. I just need your names, so I know who I'm dealing with."

"Of course, Mrs Sharp. I'm Barny, and this here is my wife, Queenie."

Chapter 43

April 1933

It took the worst row we've ever had, but I'm finally here, ready to be checked over by the doc. Waste of money, Barny says, but I don't reckon you can put a price on peace of mind. And anyway, he owes me. After making a profit on his other building projects, he's poured all our savings into a bloody block of flats. I don't doubt ours will be a beautiful flat, but a flat don't count as a family home. He's given up, and that hurts more than anything.

"I'll see you at two."

"You're not coming in?"

"You know I bloody hate hospitals. Go in healthy, come out sick."

"So, I have to do this alone, do I?"

The blood is boiling in my veins. So much for a partnership, he's no different from any other bloke once you scratch the surface.

"It's not right for a chap to be there when the doctor's looking at your private parts."

"It's nothing you've not seen before."

"I'll be waiting for you as soon as you're done, I promise."

Barny goes to kiss me, but I turn my head and storm towards the hospital. It's an enormous building, and the receptionist is less than helpful with her directions. I walk corridor after corridor with no luck. Sick people lie in beds moaning and groaning. This is no place for a healthy young woman. Maybe Barny was right, and I should've let sleeping dogs lie.

A young doctor walks past me, studying a pile of papers in his hand.

"Excuse me."

"Yes?"

"I'm looking for Doctor Graystone."

"Ah, you're on the wrong floor. You'll find him on floor five."

"Thank you."

I climb the mountain of stairs up and up. I don't trust those new-fangled lifts. I find floor five easily enough, and know I'm in the right place, for it's mainly women around, and most of them have big bellies. An old man with thick-rimmed glasses leans against a desk, scribbling notes onto a page. I cough, but he don't look up.

"Hello?"

"Yes, how can I help you?"

"I'm here for an examination."

"I see. Can I take your name?"

"Yes, It's Queenie, I mean Nellie."

"Nellie what?"

"Read."

"Hmm, we don't appear to have anyone of that name on our list. Do you go by any other names?"

"I might be down as Ellen?"

"Ah yes, here you are. An examination and an X-ray. Right, I'll get a nurse to take you to a cubicle where you can change. She'll explain how it all works, and once the X ray has been taken, I'll see you in my office to go through the results."

"Thank you."

An efficient-looking nurse leads me to a bed and pulls round the curtain. She hands me a gown and asks me to change into it.

"I'll be just outside. Shout if you need any help."

Help? Getting undressed? What on earth does she think I'm here for?

"That's very kind, but I think I can manage."

It only takes a minute to change out of my clothes and into the gown. I call to let the nurse know I'm ready. When she pulls back the curtain, she's got a metal trolley with her, holding a large needle sitting in a bowl.

"What's that for?"

"Nothing to worry about, we're just going to inject a little dye into you. It will help us see what's going on when we take the X-ray."

She's got a kind face this nurse, plump, rosy, and covered in freckles.

"Will it hurt?"

"A little, but it's really not too bad. Can you lift your gown for me?"

Lift my gown? If I do that, she'll see my privates. Bloody hell. She must see the shock on my face, for she suggests I lie beneath the bed covers and leave just my belly exposed. I do as she says and wince as the needle pierces my skin.

"Well done, Ellen."

"It's Queenie. My name's Queenie."

"Oh, that's funny, I have you down on my notes as Ellen."

"Long story," I say, and she smiles a wide smile.

"You get yourself comfy here, and I'll check if they're ready for us in the X-ray room."

She's back five minutes later with a wheelchair.

"What's that for?"

"I thought you might like a ride."

"There's nothing wrong with my legs."

"Very well, follow me."

She leads me down a long corridor and stops outside a door, tapping with her knuckles. The door opens and a stern-looking woman in overalls beckons me into the room.

"I'll wait out here," says the nurse. "It shouldn't take too long."

The nurse was right, fifteen minutes after I went in the room, I'm back out again. It's a bloody relief too, for the woman in there never spoke a friendly word, just barked instructions at me to lie still and stop wriggling.

"What happens now?"

"Well, there'll be a bit of a wait while the doctor studies the images. I suggest you change back into your clothes and I'll fetch you a cup of tea. Would you like a newspaper to look through?"

"Yes, that would be lovely, thanks."

Two hours. Two bloody hours it takes for the doc to look at the photographs of my belly. I've read the newspaper cover to cover three times before the nurse arrives to take me to his office.

"Good luck," she says, knocking on the door.

The old chap I saw at the desk is sat in the room, behind a much larger, grander desk than before. His glasses are perched on the end of his nose as he studies black and white photographs that make no sense to me.

"Sit yourself down," he says, pointing to a chair opposite his. "Now, Mrs Read, I see from your notes you have had a number of unsuccessful pregnancies."

"I've lost five babies, if that's what you mean."

"And none of them reached full term?"

I stare at him blankly. What the bloody hell does full term mean?

"How long did you carry the babies for?"

"The shortest was three months, the longest seven."

"My sincere condolences for your loss. It sounds like you've really been through the mill."

My eyes fill with tears. I mustn't cry here in this office, it's important to be strong. That's what Barny says anyway. The doc starts speaking again.

"Well, looking at your X-rays, I can see where the problem lies."

"You can?"

"Yes. You have what's called bicornuate womb."

"A what?"

"In layman's terms, your womb is the shape of a heart, and it shouldn't be. In fact, your condition is often described as a heart-shaped womb."

"Have I done something wrong?"

"No, you've done nothing wrong at all, Mrs Read. Your womb will have been this shape since birth. We often find that women with your condition struggle to carry a baby to full term."

"Can you fix it?"

"I'm afraid not."

"So, if I have another pregnancy..."

"It will be unlikely to last the full nine months."

There's a strange ringing in my ears, getting louder and louder. It's hot in here too, I fan my face, but it does no good. The doctor passes me a glass of water and a box of tissues. But I don't cry. I can save my tears for later, in private.

"Do you have any questions, Mrs Read?"

I shake my head and try to stand up. But the room is spinning, and I flop back into the seat.

"Let me get you some sweet tea. I realise this has been quite the shock. There's no rush to get up, you stay there as long as you need."

The doc disappears off to fetch me tea. What will I tell Barny? Why me? Why not one of the others? It's not like my sisters have had any problems popping out babies. I thought I'd escaped Mum and her meanness, but seems she found a way to hurt me even from beyond the grave. For if this is anyone's fault, it surely must be hers. She's the one who made me, after all.

Chapter 44

April 1933

"Queenie? Queenie?"

I look up through blurry eyes and see Barny walking towards me.

"How did you know where I was?"

"You've come to Chapelfield after each of the babies, so I guessed you'd had bad news and come here again."

"Oh."

I stare out into the gardens. It's too cold for most folk to be out, but there's a couple of mums pushing babies in prams, probably trying to get them to sleep. What I'd give for sleepless nights.

"Sorry I didn't meet you at the hospital. I just had to get away from that place."

"What did the doc say?"

"Sit down."

Barny sits beside me on the bench, and I let my head rest on his shoulder. How do I tell him I've failed, that I'm not a proper woman? Best get straight to the point.

"There's some fancy name for my problem that I've forgotten. But the doc said some folk call it a heart-shaped womb."

"And what's one of those then?"

"Just like the name says. My womb is the shape of a heart, so although I can get a baby inside it, it most likely won't last a full nine months. Maybe it's just not comfy enough in there." I manage a little smile, and Barny wraps his arm round me. "I'm sorry I'm not a proper wife."

"Don't you remember our pact all them years ago? I wasn't ever looking for a proper wife, as you put it. I was looking for a partner. I was looking for you."

"But we can never have a family. A family is what I've always wanted, ever since Julia and Henry taught me what a family should be."

"We're each other's family. And you're not short of nieces and nephews to look after."

"It's not the same though, is it."

"No. No, it's not." He kisses the top of my head.

"It's ironic really. All them years I've thought my heart was breaking, and all the while it's the heart in my belly what's breaking me."

"Did the doc say a baby is impossible?"

"Not impossible, no. Just unlikely. But, Barny, I can't put myself through all that again. All that hope, all that loss. I've had enough loss in my life to last a hundred lifetimes, I don't need no more."

"Then we carry on, just the two of us. Our own little family. Fancy coming and seeing the flats this afternoon? Looks like we'll be able to move in by the end of the week."

"No, not today. I'd like to go and see Florrie. Can Stephen mind the shop?"

"Of course. You go, a woman's shoulder will be better for crying on than mine. See you at home later on."

***

"Nell! This is a nice surprise. Come in."

"Is Joe around?"

"No, he's at work, then will be at the pub till late. Are you alright? You look like you've been crying."

"I went to the hospital to get checked over."

"And?"

"Seems kiddies won't be in me and Barny's future."

"And they know that from one hospital visit, do they?"

"They know what they're talking about, Florrie. I had an X-ray and all."

"I'm so sorry," says Florrie, cupping a hand beneath her enormous belly.

"What about you? Is the doc happy with how things are going?"

"It all seems fine for now. He was bloody pissed I'd got myself in the family way again and said I must do nothing but rest."

"And are you? Resting, I mean."

"It's hard to rest with kiddies to care for, and Joe's meals to see to."

"He don't help?"

"Not a man's job, is it?"

"Stupid bugger."

"I'll pretend I didn't hear that. Look, Nell, I know it's not the same, but there'll always be children in your life. Mine love you, and aren't you godmother to Olive's eldest?"

"Yes, bloody joke that is and all. I think she only picked me to get at Cecil. I'm hardly going to teach the poor blighter about the bible, am I?"

"No, but you see my point."

"You don't understand. How could you when you've so many children of your own?"

Florrie looks awkward, and I'm sorry I snapped. We've been getting on much better lately and I don't want to spoil things with her. She looks like she could do with me being around. If I'm honest, she don't look well. Her skin is grey and I'm sure I spotted a bald patch on her head when she bent down.

"How long have you got to go?" I say, pointing to her belly.

"Two months."

"Bloody hell, you sure you're not having twins?"

"I'd better not be. Look, Nell, I'm going to need all the help I can get with this next one. My health's not been too good lately. How about we share it?"

"Share what?"

"The baby. You'll be a special aunty. I'll make sure you get to spend more time with it than you have the others. Joe's that drunk most of the time he won't even notice. Most of the time he don't have a clue what's going on."

"I know you mean well, Florrie, but I don't need a consolation prize. I'll help you any way I can, I promise, but it will always be your baby. It can come and stay over at our new place though, that would be fun."

"You mean the new flat? When you moving in?"

"End of the week. I hated Barny for buying it, but now I see it's for the best. A chance to start again. You'll have to come over at the weekend and have a snoop around. Bring the kiddies too if you like."

"I will."

***

"I didn't think you were coming."

"I didn't stay long with Florrie. It was lovely seeing her, but it was hard to see her big belly. Either I was going to go home and cry myself into a stupor, or come and find you and try to make the best of things."

"Well, I'm pleased you came. What do you think?"

"You really helped build this?"

"Yep, poured my muscle and money into these beauties. You like them?"

I stare up at the red-brick block of flats. All have large windows, and each flat has its own balcony.

"No wonder I've not seen you for months. It must have been a job getting these built."

"Well, it's not like I've been working on my own. Fancy a look inside?"

"Lead the way."

Everything in the block smells new. Everything looks fresh and clean. Barny leads me up a wide staircase to the second floor.

"Number thirty-two. This one's ours."

He turns the key in the lock and steps back to let me inside. The first thing I notice is the light. It's dull and grey outside, but the thin winter light pours through enormous windows and bounces from room to room. The floors are covered in thick cream carpet. I take my shoes off and lie on it.

"I had your voice in my mind when I chose that. You like it?"

"I love it."

Barny reaches his hand down and pulls me up.

"I thought this could be our room," he says. I follow him into a large cream room with one wall almost entirely made of window.

"Show me more."

"Next to this one there are two spare bedrooms."

My heart twists and I swallow down tears. Those bedrooms shouldn't be spare, and we both know it. All those rows about him choosing a flat over a house, and all the while he'd been planning on somewhere big enough for our children to live too. I pinch my arm to distract the tears away. I don't look inside the extra bedrooms. If I do, I'll see a cot and gurgling baby in my mind's eye and there'll be no chance of keeping the tears at bay.

"I think you'll like this," he says, opening another door.

Bloody hell. A proper kitchen. There's a sink, an oven, worktops for chopping veg and making a cuppa.

"There'll be no excuse for my awful cooking now."

"Come through and see the sitting room."

The sitting room stretches the width of the flat. On one side lies a huge window, on the other, doors leading out to the balcony. Barny opens them and I step out to views across the whole of Norwich.

"This is almost as good as the view from Mousehold."

"Better, I'd say. More going on, more people to watch."

"I don't know what to say, Barny. This place is perfect."

"And I've even saved the best till last."

"You have?"

"Follow me."

We head back down the corridor to a door I'd walked straight past when we'd first arrived.

"I'll let you open this yourself," he says, stepping back.

I push the door open and burst into tears. What I'm crying for I can't say, for sadness jumbles with happiness, loss mixes with hope. Our own toilet. Our own taps. Our own hot water. Our own bathtub. Our own beautiful bloody bathtub.

Chapter 45

June 1933

I catch Olive's eye as she downs another glass of wine. She shakes her head in a message to say nothing. Poor old Olive, she don't look happy. Neither does Cecil. I squeeze through the mass of bodies and flop down beside her.

"You alright?"

"Fine."

"Who's watching the kiddies?"

"Cecil's mother. Mine can't be trusted not to have a drink."

She sounds bitter, spitting out the words, then taking another glug of wine.

"And don't you say anything about me turning out like her. This is my first evening out in months. I deserve a drink."

"Things no better with Cecil?"

"Nell, I know you and Barny have your ups and downs, but thank your lucky stars you didn't marry a bore. He's even boring in bed. Have you seen the way he speaks to people? Two minutes is all they can take before they move off to find someone more interesting."

"Have you thought about getting a job? It could be a nice distraction."

"Cecil doesn't like the thought of me working while the children are still small."

"I suppose that's fair enough."

"Yes, but I'm going out of my mind. Between the nanny and the cleaner, there's nothing left for me to do but while away the hours in a boring version of hell." She reaches to the small table beside her and tips the dregs of a bottle into her glass.

"You should eat something. Let me make you a sandwich."

Olive laughs, but it's a hard laugh, an unkind laugh. "Look, just because you have no children of your own, doesn't mean you can start treating me like one."

"Suit yourself," I say, and leave her to her wallowing.

"Is that the door?" Barny asks me.

"I didn't hear nothing."

"I'm not surprised with all this racket. I'll go and check." Moments later he's rushing over to me. "Alice is at the door, says Florrie needs you."

I hand him my champagne glass and rush to find Alice.

"What is it, love? What's happened?"

"The baby's coming. Mum asked me to fetch you."

"Wait here, I'll grab my coat."

***

We hear the screams from halfway down the road.

"Where's your dad and brothers?"

"The boys are at Sarah's, Dad's down the pub."

"Of course he is," I mutter, hoping Alice don't hear.

"Are any of the others at home? Ethel? Maria?"

"No, it was you Mum wanted."

"Alright. Let's see what she's up to then."

Alice opens the door and leads me up to Florrie's room. I know poor old Florrie tries her best, but this house really isn't fit for living in, especially not little kiddies. Joe's not even sorted them out with a proper bed, and they've been here getting on twenty years. A charming smile's all well and good but it don't put food on the table. Florrie would've been better off if he'd done a runner like Dad.

She's lying on her mattress, covered by greying sheets. When I walk in, she gives me a faint smile.

"You didn't need to dress up for the occasion," she whispers, before her face twists up in pain and she lets out a groan.

I'd forgotten to change in all the rush of Alice arriving. Satin and sequins aren't ideal midwife clothes, but they'll have to do.

"We were having a party," I explain, running my hand across her forehead.

"You're not half cut, are you? That's all I need."

I laugh. "No, don't worry, I was too busy playing host to have much to drink. I did bring this with me though..." I pull a bottle of brandy out of my bag. "I remember it helped Mum all them years ago. You want some?"

Florrie nods, and I send Alice off in search of a clean cup.

"How long has this been going on?"

"The pain started first thing. I tried to get on with the day as best I could, but eventually I had to give in and come to bed."

"And you only just called for me?"

"I thought I could manage by myself."

Florrie grips my hand and lets out a scream that will have woken the whole of Norwich.

"I'm sorry to ask for you, I know it must be hard, being around babies and all. But you're the only one I trust."

"Don't you worry about me. Seeing you in this much pain makes me feel I've had a lucky escape."

My fingers stroke her hand as another wave of pain floods through her.

"I think I can feel it," she says.

"Want me to take a look?"

Florrie nods, and I lift the bedsheets. "Well, that's definitely a head right there. And a fine lot of hair that baby has. You're nearly there now, not long to go."

It takes less than ten minutes before the baby slithers into the world. Alice passes me a towel and I rub it down. Blood has covered my cream dress, but holding the little dot in my arms, I really don't care.

"You have another little girl," I say. "Say hello to Mummy."

I hand the baby to Florrie and she holds it to her breast.

"You take a moment with your daughter, while I put the kettle on."

With the tea made and the afterbirth seen to, I set about cleaning Florrie up. All her energy is gone, and it's all she can do to hold the baby to her.

"You hungry?"

Florrie nods.

"Alice, can you have a look in your cupboards and find some bread for your mum?"

"There's nothing there. I looked earlier."

"You mean none of you have eaten all day?"

Alice shakes her head.

"Right, you head back to my place, and tell Barny we're in need of food. He'll know what to do."

"Thank you," Florrie says, a light flush showing beneath her grey skin. "Do you mind taking the baby? I'm worried I'll fall asleep and squish her."

"Not at all. You rest. I'll be downstairs if you need anything."

I carry the baby downstairs, pausing on each step to be sure I don't trip. As we reach the front room, the baby starts to grizzle, and I jog her up and down in my arms. She's light as a feather, her face so screwed up I can barely see her eyes.

"What's wrong, love? You hungry? Or just tired from making your way into the world?"

All I get in reply is a snuffle, and she screws her hands into fists and rests them against her face. I grab a spare rag and gently wipe down her hair. Such a full head of hair. Such tiny hands. She begins her crying again. I prop her against my shoulder and walk her round the tiny room, singing as I go. I feel the tears on my cheeks as I sing, love for this little one, mixed with grief for my own.

"I'll always take care of you," I whisper. "I'm your Aunt Queenie. You'll never be alone so long as I'm around."

***

It's six before I'm able to leave Florrie's and head home. Joe rolled in just after midnight, waking the baby with his kisses and drunken lullabies. His eyes were full of love, but he's not turned that love into action when it comes to providing for his other kiddies, so no reason to think he'll start now. I turn my key in the lock as quietly as I can, and creep through to the bedroom. Barny isn't there. I pad along the soft carpet to the living room and find him snoring in a pink armchair. There's a blanket on the sofa and I spread it across his legs and creep away.

The room is flooded with sunlight when I wake to find a steaming cup of tea beside me.

"Barny?"

Barny appears in the doorway, stooping so as not to bump his head.

"What time is it?"

"Eleven."

"Bloody hell, why didn't you wake me? I'm needed at the shop, then I have to pick up some supplies for Florrie."

"How did it go last night?"

"Not too bad. The baby is a darling. I held her most of the night while Florrie got some sleep."

Barny smiles, but there's no hiding the pain in his eyes.

"Are you alright to cover the shop till five? I've got a meeting this afternoon about the new development by the river, but I can pick up supplies for Florrie on my way back."

"Sounds a good plan."

"Was Joe pleased with the new addition to the family?"

"Seemed so, but how well he'll care for her's another matter. Stupid bugger."

Barny grins. "Don't you be passing your foul language on to your new niece, will you. Have they got a name for her?"

"Not yet. I'll ask Florrie when I see her later."

***

"Only me," I call, letting myself in to Florrie's house.

"Come on up," she calls back.

"Be up in a minute. I've got a few bits and pieces to put in the pantry first."

She must be tired, for there's no argument shouted down the stairs. I give the shelves a good old wipe before putting the food away. There's stuff that looks suspiciously like rat droppings on most of the shelves. I sweep it off with a rag and brush it outside into the yard. Before heading up, I make a quick cuppa for Florrie, I doubt anyone else will have taken her one.

"How are you feeling?" I ask, settling the cup on the floorboards beside her.

"Shush, she's finally dropped off."

"Sorry," I whisper. "You come up with a name for her yet?"

"Barbara."

"A pretty name for a pretty girl. Did you manage to get some sleep?"

"Not much. She's been wanting fed most of the day, but I don't have much milk to give her. Hopefully it will come in soon."

"Well, I'll make some dinner for you to build your strength. You need to eat yourself or there'll be nothing to pass on to Barbara."

Florrie grabs my hand. "Thank you, Nell, for everything."

"Just doing what sisters should do."

"I don't see none of my other sisters running round and making me food."

"Yes, but they have their own families, don't they?"

"For a skinflint, you can be bloody generous sometimes."

"Get some sleep," I say, and make my way downstairs.

Chapter 46

November 1933

"How's she doing?"

"Not good."

"What does the doc say?"

"That it's a mystery. They can't understand why she's not recovered from the birth. It's been months now. Instead of getting better she just gets weaker."

"You going round again today?"

"I've got to, the kiddies won't eat otherwise. I'm sorry I've not been able to help at the shop as much as usual."

"Don't worry about that. Stephen's really stepped up. I think he likes it when you're not there and he don't get bossed around by a girl."

"Well, he'd better not get his feet under the table too much. As soon as Florrie's better I'll be back ordering him around. Are you at the shop today or back on site?"

"Both. I'm on site this morning then in the shop this afternoon. There's a big race on today so I reckon it'll be a busy one."

"Alright, well, I'll see you later." I give Barny a quick peck on the lips then I'm out the door.

It's good we're only ten minutes from Florrie's, as I've practically moved in these past few weeks. Alice has done her best to help me with the cleaning, and she's not a bad cook, but there's still Florrie and the baby to care for.

"Where's Mum?" I ask Alice.

"In bed, same as every day."

I kiss her cheek and take the stairs two at a time.

"How's the invalid today?"

"Please don't call me that. I hate being stuck in this bed day after day."

"Sorry. Anything I can get you?"

"I could do with a scrub down, as you can probably tell."

I don't say nothing, but the smell hit me as soon as I walked in. It's a smell what scares me, for it's one I've met before, when I was caring for Henry. But Florrie's younger than Henry, so I'm probably worrying over nothing. I leave Florrie in peace, and heat some water for the bowl. She's drowsy by the time I make it back to her.

"You sure you wouldn't rather a sleep than a wash?"

"All I ever do is sleep. I'd like to be clean, if you don't mind helping."

"Of course I don't. Put your arms round my neck if you're able."

Florrie leans against me and for a moment I'm back in the yard, helping her lean over a pan in the dead of night. I pull off her nightdress and throw it in the corner of the room.

"Let's do your back first."

As the warm water meets her skin she relaxes further into my arms, and I wonder if she's fallen asleep. I check her face, but her eyes are open.

"Good girl. Now lie on your back and I'll do under your arms and your face."

I begin wiping water across her cheeks, but she grabs hold of my wrist.

"Nellie?"

"What is it? Is the water too hot?"

"No, it's not that. I want you to promise me something."

"What is it?"

"When I go, I want you to take care of Barbara. Will you do that for me?"

"Don't be daft, you're not going nowhere. Now, I need to wash down below, but I promise not to look."

Once she's clean, I pull the blankets up to her chin.

"I know its strange, lying there in the nud, but you'll feel much better with a clean nightdress on. You have a nice sleep now, and I'll fetch you one."

"I think Barbara could do with a change too," she says, her voice thick with sleep.

I look in the cot, where Barbara is grinning, waving her arms and legs around like she's doing a dance. She's pretty pongy too, so I hold her at arm's length and take her downstairs to find some clean clothes.

I give Florrie an hour before I go up with her fresh nightie. She's lying still as a doll, her face looks peaceful and for once not in pain. It seems a shame to disturb her, but I don't want her catching a chill lying there with nothing on. I creep over and give her shoulder a shake.

"Florrie? Florrie, it's time to wake up. I've got your nightdress here."

She don't move. Bloody hell, she's sleeping deeply. I shake her shoulder a little harder, and her head flops to one side. My belly starts fizzing and my heart pounds in my ears. This time I grab both shoulders and shake even harder. Nothing.

"Florrie," I say. "Florrie, please wake up. Wake up!"

Beside the still Florrie, Barbara gurgles and kicks about on the floorboards. I pick her up and lie her on Florrie's chest.

"Florrie, Barbara's here. She wants you to give her a cuddle."

Still Florrie don't move. Barbara squirms her way back onto the floorboards. I hold my cheek to Florrie's mouth, praying for a tickle of breath to reach my skin. I stay there till my neck hurts and I have to stretch out again. I lie beside Florrie on the bed, and wrap my arm across her. My body feels heavy, like there's a brick wall crushing my chest. *Please don't go*, I pray. *Please God, don't let her leave me.* But once again, God has ignored my prayers. I reach beside the bed and pick up Florrie's hairbrush. With her head propped up against a pillow, I brush out the tangles, leaving long shiny waves trailing right down to her belly. My lips kiss her forehead, then her cheeks.

"Goodnight, my darling Florrie. Thank you for being my sister. Thank you for being my friend." I climb up from the bed and tuck the covers neatly around her chin. "Sleep tight, beautiful girl."

***

Me and Barny walk back through the church, hand in hand. I don't know how I'd have got through it without him beside me. Olive walks behind us, a wreath of lilies in her hand to lay on the grave. It was bloody kind of her to come. She never met Florrie, but said she's heard enough from me to feel she knew her well enough to say goodbye.

It's strange having the family gathered together. Not the best of reunions, for although there's enough kiddies around to swell our numbers, it's the ones missing what stick in our minds; Mum, Dad, Arthur, Albert and of course Florrie.

Outside the church, Fred pulls me into his arms. I've promised him I'll visit him in Wales in the spring. I might make a proper trip of it and visit Julia while I'm at it. It will be good to get out of the city for a while. It seems a lifetime since I was on the road. A familiar cry pierces through my thoughts, and I head over to check on Barbara, lying beside Joe in her pram.

"You going to keep your side of the bargain?" he says as I reach them. His eyes are red-rimmed and his voice holds a note of panic. He's shuffling from foot to foot, fiddling with his tie like he's choking.

"What you talking about?"

"The deal you made with Florrie before she snuffed it."

"I've no idea what you're on about, Joe. I never made no deal with Florrie."

"She told me, she said Barbara would be alright." His eyes near enough fall out of his face, he's staring at me so hard. Sweat prickles his brow despite how cold it is.

Barny appears beside me. "Perhaps you could explain to us what this supposed deal was?"

Joe runs his hands through his hair, looking from me to Barny and back again. "She told me you'd got it all worked out. She said Barbara would be alright. She said... she said..." A sob escapes his mouth, and he turns to brush away tears. "She said..." He's jiggling round that much I want to grab his arms and pin him down.

"Bloody hell, Joe," I say, losing my patience. "Just spit it out, will you."

"She said you'd have Barbara."

"What?" Barny looks at me. "Queenie? What's he talking about? This is the first I've heard of it."

"She asked me to take care of Barbara, nothing more."

"That's not what she told me. Said you'd agreed to take her in."

"But she can't have. She only asked me hours before she died."

"Oh God, she said she was going to ask you and that you'd say yes. You have to, Nell, or it will be the orphanage for her. The others can go to my mum's. But there's no way she can look after a baby."

"But can't you look after her? You are her father, after all."

"And how exactly can I do that? I'm a working man. Fuck's sake, Nell, I can barely look after myself." He looks defeated, staring down at Barbara, a lonely tear dropping down into her pram.

I look at Barny. His face is creased with impatience, like he wants to shake some sense into his brother-in-law.

"I'm leaving now. Either you take the baby home with you, or I'll wheel her down to the orphanage on my way home. Will you do it? Please, Nell, for Florrie?"

"We'll take her," Barny and I say together.

Joe marches off, and we're left with the pram between us. "Bloody hell."

"Couldn't have put it better myself," Barny says, reaching over and squeezing my hand.

Chapter 47

December 1933

"Don't forget the decorations. We're celebrating properly this year."

"I won't, don't worry."

"And can you post the cards off to Fred and Julia? They'll struggle to get there on time as it is. I should've posted them last week."

"Well, you've had a fair bit on your mind," Barny says, reaching into the cot and tickling Barbara's chin. "Now don't you girls be getting up to mischief while I'm out, will you?"

"No chance of that. There's that many nappies to wash it will take me the best part of a day to get through them."

"Is it today we've got Olive and Cecil coming round?"

"Yes, six o'clock. I've not checked how much sherry we've got left. I think Olive might've drunk most of it last time. Could you pick up some more?"

"Yes, I might get a few beers in too, I'll need something strong to get through an evening with Cecil."

"Don't be so rude," I say, but I can't help but laugh. I wish Olive would come round on her own sometimes, but she always brings Cecil with her. I don't know why, he seems to enjoy our company as much as we enjoy his, and that's not saying much. "I'll pop in the shop this morning and check Stephen's alright by himself."

"He won't thank you for it."

"I know, but I need something other than washing nappies to occupy me."

"You know, a mum pushing a baby would be good cover for a runner..."

"I'm not having this argument again. I've told you, once she's in school I'll get back to the business. But I don't want her having no part of it. She'll grow up respectable. There's no need for her to know how we come by our money."

"She'll work it out one day."

"That may be true, but hopefully by then she'll love us enough for it not to matter."

"Right, well I'm off. See you later."

The door slams and I stare into the cot. Barbara's eyelids flutter in her sleep, and I wonder if she's dreaming of Florrie. I do. Not every night, but now and then she pops by for a visit, just like Henry. I know they're in my imagination, but even if they were ghosts, I wouldn't mind. I can't think of two kinder ghosts to have watching over you.

I'm falling asleep myself when Barbara stirs. If only she'd sleep at night, we'd all be better rested and less grumpy with one another. But I know these days are precious, and will be gone all too soon. The purple bags under my eyes are worth the life she's brought into our home.

The day goes by quicker than I thought it would. Barny was right about Stephen not welcoming my interference so I don't linger at the shop. I take Barbara for her first visit to the market, show her where me and Barny met all them years ago. She don't understand, but coos and grins like she do.

The nappies take me all afternoon. How such a small kiddie can produce so much filth is a mystery to me. At least I've got a bathtub to wash them in. I'll have to unpeg them before Olive arrives. I don't suppose Cecil would approve of nappies and underwear drying on the balcony.

Thankfully, at half past four Barbara decides to go down for a nap. It means I can take my time getting ready, I even manage a bit of makeup and a quick whip round the house. Not that it was messy before. I love our flat. It's the same pinks and creams as our old house, but now I can afford to add in touches of gold. A gold clock what chimes on the hour, gold tassels on the cushions, teacups painted in pink flowers with gold along their rim. I'm plumping up the sofa cushions when Barbara stirs.

"Hello, sleepyhead. Blimey, you stink. Let's get that dirty nappy off you and tuck it away in the bucket so the house don't smell when the guests arrive."

With Barbara changed and fed, I lay her on the bed and climb up beside her. Barny comes home to find us both playing with her tiny toes. Barbara thinks it's hilarious to shove them in her mouth, and even funnier when I pull them out again.

"You look nice. You smell nice too."

Barny climbs onto the bed and leans over Barbara's head to kiss me.

"You know, it's funny..."

"What is?" he asks.

"Well, it's just that I've had so many names over my life; Ellen Hardy, Nellie Westrop, Queenie Read. But the one name I wanted, I never thought I'd get."

"Oh? And what's that then?"

"Mum."

Barbara gurgles and smiles up at us. She reaches her tiny hand towards me, wrapping her fingers round mine, like she'll never let go.

Author's note

Queenie Read died in 1999, four months before her 100th
birthday. She outlived Barny and Barbara, but remained
close to her two granddaughters and lived to see the birth
of six great-grandchildren. I knew her as Queenie Nanny,
and remember visiting her as a child in Norwich. Her story
is legendary in our family, and one I've always wanted to
tell. If she knew a book had been written about her life, her
response would probably be -
'Bloody hell!'

One last thing...

Queenie

Me

One thing authors love is reviews! Why? Because they are the best way of helping other people discover the book. As an independent author, reviews are even more important to me as I don't have the weight of a big publishing company with a big marketing budget behind me. If you can spare a couple of minutes to review this book I'd be very grateful. I read every review - the good ones put a spring in my step (or make me do a little dance), the less good ones help improve my writing!

Finally, if you'd like to get in touch, find out more about my writing, or follow the progress of my next book The Wives Left Behind, you can find me at-

lkwilde.com
(Sign up for my readers' club via my website)

facebook.com/lkwilde

twitter.com/lkwilde
Thank you for reading Queenie's story!
LK Wilde x

Acknowledgments

This book has truly been a team effort. So many people have given up their time and expertise to help me get Queenie's story down on the page. Firstly, a huge thank you to Queenie's granddaughters Jo Egleton and Gillian Middleton (known to me as Mum and Aunty Bean!) who not only dredged their memories for invaluable information on Queenie's life, but also provided support, wine, and a wealth of editing advice during early drafts of the book. Thank you to Neil Middleton for sharing your memories of Queenie and encouraging me to dig deeper into our remarkable family history. Thank you to Ian and Leanne, for reading one of the later drafts and giving me the encouragement to send this book into the world, and to Bridget for being far better at telling people about my books than I am.

When the brilliant Tom Fosten agreed to edit this book for me, I knew I was in safe hands. Without his wise insights into character and plot, the book would not have done justice to the remarkable life Queenie led. Thank you for pushing me and the story to be the best we could be.

Thank you to the brilliant Julia Gibbs for your eagle eyed proof reading. I promise I'll learn from my mistakes before sending my next book to you!

I relied heavily on both the British Newspaper Archive and the Ancestry website for research. The moment I finally traced the couple (Henry and Julia Westrop) who had adopted Ellen into fairground life, I screamed with joy. All the hours of cross-checking and drawing blanks felt worth it for securing that one puzzle piece. Once I knew their names, I was able to track the journey of their shooting gallery around the country. Thank goodness for modern technology!

When researching the Norwich Yards, the fantastic book The Old Courts and Yards of Norwich by Frances and Michael Holmes proved invaluable, as did the video recollections on their Norwich Heritage website (http://www.norwich-heritage.co.uk/). I'm incredibly grateful to Frances and Michael for reading through sections of this book and checking historical detail.

When researching life as part of a travelling fair, two books helped enormously - Showfolk - The voice of travelling fair people by Sally Festing, and The Travelling People by Duncan Dallas. Thanks also to Guy Belshaw from The Fairground Heritage Trust for helping with my research into early 20th century shooting galleries.

Any historical inaccuracies are down to me, either due to missing information or artistic licence!

Thank you to all my friends and family near and far for your constant support and encouragement, especially my 'boys', Pete, Joseph and Tom, for putting up with me being locked away writing for hours and providing tea and hugs.

Finally, thank YOU, the reader, for picking up this book and giving it a go. It means so much to me that Queenie's story is finally out there in the world, and that you have taken the time to read it. Thank you! x

Also By LK Wilde

In 1895, a Northumberland island welcomes two new residents. Clara and Jimmy are born on the same night to families poles apart. Clara is an islander through and through; Jimmy longs to escape.
When tragedy forces them from their island and each other, they join the herring season in a bid to survive. As they follow shoals of silver darlings to Lowestoft, their paths are dogged by war, injury and misunderstandings.
Will they be reunited? And will they ever find their way home...?

Made in the USA
Monee, IL
05 December 2023

48307214R00217

Kate is stuck in a rut, She works a dead end job, lives in a grotty bedsit and still pines for the man who broke her heart. When Kate inherits a house in a small Cornish town, she jumps at the chance of a fresh start. A surprise letter from her grandmother persuades Kate to open her home and her heart to strangers.

But with friends harbouring secrets, demanding house guests, and her past catching up with her- can Kate really move on? And will her broken heart finally find a home?

Coming soon...

1840, Cornwall. A murderer, a victim, and the wives left behind.